CW00864743

A PRISON STORY
IRAN

A PRISON STORY
IRAN

A MEMOIR

Mehri Dadgar

HAAS-PUBLISHING-HOUSE

UNITED STATES – FEBRUARY, 2016

HPH

February 6, 2016 Haas-Publishing-House
Copyright © 2007 by Mehri Dadgar

Attention: Permissions Coordinator
Haas-Publishing-House
201 Kent Ave. Unit 1
Kentfield CA 94904

Ordering information:
Quantity sales and special discounts are available on quantity purchases by corporations, associations, and others. For details, contact the publisher at the address above.
Orders by U.S. trade bookstores and wholesalers. Please contact:
 haas.publishing.house@gmail.com

Published by Haas-Publishing-House in Kentfield, California.
Printed in the United States
www.haas-publishing-house.com
A Prison Story Iran: a memoir by Mehri Dadgar
Book Cover: Mehri Dadgar
Photography: H. Mahmoudi
First Edition
ISBN-13: 978-1522719533
ISBN-10: 1522719539

The First Murder

[5:27] Recite for them the true history of Adam's two sons. They made an offering, and it was accepted from one of them, but not from the other. He said, "I will surely kill you." He said, "GOD accepts only from the righteous. [5:28] "If you extend your hand to kill me, I am not extending my hand to kill you. For I reverence GOD, Lord of the universe. [5:29] "I want you, not me, to bear my sin and your sin, then you end up with the dwellers of Hell. Such is the requital for the transgressors." [5:30] His ego provoked him into killing his brother. He killed him, and ended up with the losers. [5:31] GOD then sent a raven to scratch the soil, to teach him how to bury his brother's corpse. He said, "Woe to me; I failed to be as intelligent as this raven, and bury my brother's corpse." He became ridden with remorse.

Grossness of Murder

[5:32] Because of this, we decreed for the Children of Israel that anyone who murders any person who had not committed murder or horrendous crimes, it shall be as if he murdered all the people. And anyone who spares a life it shall be as if he spared the lives of all the people. Our messengers went to them with clear proofs and revelations, but most of them, after all this, are still transgressing." Quran, Chapter 5:27-3

AUTHOR'S NOTE

I experienced moments in prison that other prisoners did not witness. *A Prison Story **Iran*** is my story and I have endeavored to tell it accurately and truly. Truth and honesty protects the soul of mankind and society. I've tried to portray characters and events as they happened. Even so I have changed most of the names including those of the prison personnel, in the case of the latter, to allow for the possibility that they have learned to live in peace with themselves and others. My story is one of the many told to contribute to understanding of the Middle East and Iran, its goodness and miseries, and of Iranians and the reasons behind Iran's failed revolution.

CONTENTS

PART 1

During the time of the King

(1977)

In 1977 what seemed to be a small event sparked a momentous change in my life, a change that realigned everything for me from that point forward. It was still during the powerful reign of the King of Iran, the Shah, and Jimmy Carter was the President of the United States when I had finished two years of special training to become a teacher. My life up to then was that of a normal Iranian girl, that is until I met one of my relatives. She had come from Tehran with her mother to propose to my sister on behalf of her brother.

She had abandoned fashionable sleeveless dresses in favor of headscarves and a robe-like manto. When she introduced me to a new face of Islam, which contrasted with the fanatic old version, I found myself attracted to this world. In pursuing answers about the purpose of life I clashed with my mother and her generation who had been raised to love the Shah, his modernity and dynasty.

After reading many poetic writings about Islam, I conquered my love for fashion and began wearing a scarf and a loose manto, as it was the unfamiliar attire of girls in the new Islamic movement

I must add I became confident and reassured in my views of life, for faith and truth had greatly affected me. But I must admit also that I was not aware of the twisted information imbedded within the political Islam that had been introduced to me. Neither did I have enough life experience to understand that my attraction towards the truth was not enough and the means of how to approach the truth was critical as well. I didn't know how to deal wisely with the reality of the world I was living in.

As a result, I couldn't recognize the true nature of the darkness that was hidden deep under the layers of confusing words within the mix of religion and politics. Alas, the path I was taking was going to set me up in an evil world and I was going to learn a great lesson at a great cost.

When the Iranian people started to turn against the Shah and his dynasty, I was part of small political gatherings before the mass demonstrations against the Shah attracted hundred thousands of people.

At this historical time Ayatollah Khomeini's fame grew through underground flyers sent first from Iraq, and then from his place of exile, Neauphle-le-Chateau in France. The myths of his heroism spread all over the country and led to many blindly following.

On one of those days that I set out for a demonstration against the Royal regime, my mother blocked the door and cried out, "You don't know what you're doing. Are you aware that you're helping the mullahs come to power? The illiterate men? It's nonsense. This is not a joke. You'll be in trouble. You have no experience. Oh, you young people. You want to turn the country upside down. Don't you know? Don't you know what the Shah and his father have done for the country? We owe them for making our country secure." At that moment, my mother was frustrated. She then sat down to control her anger and lowered her voice.

"I knew reading those books would brainwash you. I just knew it."

At the age of nineteen, I was too young to understand why the absence of democracy was not important to my mother who was born after Reza Shah overthrew the former chaotic Ghajar monarchy in 1925. For her, the Shah and the Pahlavi dynasty were a symbols of stability and wealth.

"But Mom, you yourself don't like injustice. It's not what you think. We want a better Iran, a better life for the people. Please let me go."

I walked past her, pulled open the door and said, "Good-bye." I ran down the alley to get to the main street as quickly as possible. The streets were filled with people walking in one direction. Along with the throng, I entered the largest mosque, called the Shah

Masjid, where the gathering was supposed to take place. I found my fellow teachers and friends and walked to join them with a happy smile on my face. People waited for a while then moved out of the mosque in silence, like a calm flood overflowing on streets.

Everybody else, including my mother, criticized the changes in my appearance and clothing, but what I experienced in turning to God was pure joy and happiness. I was only nineteen, yet I was striving to purify everything in my mind and my heart. That was when I became a solid believer in God and read the scripture of the Quran and felt truly happy inside. I practiced the commandments as I understood them. None of my family or close friends practiced the rites of Islam except my father in his simple way.

One winter day, my young co-teachers and I wanted to go back home from the village where we taught school. No car was available due to the heavy snow which had locked us in the village for two nights. We had to walk along the unpaved road covered under snow up to our knees.

The reflection of the sun on the vast farms at both sides was blinding, but we were determined to go back to the city. We were still a few miles from the main road when a jeep pulled up. It was rare to find any vehicles on this road. Three of us sat on the back seat. The driver seemed about fifty years old and wore a Jewish top hat. The car took off, but stopped after a few moments.

"Pardon me," the man said. "I have forgotten to do my prayers. I need two minutes of your time to do it, with your permission," He grabbed a small booklet from his inner pocket, read a prayer then drove quietly on the road that narrowed into the main way. The man's prayers lifted me and put tears in my eyes. By his simple act the man had confirmed my faith in God. It was a turning point for me, making me more serious in my practice of getting close to God.

As we arrived, I said good-bye and stepped out onto the sidewalk. Cars moved slowly in the calm city. Relaxed pedestrians passed by the main square. The pool, the fountain, and the white statues in front of the city hall were signs of wealth, culture and civilization.

Right after I passed the pool, the mild sunlight and gentle breeze touched my face in a strange way.

I gazed at the sky and saw that the air was clear, the leaves, breeze and the sun-rays were unusual. Everything around me seemed elevated to a higher quality, a quality that I had never seen before. I was surrounded on every side and suddenly became one with everything around me as if one with the whole universe. I heard a chorus of harmonic chanting, so joyful and so real.

Perhaps I became aware of this unknown world because I had let go of all attachment I had. No matter what others would do or say, I was at peace, surrendered. I purified myself from the smallest wrong thoughts and I respected my parents. My days were so filled by prayers and practicing goodness that I felt God's constant presence.

My focus on religion shifted during the last months of the Shah's rule and I spent a great deal of time on political activities and traveled more frequently to Tehran to join the large number of people who climbed to the rooftops to call Allah o Akbar, God is Great, after the sunset. Our shadows in the dark appeared and disappeared from time to time masking our faces so we would not be recognized by SAVAK, the Shah's secret police. In the last effort to stop the voices of the demonstrators, the army fired on the crowd in Tehran's Jaleh Square the day after martial law had been announced. At the same time, there was a general strike to shut down the petroleum industry to destroy the King's economy.

In Borujerd, I actively participated in the teachers' strike at the school where I taught in a village half an hour away from the city. The day a group of soldiers followed the crowd who had gathered for a rally, my friend Pari from school and I turned away towards an alley, where many people ended up hiding in a house. Pari poked her head out of the door and reported that a soldier was at the end of the alley straightening his gun, putting it to his shoulder to shoot at anyone across from his position. Pari suddenly walked out, saying to us, "I don't fear him," as if life was worth nothing to her or this was such a worthy cause that she was willing to give her life for it.

Whatever she had in her mind, offering her life or embracing death, there was no fear on her face. There was an unnerving pause for both the soldier and my friend until the soldier shot his gun once, then twice in the air.

A strength greater than my fear pulled me out from behind the door to stand by my friend, not sure of the next moment. It was great to be brave, just like her. Gradually, second by second, everyone came out of the house and formed a chain at the end of the alley. On the other side the number of soldiers increased. Their guns glaring sharp white under the sun; they sat about thirty feet away ready to shoot. Then suddenly a middle aged sergeant ran in front of his troop, his thin body shaking. He commanded with all the force that could come out of his lungs, "Don't shoot!"

The authority in his voice saved us.

Killing in the streets, squares and alleys was not working anymore. The Shah's secret police SAVAK and his well-trained army no longer intimidated the millions of people who now chanted in rhyme, their voices rising without fear, demanding the release of political prisoners.

The Shah's appointing a new nationalist prime minister was too late, the people of Iran wanted the King to leave and Khomeini to return.

Tehran in the winter of 1979 was more a fantasy than reality. Six million people came into the streets and looked up to the airplane that carried Khomeini back to Iran. We were so sure of our future with him that our emotions reached up to the heavens. We walked with certainty for hours on the streets to welcome him.

The first night after the victory of the revolution my sister's mother-in-law, an educated experienced Tehrani woman, walked across the room, waved her hands in the air to the words of the national anthem broadcasting on the TV and sang with joy and even more with pride.

oh Iran, oh bejeweled land!
arts originate from your soil!
far from you may at the thoughts of the wicked be
be you eternal, be you infinite!

PART 2

Tehran, Beloved Capital City

(1979)

The revolution brought the blazing gleam of democracy. I yearned to be in the middle of all activities, from political gatherings in the city to joining the volunteer groups assisting the farmers harvesting wheat in the villages and countryside.

Six months later, I saw a great opportunity to live my life according to my revolutionary ambitions for liberty. Even though I knew my mother would object, I was determined to move from Borujerd to Tehran. Two days after I had made up my mind, my cousin Hussein and I, both of us in our twenties, drove towards my sister's house in the capital city, just after the crack of dawn.

I needed official permission to work in Tehran, but my sister was skeptical for she, herself, had to wait an entire year to transfer her teaching position, and she had the legitimate excuse of moving to be with her husband who lived in Tehran.

Nevertheless, Hussein and I headed towards the ministry of education the next day. I waited in the car while Hussein climbed the stairs to the second floor to ask about the process.

About an hour later, he rushed into the car, a triumphant smile brightening his face.

"Good God, Mehri, they signed all the papers for you to be transferred to Tehran immediately. Can you believe that?"

I said excitedly "It's impossible! How?"

Apparently the clerk had left his office, and Hussein had covered for him, answering an important phone call from the man's boss. In exchange, the clerk had made an exception to the rules, and authorized my work permission for Tehran's suburban schools.

Free of my parents' house, in the middle of the large beloved capital city, I could now make my own decisions. It was during the last days of summer and the school term was going to start soon. I rented a room in an old house on a busy popular street, under the Pol-Choobi Bridge and got up my nerve to call my mother with news of my move.

"Maman."

"Oh my dear child, why don't you come back? The schools will be open in a week and you are still in Tehran."

"Mom, I….'m going to stay here."

"What do you mean? You don't want to come back?"

"I am going to live in Tehran."

"What? What's the matter with you? What about your work? What about us?"

"Maman, I've been transferred to teach at a school in Tehran's suburb."

"How is it possible? I can't believe it."

"Yes, Maman. The school district agreed. It's done."

"Are you going to stay with your sister?"

"No, Maman joon. I've rented a room in a house belonging to a kind woman. Don't be worried Maman. I'll be fine here."

"Oh dear, oh dear," she cried.

"Mom, I'm here. It's done. I've already been transferred."

At this point my mother didn't have any other choice but to accept my decision. I drew a long breath since she didn't seem as upset as I had expected. She had to deal now with the task of cultural expectations, explaining my decision to others. Back in 1979 it was unusual for a girl to live apart from her family in another city.

The old house was in a short alley under the famous bridge, where all the shops on either side belonged to carpenters. A recently widowed woman with a two-story house rented out her rooms to earn some income. Three university students, supporters of a communist group named Hezb-e-Toudeh-e-Iran, resided together in the larger upstairs room opposite to mine.

I was the only one wearing a scarf since I still practiced the understanding of Islam that commanded me to cover my hair, but I didn't take it as seriously as before. In fact, something was not working well for me. After the revolution had taken place I had some doubts so that I didn't enjoy my religious practices even though my belief in God was strong.

Our rooms opened to the small upstairs corridor, which we used as our kitchenette. The walls and hallways were covered with pale yellow wallpaper entwined throughout with bright rose blossoms. The only bathroom was at the left corner of the yard, behind an enormous persimmon tree loaded with ripening fruit.

Even though the first thing I saw in the morning through the old window was the bleak tall brick wall of the neighbor, I felt as happy and splendid as the Queen of Sheba, in my room, furnished with one wooden chair and a single bed.

I extended my freedom by purchasing a new five-speed sport bike that I had always wanted. With my bike I could explore the streets of Tehran and attend many political events and speeches throughout the city. Riding a bicycle on streets was not a norm for women, but I didn't want to miss out on these joys of life because of societal restrictions.

Riding my bike as a vehicle also burnt the calories that I now consumed in the delicious meals my landlady often provided. The large plates of basmati rice, its top covered with gourmet stews like Fesenjan, Ghaymeh or Kaleh-Gonjishki, caused my housemates to roll their eyes and complain, "She only gives you these favors."

It wasn't far from the truth. I had purchased a patterned cotton fabric from the bazaar as replacement for her mourning dress, gave her a souvenir of the best grape syrup from Borujerd, and became her favorite tenant.

On November 4th of 1979, I had just returned home from work and was climbing the old stony stairs to my room when I heard a loud gleeful voice emerge from the other room.

The youngest of my three housemates rushed out of the room. "Did you hear the news? The Americans are under arrest and are being held in their embassy by Imam Khomeini's followers."

"Embassy?" I stopped for a moment.

"Yes, they have taken the Americans hostage."

"Really?" I asked as I turned the doorknob to enter to my room.

My housemate's voice changed, carrying a tone of unexpected disappointment,

"Don't you know? The embassy was a nest of CIA spies and organized to overthrow the new regime. I am going to join my friends at the embassy to support the students."

"Wait!" I told her and from the top of the sconce, I grabbed my black and white Russian camera. I ran to join my housemate, tall and tight in her jeans, intellectual-looking with her round eye glasses and modern in her short brown hair. She walked one step ahead of me as I adjusted my scarf when we went on to the embassy, a mile away from our home.

Tehran streets were loaded with cars and pedestrians. The rows of sycamore trees along the sidewalks ranged from green to red then to orange-yellow in the chilly autumn.

We reached Takht-Jamshid Street where a crowd of about 800 young men and women belonging to different political groups had blocked the traffic by standing in front of the main gate. Some were still advancing towards the entrance to the embassy, pumping their fists in the air chanting slogans against America. Others had formed small circles at corners discussing their political views on the hostage taking.

The oldest far left political group since 1941, the Hezb-e-Tudeh, openly supported the attack on the American embassy. The Mujahedin, a paramilitary Muslim group, mobilized their young supporters to engage others in political discussions and to set up bookstands in front of the American embassy. Their female followers dressed neatly in mantos, their hair covered with small dark-blue scarves. The men were cleanly shaven and neatly dressed. The leaders of these groups had spent years in the Shah's political prisons.

Perhaps I was most impressed by the Mujahedin because its members had claimed Islam and at the same time were exploring the possibilities of a shift to democracy. No one including the Mujahedin dared to publicly criticize Khomeini, the far too important religious leader.

I walked closer to the building to look through the embassy's crafted iron gate. At the time people were not permitted to own guns, however the young students who had locked the Americans and themselves inside were well armed. I sensed a familiar face among the guards, but I was shocked when I recognized the bearded young man. He was my sister's brother-in-law, his face enclosed in his warm, knitted hat. When he saw me gasping at the gun he held at his side, he disappeared behind the others.

The next few days I taught school until 2 p.m., and then rushed to the embassy's front door to listen to the political discussions of the smaller crowds who gathered around small fires and stayed awake through the cold Tehran nights to the morning. The tables of books and flyers and the intellectual atmosphere were irresistible. The food-stands sold hundreds of sandwiches and sodas.

I didn't know if taking the embassy was right or wrong, but I felt hope waning, sensing the revolution was heading in the wrong direction.

During the early months of Iran's historical shift from monarchy to republic, Khomeini was at the height of his popularity and power. Every week, thousands of devoted followers entered his place in the famous Refah School, located in an old part of Tehran, to see him seated in a chair on the balcony waving his hand in response to their emotions.

On the other hand, his restrictive religious laws and fatwas didn't satisfy the thirst of the young men and women for a democratic revolution. Even though the majority of people still supported the regime, the situation deteriorated among the younger generation just as the reality of Khomeini's policies surfaced.

The Islamic regime's violation of human rights began when the new leadership executed the former regime's prime minister and the army generals without public trials. Many of us, delirious from the success of the revolution and over throwing the Shah, were unaware of the violation of due process and of the rights of the vanquished leaders of the former regime.

Deep political rifts divided family members, friends and classmates. Thousands of young energetic Muslim youths joined the People's Mujahedin of Iran, which became the largest group opposed to the new regime. In my family, my sister remained a supporter of the new government and Khomeini; two of my cousins became communists; and my cousin Hussein had already joined the Mujahedin.

I had lost my hope in the new regime and turned my back on Khomeini, the revolution's leader who had no commitment to democracy. In my search for an alternative party among the opposition groups, I gradually was convinced that the Mujahedin favored democracy and rejected the fundamentalist interpretation of Islam.

A university student introduced me to their education branch to volunteer for them selling their books and newspapers in the afternoons after my work. Alas, I didn't fully realize their basic philosophy until some years later.

Within less than a year of the ascent of Khomeini, my mother's prediction came true. Local Mullah preachers became mayors, university deans, army sergeants, judges, and senators, leading the country back to the dark ages.

Sadly, the liberty in Iran did not last longer than the blossoms of the cherry trees in spring of 1981. Everything we had fought for in the streets was going to be swept away over years of sorrow and with great loss of lives.

PART 3

My Secret Fiancé

(1981)

At the beginning of spring I took a bus ride back to my parents' home in Borujerd to celebrate the Persian New Year. We had planned to go on vacation to Esfahan, one of the tourist cities in Iran and see the historical Chehelsetoon Palace, the Shah Mosque, Seeosepol and Khajoo Bridge. We then would travel to Bandar Lengeh, a harbor city on the coast of the Persian Gulf in southern Iran, where my father had lived and worked for years as a shoemaker and a minor merchant importing sheepskins for leather factories in Tehran during the hard economic time when he had to seek work outside Borujerd.

Before we left, I went to visit my auntie and her family at her house and found my cousin, Hussein, lounging on a fine Persian carpet in their large living room immersed in a book. It was hard to believe he was the same slender boy who had reenacted the roles of movie characters, changed his voice to make the sound of shooting and punched the pillows to create a fighting scene.

As Hussein and I grew out of childhood, at eighteen, our relationship changed. He was the only boy with whom I had gone out to parties. We had the privilege of dancing together without a problem at wedding celebrations without it being seen as breaking the strict cultural rules governing interaction between the sexes. It was also all right with my family to let me go out with him during summer evenings since he was my cousin.

I was flattered to wear nice clothes and stroll with him on the streets swarming with people. Later in the evening when the streets were not as crowded, Hussein with boyish pride gave me a ride on his luxurious motorcycle. Laughing loudly with excitement, I let down my hair to twist wildly in the wind. The warmth of the streetlights, new shops and boutiques, in addition to the smell of corn roasted on coal barbecues and the scent of fresh summer fruit that wafted in the air satisfied our youthful desires for freedom. We passed the time carelessly and joyfully.

However when I turned nineteen and changed my views, I avoided him, knowing that he had a crush on me from the time we were fifteen. Marriage between cousins was common in Iran, for knowledge of a spouse's family was considered the most important matter in an alliance between a man and woman. Yet, I had refused to accept Hussein's proposals when he sent his mother and my aunt as his messengers. I loved him only as my cousin, I told them.

Everything, including my relationship with Hussein, confirmed that I had changed and now needed to conquer my materialism and vanities. Even though his gentle manner towards me continued, my strong curiosity and my desire to build an ideal world were my all-consuming focus.

I had even hastened to talk to him the day he came to visit me in my room. I looked up into his face searching for words to express my thoughts. A record from the most popular singer, Googoosh, carried my message more strongly than my own words.

> whatever was between us, is all over
> the love of our time doesn't last long
> whatever was between us, is all over

I was astounded at how he responded. He reached his hand for another song. His tall figure was bent over his knees, his face towards me with his eyes downcast, when he played the song.

> I don't know where you come from
> or to what story you belong
> no matter who you are,
> my love for you is a habit
> not being with you, will bring sadness

being with you is peace
whichever land you belong to
or wherever you come from
you bring the reasons for blossoming
take me with you…wherever you go
take me with you

Now, three years had past since we demonstrated against the Shah. The revolution was won with the efforts of millions of participants. Many people and many lives had changed.

Hussein had also changed.

In recent months a vague sweet feeling rose up within me whenever I saw him. I was charmed by everything about him, his look, his gentle manner and his thoughtful eyes. He was unquestionably one of the most handsome among all the men. His lyrical tenor voice with its reflection of his pure honesty had touched me many times while trekking up the mountain trails with groups. His interest in reading theology and politics added to his charm and soon led him to assume leadership in the Mujahedin organization.

He was twenty-three years old now, more than six feet tall, with straight shoulder length hair.

I wondered what would he say if he knew my thoughts and feelings for him had changed? I decided to tease him and to let him know how I felt about him.

"Drowning; a handsome man is drowning!" I whispered poking my head into the room.

Hussein looked up from his book and laughed at me.

"I meant drowning in a book." I walked in.

"Sorry, I didn't see you, Mehri. I heard you were back. When did you arrive?"

"Two days ago," and before he said anything I continued. "But I have to go back home and cry since you haven't paid attention to me."

He laughed again.

"Where is my auntie?"

"There she is," Hussein said. I followed his eyes and looked out the window to see my auntie in the yard. After a warm chat with Hussein I went to spend some time with my auntie, but before I left the room, I turned back and looked into Hussein's kind, intelligent eyes. It was as if I had truly seen him for the first time.

Two hours later, Hussein rang the doorbell of our house. I ran to open the door and invited him in. In his fine gray suit, he looked like a model who had just stepped out of a high-quality fashion show.

My mother was sitting in the living room by the radio, listening to the latest news.

Walking through the hallway, he greeted her and followed me into the next room. He became more serious when he sat down.

"Mehri, I know you are about to leave for vacation," he said, "but I needed to talk to you before you left…"

He wasn't looking at me but at the floor.

"Well…" I waited for him to continue.

"You know how I feel about you. There is no one I could love more than you. Yet friends and family have their ideas about whom I should marry. Even our organization advised me to choose a wife for myself from among the members, but I didn't respond to any of them because I was still thinking of you."

He was good at getting straight to the point. As he paused his eyes became intense. I shook my head knowingly for I had seen how the Mujahedin matched up their higher-ranking females and males. In an important political role, it must have been hard for him to be truthful to his own thoughts and feelings, a rare natural excellence.

"I came here to ask you to marry me." He looked into my eyes. "But I want you to know that this time the quality of my proposal is totally different from the time I sent my mother to propose."

He then waited for my answer while deep lines of worry appeared on his forehead.

Ever since my teenage years, I had wanted to experience romantic love. At that moment, I was certain I could love Hussein dearly if I allowed my feelings to grow. His qualities were the ones I was looking for in a man. Above all was the sweetness of his presence. Since becoming a human-rights activist, he had grown spiritually; I respected him and wanted to have him in my life. I couldn't find anything in him but goodness, but I thought it was necessary for us to experience our relationship in a new way before we tied the knot. I needed at least a year to make sure I had made the right choice.

"Hussein...," I called him. He looked at me intently, "My answer is 'Yes', but only on one condition."

His handsome eyes gleamed as if he was tremendously relieved and he kept breaking into a smile as we continued to talk.

"Let's keep it a secret," I requested. "I think I need to spend more time with you and get to know you more deeply before we make it official."

Even though I had set a condition, I could tell how happy he was at hearing the only thing that mattered to him, "Yes."

I heard him say, "I wish I could come with you all to Esfahan, but I'm too busy. I need to do a lot of work in the next few weeks."

Then he helped me to carry our piled up suitcases to his car to take us to the bus station. At the station, flushed and joyful, he stood outside, just next to my window when the bus driver was getting ready to take off. As the bus pulled away slowly, Hussein strode up to the sidewalk and shook his hands in the air. He then walked towards his car, putting his hands back into his pockets. As we rode away his eyes filled with sadness and his gentle smile disappeared.

On the way to Esfahan, I thought of Hussein. Since I had become a teenager, suitors of all kinds had appeared at our door, with or without notice. Young men in our neighborhood, sons of relatives, my friends' brothers or strangers would send their mothers, aunts and sisters. I refused to see the nominees, who usually were absent in the first visit, when women came to negotiate the matter. My best friend in high school and I had both made the decision to marry only if we first fell in love. But in the end I found my secret fiancé where I had not looked, among my childhood playmates, even before falling madly in love. There was no thought in my mind except to see if my feelings for him were going to mature into love and overcome the anxiety that tinged my certainty.

PART 4

The Iran-Iraq War

(1980-1988)

My parents, my younger sister, Ziba and I stayed in a hotel for five days. On the morning of our last day there, my mother and I went out onto the large balcony, which connected to the Café where they served breakfast.

A thin young man from a border city in the west of Iran was sitting alone at a table perched at the edge of his chair. He had small eyes, an Afro, and dark skin and he was dressed in military clothes covered with dirt. He seemed distressed, looking at faces as if not comprehending why those of us around him were so relaxed. He then spoke loudly to me.

"Iraqi forces have attacked the borders of the state of Khuzestan. Cities are being destroyed. Our beloved Khuzestan is red with blood. I can't understand it. I don't know what to do, but everything seems meaningless to me when I know people are dying."

My father and my sister joined us and listened to the young man who had been on the front lines and continued to lament the Iran-Iraq war that had started six months earlier, in September of 1980. My mother's face filled with fear and she sighed heavily. My sister grew tense and my father listened silently with sorrow in his eyes.

I waited for an opportunity to say something sympathetic.

"Yes, yes, I agree with you about the war," I finally said, "I think the new government doesn't seem to be able to manage the matter properly. As things are now, no one can predict the next disaster in Iran. This war is just another phase of the ancient Persian-Arab conflict over borders. If we had a wise government we wouldn't get into such wars."

It seemed like he had not heard a word of what I had just said. He talked about the threats to the people and the ancient cities in the southwest of the country and prayed for a miracle to stop the bloodshed.

No one paid much attention to him. The men sitting at the next table walked out. The hotel's manager ignored him completely. We apologized to him, saying that we had to leave the hotel to continue our trip and finished our breakfast in a hurry.

The young man had seen the war with his own eyes and wanted to convince people of its pointlessness. As we left, I glanced back and saw him desperately looking around for anyone who would care about the slaughter of warfare.

People from other states including my family and I had not been affected by the war yet. In spite of the massive destruction in the border towns close to Iraq, people in the other states lived their lives denying the existence of the war, no matter how harsh the circumstances were in the war zone.

The streets were filled from morning until late into the night with cars, crowds of shoppers and people going about their daily lives. But the steady stream of refugees flowing in from the border cities was a persistent reminder that life was not really as we wanted to believe it was.

We left Esfahan for the sunny, exotic cities of Southern Iran. In Bandar Lengeh, we stayed at my father's rental house and visited his friends. In the noon heat, we walked to a luncheon at the house of my father's friends. As we passed through the Bazaar, lean, dark skinned women walked hurriedly in floral patterned garments. Their long skirts covered their colorful cool cotton trousers. Some masked their faces with shimmering fabrics embroidered with golden lines of thread. These stood stiff across the bridge of their noses. An open gap let their honey colored eyes see as they carried out their daily tasks.

After spending days of pleasure with my family, I went back to Tehran to the apartment I rented a few months ago. During my absence, my roommate married her fiancé, a member of the Mujahedin and was in the process of moving out.

When I didn't hear from Hussein for a month I wondered what was happening. Thinking about him was my greatest delight every day. With him being seven hours away by car, a long silence might be expected, but not from Hussein. He had swum against the stream and broken the norm of the organization. He waited for me for more than three years and since it was so, I waited for him to explain. There was no telephone at his house so I planned ahead of time to talk to him at my uncle's.

"Well, is this how it is going to be, Hussein? No visit, no phone calls, no nothing?"

"No, no, I'm so sorry Mehri." He responded with all his sweetness.

"I would love to visit you, and I will. Yes, I'll manage my work and take some days off very soon, I am even thinking of moving to Tehran."

"Are you serious, Hussein?"

"Yes, yes," he said, obviously afraid that he had hurt my feelings. "I tell you I can't wait to see you. Don't you ever have any doubt about my feelings for you. Never, please."

Since I volunteered for the Mujahedin I knew how hard it was making time for personal matters. Members who worked long hours in Mujahedin centers had to decide their lives according to the needs of the organization, and Hussein, a high-ranking member, couldn't easily give priority to his own wish to travel to Tehran.

In a free society there are laws ensuring that the rights of the people are protected. In America these rights are enshrined in the Constitution and are declared to be inalienable.

But this is not the case in authoritarian nation-states. In an authoritarian system, unquestioning obedience to the state and its leaders is not only demanded, but harshly enforced by the regime's police, its military and judiciary. Individual freedom is an anathema because it allows for dissent, and dissent leads to rebellion. Neither can be tolerated. Both must be crushed. Those who speak out are swiftly and mercilessly punished. Soon the word spreads and people watch what they say or keep their mouths shut.

I didn't really understand this when I was 22, nor did many of my generation.

The same week that Hussein planed to visit me in Tehran, the axe fell on free speech as the Iranian theocratic regime issued new laws banning the free exercise of publishing rights. As if to leave no doubt about its willingness to enforce the new laws, the government targeted three popular newspapers that covered political opinion and dissent. Meanwhile, political gatherings throughout the city were being disrupted or even attacked by supporters of the regime. Opposition groups decided to fight back, believing that if liberty were to survive, passivity was not an option. Ignoring the newly instituted laws, the Mujahedin enlisted teams of young activists to find subscribers for their now illegally published newspapers.

Of course, I volunteered.

I believed it was the right thing to do. We had to do something. And if not us—who else would step up? I was 22 and starry-eyed. I had not even dreamt that there could be some grave connected to what I was about to do. How bad could it be to go door-to-door, trying to sell subscriptions? Yes, illegal subscriptions. But still...

Perhaps I might have stopped in my tracks had I known more about the strange man whose forbidding face glowered down from a hundred giant murals and facades throughout the city of Tehran.

But I knew very little about Khomeini or his strangeness. It seemed many of my countrymen were suffering from the same malady: acute ignorance. We Iranians, who had been so joyful and full of hope after the 1979 Revolution, had believed we were on the verge of a new era. An era of freedom wherein the rights of the people would be protected. Rights which, as the American Constitution declares, cannot be morally taken away.

Yet, by now it was becoming apparent that the regime was not especially interested in freedom or human rights. Some may have thought that it had changed, that it had strayed from its original good intentions. This of course was not the case. Like a vulture that is oblivious to its carrion-stained head, the regime was merely now revealing what it had always been. In the two years after the overthrow of the Shah, the Khomeini regime hadn't publicly exercised the ruthless control that would soon follow. We later learned that behind the scenes it was busy consolidating power via liquidation of its enemies. My mother's warnings about the mullahs, delivered some three years earlier to a doubting nineteen-year-old, were beginning to seem prescient.

PART 5

Good Bye Freedom

(1981)

It was a hot afternoon of May 1981, two and a half years after the Islamic Republic was declared. I had just arrived home from work at 2 in the afternoon, when hot air blasted through the open window indicating the spring was about to end.

I had to hurry. I grabbed some money from my purse, shoved my apartment key to the bottom of my pocket, covered my hair with a small blue scarf and rushed out the door. I flagged down a taxi and rode towards Tehran University where I was about to meet two members of our advertising team. We were going to sign up subscribers for a pro-democracy newspaper, even though it was banned by the new regime.

The driver pushed his way through the heavy traffic, squeezing into gaps between cars that belched blue grey exhaust. People hurried down the crowded sidewalks alongside Tehran University, where more than one hundred small bookstores displayed piles of books by Kafka, Dostoyevsky, Marx, Lenin, Tolstoy, Marquez, Hemingway, and Jack London. This crowded part of the city was the most popular place in the heart of Central Tehran.

In the circles of young people heated by political arguments, I spotted Nasim's tall figure in a black chador, an outfit often worn by women who supported the Islamic regime. I cautiously walked down from where the taxi dropped me off. She looked up at me quickly and we both hurried to Kati at the corner of the intersection, to find her glancing around for us.

Nasim stood in her chador, at the corner of the block as lookout to survey our surroundings for any possible threats by the Revolutionary Guards. Kati and I went to ring the doorbells. We talked to people with no success until we arrived at the tenth house.

A man of about twenty-six in a white t-shirt and blue jeans opened the door. He leaned his tall torso to one side and poked his head out of the doorway, pointing to his left, "The neighbor a few houses down is the head of a jail run by the Revolutionary Guards." He then dodged behind the door and continued, "You must be careful, if he knows why you are here he will cause you trouble, for he hates the opposition groups."

The neighbor he referred to lived in the first house we'd approached where a rough-looking bearded man had chastised us. We thanked the young man and turned around to cross the street in search of more subscribers. We both knew well that no matter what happened, we wouldn't quit our work as long as breath was in our lungs. We were determined to complete our task as believers in democracy and a better life for the people.

People heading home from work crowded the sidewalks, honking cars whizzing by in both directions. We were about to reach the sidewalk when an old white car screeched to a stop beside Kati and me.

Five men dressed in black stormed out and surrounded us. We both stepped to the sidewalk to get away. One of them pointed to the opened door of the old Iranian car and yelled, "Get in. You stupid girls, get into the car,"

"Why?" I asked.

"You are upsetting the residents in this neighborhood."

"And who are you? What we are doing has nothing to do with you," Kati said.

A young man saw us argue and confronted the men in black, "What are you doing? Leave them alone."

The men in black pushed the young man several times and tightened the circle around Kati and me. Other pedestrians gawked, encircling us, but Kati, the young man, and I were forced through the crowd into the backseat of their car. Two of the men in black jumped in the front and the driver raced the engine, changed gears and pulled out into the street.

Through the window I saw Nasim walking in the same direction the car was traveling. She tried to run, but struggled to move her feet fast enough inside her chador. Surely she was going to call and report our arrest to the Mujahedin, the organization we volunteered for as their sympathizers.

In the backseat, I was in the middle, and Kati and the young man were on either side. When the car turned onto the main street towards the jail, the driver slowed down, passing through the crowded street near the bookstores.

As usual, people and students were standing around in small groups discussing politics. Because the sidewalk was too crowded, they had moved into the street. The driver had to stop, as the street was jammed with people and cars.

Suddenly, the young man and then Kati opened the doors, jumped out, and disappeared like two drops of water in the ocean.

I slid towards my right to reach the opened door, but before I could, the men in the front got out, shoved me back and sat on either side of me. I saw a number of people move towards the car to help me. The men locked the doors. The driver stepped on the gas forcing his way through the crowd.

One of the men grabbed my scarf and pushed my head down hard. My neck hurt. I tried to break away by twisting my head to the right.

"Don't move." The man on my right side said and punched me in the face. He pressed my head down even harder. I struggled for breath. The man's hand, wet and coarse, kept pushing my head down. I struggled, humiliated.

A few minutes later, the car stopped in front of the closest jail. The men hustled me inside a yard, into the custody of a bearded young guard and left.

A one story old house with tall brick walls had been altered to become a jail. From the jail yard, the guard walked me to an office where a middle-aged man in an army uniform was busy talking on the phone at a desk. He ignored me and continued his conversation.

I sat by the window. Many metal chairs were scattered around the room but no one was there except me. I waited for the man to finish his call, so I could object to my arrest. The guard stood by the door, watching his boss. A few posters were hung on the walls. The largest was Khomeini, in the center behind the man.

I touched my face where it was sore and noticed that my nose was bloody. I asked the guard to let me go to the bathroom to wash my face. He nodded his head and pointed to the door. On the way to the bathroom, I noticed there were no guards in the narrow hallway. I whirled around, walked deliberately towards the door and stepped down the three stairs to the jail yard. A guard with a gun in his hands had blocked the gate to the street.

As my foot touched the ground, I heard a whistle from behind. I didn't turn around, but saw the armed guard move to one side. I continued to walk.

As I got closer to the door, I saw cars and pedestrians. They weren't going to stop me. I walked right by the guard and out of the jail compound in disbelief.

The only thought in my head was to get out of the area. I waved at several empty taxis passing by me on the busy street, but they didn't stop. It was unusual. Suddenly I realized my bloody face must have scared them and they didn't want trouble. Finally, a minibus stopped.

The moment I stepped up on the first rung, I noticed a few men about seventy yards away. I rushed to get in when I saw they were the same men who had arrested me. I had no idea what they might do after they had just seen me getting on the minibus. It was too late to change my mind. The minibus started up.

I took a seat in the middle of the bus and waited. Through the front window, I could see the men in black step into the street to wave down the minibus. I knew then they could recapture me, but I had no choice except to wait and see what would happen next.

When they moved to block the minibus, I stood and urged the driver, "Please don't stop. Those men will hurt or arrest me." The driver looked at me through his mirror and laughed sarcastically and stopped right in front of the men. I turned around to ask for help from the passengers. Then I noticed I was not in a normal transportation minibus. There were no women and all the passengers were from the countryside and under eighteen. They must have been members of the Basij, a paramilitary volunteer militia, established by the Islamic regime. In a normal minibus, I would have found men and women to help me.

Men from the gang rushed onto the minibus and blocked the exit. One of the men ordered the driver to carry on. A half mile farther, they told the driver to stop in front of the main entrance to Tehran University. I checked out the window on my side. It was impossible to get out. The men in black pointed to me and moved aside to escort me down.

I studied the innocent faces of the young country boys who had no idea what was happening and laughed as if something funny was going on. I walked reluctantly towards the exit. There was no room for protesting.

The main university gate was occupied by about twenty men in black with shaved heads and heavy bodies. Men cursing the enemies of the regime walked in and out of a tent set up outside the gate. The university's fenced wall prevented people from entering. A brand new black Mercedes Benz was parked near the entrance.

The sidewalks were strewn with shredded books, magazines, and circulars of pro-democracy newsletters the men had already destroyed. As people hurried by, the torn up papers that covered the ground flew up into the air like autumn leaves. The thoughts of my longing for a better country choked my throat. How could I ever imagine during the demonstrations against the Shah that this would happen? Only two and a half years after the Shah, horror was back in new cloth.

The black clad men transferred me to the Mercedes Benz and put me in the backseat then five of them got into the car. Two of them pressed into the passenger's seat beside the driver. Two heavy-set men about thirty-years-old sat on my right. Their rounded stomachs caused their shirts to stretch to the point that the buttons appeared ready to pop off. Their sweat made big wet circles under their arms.

A sturdy man in the front seat turned towards me, his eyes wide open under two thick black rising eyebrows, "Those useless

Revolutionary Guards couldn't keep you in jail, but we have a better idea. I promise you! You will be better served at Evin!"

The man's yellowish teeth that showed off in his crooked mocking smile disappeared as he rounded his tongue over his dry lips.

The car moved towards Evin up near the line of mountains in Northern Tehran. Evin, known as a prison of torture, ironically means "home" in Turkish. This infamous prison was filled with political prisoners and intellectuals for decades under the Shah.

How had I ended up here in one of the worst prisons in the world? A young teacher, raised by loving parents in a society which shelters girls. What brought me to this dangerous place?

The driver passed the Tehran University, which used to be the center of democratic meetings and speeches right after the revolution. Now Tehran's best university was the stage for men in black.

The new regime purged the universities for the government's "Cultural Revolution" in education in the first few months of their theocratic rule. All of the universities in the country were closed indefinitely. Numerous professors were fired and considered as either disloyal or intellectual. That was why I, like many, lost my teaching position at school. I was reassigned as an office secretary in another school where my students would not be able to contact me.

And now, I was simply in the hands of hoodlums riding towards a prison under the new regime, not at all aware of the bloody blister that would soon burst all over Iran from home to home, street to street, and city to city.

I looked out of the corner of my eye at the two men beside me. Their faces were puffy and their clothing disheveled. They were not religious looking. They had no beards and they didn't look down around women, as did the shier supporters of the regime. I pulled myself away from the man at my side and caved silently into the seat. When they leaned towards each other whispering something I couldn't hear, a fear grew within me that they were kidnaping me.

I looked out the window and noticed we had left the metropolitan area. I was unfamiliar with this part of Tehran and was not sure where we were going. Cars sped past us on the highway.

The younger man in the front seat had a darker complexion and Afro hair and seemed to come from one of the three famous cities in southwest Iran. To distract the men, I asked him if he was coming from Ahvaz.

He turned to face me, his small dark eyes round with sudden fear, evidencing that I was right. He had panicked.

"How do you know me?" he inquired in a southern dialect. The others stopped whispering.

"That's it. She knows him," the man sitting next to me said and nodded with regret.

"I have relatives in Ahvaz and know the accent," I told the men even though they didn't seem to believe me.

My throat became dry and I was aware of my fast heartbeat. From the impression they were making I didn't know what these men were going to do. Until the long walls of Evin Prison appeared I didn't take my eyes off them.

The sun was about to set in the late afternoon. From my window I saw the road I passed by every Friday with my friends to reach a hiking pathway towards the Alborz mountain. Hiking was a national pastime in Iran, and Darake had become the most popular trail after the revolution. Hikers increased in numbers and young people walked the road in groups. While many hikers went up in late morning, the early birds came down. Some of us had trekked through the Alborz before the revolution and looked back over the city as we sang revolutionary songs for the freedom of our country.

Along the trail, there were many cozy traditional restaurants. The air was always filled with the smell of barbecued beef and chicken. A narrow river of clear cold water flowed through the mountain and cascaded over rocks. A row of poplar trees was drenched in sunlight, their leaves flickering with the cool breeze.

The Mercedes entered the canyon road and the driver slowed down in front of the prison gate and honked two times.

The men in the front seat stepped out to talk to the guard. The sentry dressed in army clothes rubbed the rifle he cradled in his arm then opened the small door located at the side of the gate, poked his head into a room and talked to someone. A man in civilian dress with a strip of long grayish fabric in his hand came out and walked towards us. He nodded to the men, passed the coarse rag through the window to the guy next to me.

"Blindfold her." He said.

The huge iron gate screeched and the car engine started. The car entered the prison grounds then stopped again. Someone from outside opened the door on my side. Blindfolded and alone, I walked into Evin, a prison no one should ever see.

PART 6

Early Days in Prison

(1981)

Inside the prison a man guided me into a room, left and locked the door behind him. As soon as I took off my blindfold the reality of old Evin surfaced in the silence of the empty room. My first thought was, "How long will I be imprisoned here?" I had already learned about the struggles of political prisoners in the Shah's prisons, but I had no idea what lay ahead of me in the not yet officially established institutions of Islamic law. I understood quite well that it was not easy to fight men who made their way by force, with no concern for others' rights.

I paced from one end of the empty room to the other. It was the time to think of what I had been told to do if I were arrested. Following the instruction of my team leader in the organization, I had to object to my arrest and give the guards a hard time.

I knocked on the door and waited. It was sad, but true, that I heard nothing from the other side. I knocked on the door again for almost five minutes, the knocking making a coarse noise that echoed in absolute silence. I debated if I should continue knocking on the door or remain quiet. When I knocked nonstop and insistently with the heel of my shoe I finally detected faint, barely recognizable words through the noise I was making.

"What do you want, my daughter?" a voice asked me.

I stopped knocking and from the other side a chunky old man with bright blue eyes, dressed in army clothes, appeared at the doorway.

"Books," I said. "I'm bored in here."

"What books would you like to get?"

After I gave myself a moment to think of a writer whose books would be possible, "Mr. Taleghani's interpretations of the Quran," I said.

Mr. Taleghani was considered a progressive mullah, famous for his advanced understanding of Islam, so I wasn't sure if the guard would bring me the book, but a few minutes later, he returned and handed me the first volume of the series I had asked for.

I spent much time reading the book, but in spite of all the respect I had for the writer, I found it too technical and wordy. For each simple verse there were many pages of written description. This may have been my tenth time reading his books, considered as the best exegesis of the Quran, yet it still didn't make sense to me. This was a problem. The truth of the Quran was kept hidden by religious leaders and scholars out of their own ignorance. They had created false doctrines based on indefensible nonsensical traditions.

It was harmful for a religious society like Iran to follow any leaders' opinions instead of the Quran. At the time, I myself was led by books and leaders. I didn't know the extreme significance in the Quran of advocating peace, demonstrating tolerance and patience. I didn't know that it says I should never engage in any aggressive step and that I was individually responsible for my decisions.

With mixed feelings about bothering the old man who had unexpectedly acted like a father rather than a guard, I continued knocking on the door under one pretext or another.

At night the kind old guard gave me three grey army blankets. I folded one in half and placed it on the floor against the wall and rolled one into a pillow. I slept on the floor to wake up in the morning with a stiff body. I stretched and exercised before a new guard brought me a breakfast of white bread, butter, and tea.

I then heard a knock on the door by a guard who commanded me to put on my blindfold and go with him into a large office with about ten men sitting behind separate desks. One in civilian clothes in his late thirties sat opposite me. His sparse hair was combed from one side to another to cover his baldness. A brass ashtray, some papers and a black telephone sat on his desk.

"Your name?" he asked me.

I made no answer. Staring at me, he waited. I wondered if he knew the strategy of the Mujahedin's followers. Just before I was arrested, our team leader told me. "If you get arrested, don't even tell them your name. Take the upper hand. Give them no right to question you."

"The reason for getting arrested?" The interrogator asked while he controlled his frustration with a fake smile.

I looked around. Nobody else paid attention to us. When the light in his eyes began to disappear, I looked into his face and began to talk.

"Isn't that why we opposed the Shah, to bring freedom? Why are you arresting us for speaking out? I won't tell you anything, even my name. I must object to my illegal imprisonment."

He inhaled his cigarette smoke, puffing out small circles with a mocking gesture. Like a young father dealing with a rebellious daughter, the interrogator smoked his cigarette to the end while I confidently repeated the Mujahedin line.

I was unaware that the last lights of freedom were flickering and would soon fade away altogether and that I was giving the wardens more excuse to justify my imprisonment.

"Brother," the interrogator called for the guard as he walked towards the door to open it, "Take her back to the cell."

Life was going on without my knowing what my next day would be like. I was in prison, where my mother feared I would end up for reading books. She had often yelled at me when, as a fifteen year old, I read novels late at night, "Do you want to be political and end up in jail?"

I awoke on the second day in prison to spend the day doing nothing but trying to find means of disturbing the guards with the hope that they would release me. In the evening I knocked incessantly on my cell door for ten minutes, until there was a sudden noise of the door opening.

A tall, handsome man in his late thirties, dressed in beige colored jeans stepped in to find me right at the door. His large eyes coarsened with anger. He raised his hand and slapped me hard across the face.

"Are you making noise in Evin?" He said then blindfolded me with a fast movement and pulled me out of the cell.

"I am going to take you to Ghasr, a suitable prison for *monafeghin.*"

He, as all the regime's men did, called the Mujahedin and their supporters, *monafeghin*, an Arabic word for "hypocrites," believing that the Mujahedin had mixed Islam with Marxism.

I utterly forgot the pain and shame of being beaten, for the prison he mentioned was a place for criminals, thieves, and prostitutes, a much more frightening prison than Evin. I worried about how I would deal with the type of women I had always been warned to avoid. Making my way through the hallways to the back of a covered truck or van, I had no idea that this man was the first post-revolutionary warden of Evin prison, Kachwie, who would be assassinated a few weeks later.

Kachwie drove the vehicle off quickly. I had no sense of place or direction, but I heard the noise of the traffic and honking for about an hour until the car stopped, and the creak of heavy doors opening replaced the traffic noises.

Kachwie guided me out by pulling my sleeve, and we passed through several doors and hallways. When a guard asked for my belongings, I handed him my watch and money and kept my apartment key hidden in my pocket to drop it in the toilet at the first chance.

"Silence is the rule in here," Kachwie said before he slammed the door and locked it.

I took off my blindfold in a bare old cell, its length twice my height. The dirty windowpane hadn't been opened for decades and no sounds from outside came through the thick dirty walls. I began to understand that I wouldn't be returned to my home, and I should get prepared for not seeing my fiancé, my family and friends for a few months. I gradually recollected the last news I had heard in the days before my arrest. The Islamic regime had announced a maximum prison sentence of six months for selling banned newspapers. Even if I did not carry any newspapers, I assumed that would be the greatest length for my prison sentence.

I decided to say my night prayers and not to poison my mind with despair. I needed first to wash my face, hands and feet, a mandatory preparation for the prayers. I took off my pair of thin socks and knocked on the door once. I walked away from the door and waited.

Kachwie returned and looked me up and down under the cell's fluorescent, staring at my pair of tasteful leather-strapped shoes showing my toes on my now bare feet.

"Ohhhh," he said as if he was speaking to others. "She is a fashion girl,"

As traditional Muslims believe women must keep their feet covered, his judgment of me as even worse than a possible activist showed in his mocking voice. I took my socks out of my pocket, opened my hands, and murmured, "I wanted to do my ablutions."

After I finished my prayers a good-looking young man with a sparse beard and innocent large eyes, like those of Jesus in his depictions, brought me a bowl of soup and some water in a plastic cup. When he came back for the empty bowl, gently and carefully he sat down on the bare grayish floor, pushed the hair off his forehead and adjusted his back against the wall.

"What do you care for Mujahedin?" he asked me softly, pronouncing the word Mujahedin with disgust.

"Because they defend the poor," I said.

"You're speaking of the poor, but Imam Khomeini is the one who really cares for the poor," he responded.

"Let's say that is the case, but why doesn't the regime honor people with the freedom our revolution deserves? Why are political prisons in use if we have a democratic society? How do you guarantee our country won't fall back into a dictatorship when the new government doesn't allow liberty for all the different groups?"

"But the Mujahedin are enemies of our leader rather than human right's activists. They are not Muslim as they claim, but hypocrites. The political groups are being deceived by foreign countries. They want to overthrow our godly regime with the dream of a social system like the Russians want."

"All we want is a better society for all. That's all that matters to me and I don't understand why we should be oppressed for demanding our rights."

"You're honest in what you are saying," he said shaking his head as if his remorse had increased. He left the cell after a half an hour, a gentle tenderness spreading in his face.

May 25, was my third day in prison, a day I remembered well because the founders of the Mujahedin were executed nine years before on that day in 1972, during the Shah's time. The organization had made this day a memorial day, exclusively in memory of the founders.

It was an established ritual among Mujahedin followers to sing in their honor. I stood up and straightened my shoulders to sing a revolutionary song. Only a few seconds later, three men stormed into my cell. Before I had a chance to see their faces, one of them struck my face hard with the palm of his hand. A strange sharp light flashed behind my eyes and my head jerked to one side, pain exploding in my face. The same man shoved me onto the floor, straddled me and continued slapping me, left and right. He then rolled me onto my stomach, tied my hands and feet and blindfolded me. He shoved a rag in my mouth and lashed a stack of small towels onto my face tightening them with a rope.

The binding of the rope around my head and face was so tight that it cut into my skin at the temples. I could hardly breathe. I was left on the floor and the door was locked. I heard a death rattle from my chest as if I were taking my last breaths. I couldn't think, but felt each passing second more acutely. I was in the last moments of my life and counted every second with the sound of each weak breath, each slower than the one before. Suddenly the door banged open and the voices and footsteps in the room brought me back to the world.

I was still alive.

Someone quickly untied the rope that had clamped the towels over my face. I gulped the air for a few seconds before he put the rag back in my mouth. After unfastening my feet, he took me out of the cell, blindfolded, and dragged me down a narrow stairway. On the way, an older voice picked on someone in a jeering tone, "Look at him! Wipe your tears, man."

One of the guards was crying, but who was he? I wondered. Perhaps the young man who gave me food, talked to me, and looked like Jesus. The one I never saw again. He must have believed I was not an enemy of the people.

Descending many more stairs, they took me to a room and tied me to a metal bar in a spread-eagle position. Gagged and blindfolded I was left there thirsty and hungry.

I was exhausted, drowned in my own thoughts for what must have been hours. Suddenly my body trembled and I stiffened when all at once I felt two hands move over my breasts. I tried to scream. But the only sound that came out of my mouth was, "Mummm... mumm." The rope was strapped too tightly across my mouth. Again, I tried to yell, but my voice came out muffled. Then I heard quick footsteps leaving the room. It was terrifying. I would never have thought that a conservative government would use sexual abuse as a method of torture. I had trusted the guards in this regard, and all the men I had met in prison seemed to be religious.

I heard other footsteps coming towards me. Sweat dripped down my back soaking my clothes. Two hands removed the ropes and rags from my face, but didn't remove the blindfold. I shivered, and wished someone were here to help me. Alas, no one, not even my family, knew where I was and what was happening to me.

"Are you going to break the rules again?" a man's voice said through gritted teeth as he grabbed my scarf and hair and banged my head against the bar. My lips quivered and my eyes filled with tears, but I said nothing. He untied my hands and led me out by pulling me by my sleeve.

Relief.

I had thought this moment would never come. I let my arms down and placed my feet together. My body was in pain, but I was grateful to be unbound.

It had been three days since I was arrested. The cells were hot and I needed to bathe badly. As the man who had untied me led me out of that place, I asked with hesitation if I could take a shower. A few minutes later a woman's voice ordered me to remove my blindfold.

I found myself inside a very small shower stall, where a tall young woman with dark skin stood just outside. She had short wavy hair under a gray print chador placed far back on her head — a blank expression on her face, her eyes cold and indifferent. "She must be one of those women," I thought, remembering that Kachwie told me he would put me in Ghasr, the thieves and prostitute's prison.

"Hurry up," she said.

There was no door on the shower stall. "What if that bad man comes in?" I thought and asked the woman if she would stay at the door. "I will be very quick taking my shower. I promise."

"Would you, please?" I asked the woman again.

"I'm here," she replied in a curt voice and handed me a white towel. I couldn't really trust her, but I had no choice. I quickly unbuttoned my manto, took off my jeans and left them on a chair in the corner. I walked into the shower in my underwear and turned the knob to let the water run on my face and drank from the hot water feeling each drop sinking into my flesh. Looking back, I noticed that the woman had disappeared. I stared at the entrance, fearing the bad man's return. I used the soap in one fast movement over my body then washed my hair. I didn't blink until it was all done in less than three minutes.

I used the towel, but my body was still wet and water dripped from my hair as I secured myself in the same manto and jeans I had worn when I'd been arrested. Then I noticed a blurred image of a pale face with crimson spots under the eyes appearing through the steam. I touched my face. My left eye was blood shot and a purple bruise had spread across my cheek. I was looking at myself in the shower's steamy mirror.

A short, heavy woman covered in a chador showed up. The long line of an old, deep scar on her cheek was a sign of injury from nasty violence, either by a knife or an another sharp object. Surprised at seeing me dressed so soon, she jerked the wet towel from my hand to drop it over my face. Her eyes disappeared as she quickly covered mine.

"What time is it?" I asked.

"Eight," she replied indifferently.

No wonder I was so hungry. I had been tied to the bar for eleven hours. She dragged me out of the shower into another room.

"Wait in here," she said into my ear.

I didn't dare remove the towel on my face, feeling that it wasn't something I should do. Pushing my eyes wide open under the layers of the wet towel was in vain. I could see nothing.

In a few seconds, I felt a presence. The towel covering my face was slowly removed as a groom gently removes a veil from a bride's face.

A pair of lustful, carnal eyes appeared gradually from behind the towel. My heart dropped. A man with a shaved head was leering at me. A smile had spread on his face and desire filled his eyes; it was similar to what I had seen in a movie and had never forgotten. After a close up of the actor's glossy eyes, the scene had shown a girl falling to the floor, sobbing after being raped.

My whole body was shaking. The man standing in front of me had big muscles. He stood with his face close to mine. Now, I was certain he was the same one who had touched me earlier when I was tied up.

In a second, the noise of footsteps from outside the room prompted the man to drop the towel back onto my face and run out. I was still shivering in fear, my eyes peeled for someone to enter. The smell of hot food and basmati rice filled the room. A familiar voice told me to remove the towel.

"You must be very hungry," he said.

His soft tone of voice made me feel better. I lifted the towel off my face. A man with an olive complexion, light brown hair, and amber eyes handed me a plate of food and left. After he locked the door, I fell on the old wooden chair in the empty room. Piles of gold and silver could not have made me happier than that moment of relief — seeing the steam rising off the rice, and the eggs, with a froth of bubbles in the whites, as they lay on the top.

After I finished swallowing the food, the man with amber eyes came back with another guard. They blindfolded me and took me inside a very strange, dirty cell and left. The ceiling of the small room was as high as a three-story building with no windows, a sloppily painted narrow door in the corner.

"This cell opens to the guard's room," the man said from behind the closed door to reiterate that I should be quiet.

Whether it was part of my punishment or not I felt grateful that the guards were nearby so that the man whom I feared wouldn't get into my cell. Later, I realized that the bad man, the tall woman who took me to the shower, and the woman with a deep scar on her cheek must have been common convicts who were trustees and worked there.

I drifted off on a grey army blanket until morning. Early the following day a guard knocked on the door, took me out so I could do my ablutions, and returned me to the cell for the dawn prayer. I got some bread, butter, and a cup of tea for breakfast and swallowed them all.

Three more days passed before I thought I shouldn't let them think I had given in, and decided to continue singing revolutionary songs even though I knew it would result in punishment. The song that came to my mind was the one my friends and I used to sing hiking in the mountains, back in those hopeful days. The verses told of commitment in the fight for liberty. "Sing. Sing with me my friend. Sing with me a song. Sing until the night. I would paint the walls of darkness red with my blood." My voice resonated from the high ceiling. Since I didn't see any reaction I continued to sing two more songs until the door swung opened suddenly.

A young man with a full curly black beard, dressed in an army uniform and boots, rushed to get into my cell, but the man who had brought me eggs and rice the previous night blocked his entrance.

The guard in army clothes obeyed him after his physical challenge and complained. "She's singing all the time."

With my back against the wall, I sat on the blanket on the floor, my hands laced together over my knees. The man with the soft voice, sat just inside the door as if he had authority over the other.

"What are you doing? Are you practicing singing?"

I shrugged at him ignoring his question, for I felt embarrassed, and demanded some paper and a pen.

"Paper and pen? What are you going to do with them?"

"Write poems."

As he stood to leave, I asked him for a toothbrush. "It's been a week since I have brushed my teeth."

Morad was the warden of the prison. He was always wearing jeans and sneakers. The next day he brought me two sheets of paper, a pen and a toothbrush. He then took me out of the cell with my blindfold in place. I was led to where a doctor tended to me and gave me simple instructions to use warm water and salt to cure my nose, which still hurt. When I was leaving, I heard a girl with a northern accent cry out to the doctor.

"Doctor, I haven't seen the sun for ten days," she said. "Please, it's so difficult, Doctor. It's so difficult," she repeated.

"Not seeing the sun is the least price we can pay for restoring our freedom," was all I could think of.

The guard took me to the bathroom three times a day, and I washed my injured nose with salt water until it healed.

A week had passed since Kachwie transferred me from Evin.

Morad, the warden, came back and sat right at the door asking me what I did with the pen and paper. I handed him two pages of poems, expecting a harsh reaction for writing in defense of liberty against the regime. He read it quietly and smiled.

"We should send your poems out to get published," he teased and returned the papers. I had little hope that he would.

Despite his kindness, I knew I would never tell him about what the pervert had done. I was twenty-two, but like many Iranian girls, I didn't have any sexual experience. It was a rule that girls and boys did not have relationships with the opposite sex before marriage. This religious value had become an Iranian cultural tradition. Even non-religious families respected the matter and took it seriously. I was too embarrassed to describe to him what had happened and I didn't want to give the enemy any idea about what disturbed me the most, my "Achilles' Heel". I had learned from books that the enemy used such methods to break prisoners.

I couldn't continue ignoring the prison rules after Morad had treated me in a friendly manner. Because of his kindness, I felt uncomfortable singing and breaking his rules.

In my cell I looked at a narrow piece of blue sky through a one-foot long crack in the high ceiling or at a few words written and scratch marks from past prisoners on the old dirty wall. From those aged remarks, I learned to carve a line to represent each day I remained in prison. I spent most of my time dreaming about escaping from prison and surprising everyone who hadn't heard from me for weeks. It became the normal routine for the next days to think of Hussein, and the simple sweet things I had argued about with my mother.

In prison, I was completely out of touch with the outside world. I didn't know if my friends, my family and fiancé knew where I was. I paced in my cell thinking about escaping. But the thick walls, the solid ground, and the locked doors showed there was no way out.

A few times Morad came to my cell to talk to me about the revolution in a forthright and calm manner. I didn't understand why these subjects couldn't be discussed in a civilized way outside of the prison. Why wasn't there room for opposing points of view? Would any of these people who were now in power take responsibility for taking us back to another dictatorship? Under the circumstances, it was difficult to answer these questions. Caught in the midst of the upheaval, I didn't have enough knowledge or perspective to comprehend the reasons behind all this chaos.

It was difficult to work out in that hot humid cell, for I could only take quick showers once a week. Yet, I exercised every day, did my daily prayers and paced in the cell for hours. There was nothing else to do except dream.

Three times I had to put the same unwashed manto on after my shower until the curly bearded guard gave me a loose grayish manto so I could wash my own.

Aside from a guard who brought me food three times a day and took me out of the cell to use the bathroom, Morad was the only person I saw and then only when he came to my cell. On one of those days a sudden flashback to the man who had beaten me appeared in front of my eyes.

"Oh, my God," I said when Morad was talking to me. "It was you who beat me the first morning. Now I remember your face."

Morad's face suddenly flushed red and his smile vanished. He denied that he was the one, but his timid tone of voice confirmed that it was he. I had no doubt.

Morad left and he didn't return again.

Twenty-eight days after my incarceration, I was sitting alone in my cell when I noticed the smell of burning rubber. A faint sound of a crowd chanting in the distance sounded just like the rallies of the days before the revolution. The voices of people faded in and out. I couldn't understand the slogans, but without a doubt, the smell of burnt tires was a sign of protest.

The following day they transferred me to a cell with another prisoner of about twenty, dressed in a colorful blouse and blue jeans, but no scarf. I could not help asking if she smelled the burnt tires or heard the chanting of the people the day before. She hadn't, but her eyes shined with happiness for she believed people were protesting against the regime. She surged forward and hugged me. She put her hand over her short hair and pushed it behind her ears. Her white skin looked brighter on her delicate face.

"My name is Sahar. I am from Tabriz," she said proudly.

"No, please don't tell me your information. I haven't given my name to the wardens."

"No worry, Sahar is not my real name."

She then put her hands in her pockets and gazed at me with thoughtful eyes. "We should find you a name. Solmaz! I'll call you Solmaz, a flower that never dies. That's what it means in my mother tongue, Azari."

In fact my official name was Fatemeh, but before I was born my mother had wished to call me Mehri.

Sahar was supporter of a small guerrilla group. She hadn't succeeded in getting her family to support her belief in communism and left her parents' home in Tabriz without permission to join her group in Tehran. She was amazingly pure, energetic and a good human being.

When I read my poem for Sahar she listened to it eagerly and wanted to tuck away the poem with the hope that we could find it after our release when prisons became historical museums. That was our prediction. The new Iranian government would collapse soon and the peoples' wishes for a democratic regime would become a reality.

There was a small hole, a bit larger than a quarter, in the screen of double-glazed window. Sahar, who was light and agile, stepped into my clasped hands to drop the poem into the empty space between the two panes, while I was swaying to the left and right.

Two days later when Sahar and I knocked on the door, to use the bathroom outside of the regular scheduled times, it caused us a problem. The guards removed me from her cell while one of the escorting guards was cursing me.

"Damn you. If you were my sister I'd cut your head off with a knife, for you would be my shame."

"Leave her alone, Brother," I heard the other guard say, preventing him from attacking me. They tied me up to a bar for hours, to the point that sweat broke out on my forehead. I was about to faint when a guard gave me some water, untied my hands and put me in a new cell at last.

Three days later a tall skinny man, covered with a white hood over his head giving me no chance to see his face, came into my cell. His striped shirt was hanging out over his dark trousers. He stared at me with his brown eyes through small holes. A deep breath of air showed his struggle to begin.

"Do you confirm that you're a supporter of the Mujahedin?" he asked.

"Yes," I replied.

"Do you agree to write this down on paper and sign it?"

"Of course."

Oddly, he seemed satisfied with my answer and rocked his head from side to side, hastily to avoid eye contact.

"All right. I'll be back with the paper."

Before he left the room in a hurry, he gave me a look full of horror.

I waited, but the man with the hood never came back. There was no reason for me to hide my political persuasion even in front of a deadly beast in a white hood.

A few days later in the middle of the night, the guards took me out blindfolded to the back of a van or a truck where I sensed the presence of others. In the complete darkness, the sounds of other women breathing made me feel comfortable. At least I was not alone.

The guards' worried voices sounded as if they were about to carry important hostages. The car took off with many security precautions and the guards spoke in low voices, expecting an attack.

After a while, they relaxed and started to talk to one another. I heard Morad talking and telling the other men, "One of these is truly a good girl."

"Which one?" a man asked.

"This!" he said while hitting me on the head with a rolled up sheet of paper.

I forced myself to say, "I'm ashamed to be called a good girl by you."

Morad gave a short laugh while everybody remained quiet.

According to the lines I'd scratched on the wall as a makeshift calendar, I was leaving that prison after forty days, with no idea of where we were heading. We traveled for about an hour until the van stopped.

The men jumped out and someone yelled, "Everyone out."

We got out of the vehicle and walked in line with the guards for some minutes. The sound of footsteps and breathing broke the silence. When we stopped, I overheard Morad talking about a "good girl" with a man he called Haji who seemed to be in charge. Their voices grew weaker and weaker as they walked away.

Standing in total darkness, a man with a mean voice whispered in my ear, "Stay where you are. Don't move."

I stood blindfolded there for a long time with no sign of the other women or the guards. They had left without any explanation. It was as if I were in the middle of the wilderness. All I could hear in the hushed night was the chirping of crickets and the croaking of frogs.

As I stood there I began to feel a snake slithering towards me. I got goose bumps imagining the snake coming closer and closer. My whole body tensed and became attuned to the noise. Time stretched on and I waited fretfully. The sounds of the outdoor night continued, until I realized there was no snake and began to feel comfortable. It was chilly even though summer had already started.

After some hours had passed, I heard the murmur of a woman's voice. Cautiously, she said, "No one is here. Take off your blindfold."

I peeked from under my blindfold to see if she was talking to me. Gradually, my eyes became accustomed to the dark and I saw a little bit of light. I realized I hadn't been outside but standing in the middle of a very small cell. On my left, there was a three level bunk bed and behind me a light was coming in through a window. Opposite the window there was a sliding barred door. Through the bars, I could see other cells. We were in a very old prison. From across the hallway a girl waved her blindfold at me with a cautious smile on her face.

I couldn't believe I had been standing in one spot inside a cell all night when I could have been sitting or lying down. Soon the first rays of dawn filtered through the windows.

As my eyes adjusted to the new surroundings, I saw that the sliding barred doors to all the cells were open. Prisoners were free to venture out of their cells into the common room. We were inside a cellblock by ourselves with no one guarding us. I saw Sahar coming out of the last cell. We ran to jump into each other's arms and hugged as if we were long-lost friends.

I learned that the man had whispered to everyone to remain standing motionless. Within a few minutes of freedom, all the prisoners knew the names or aliases and a brief story of how the others had been arrested. Five giggling young girls from a northern city were friends from the same high school. The youngest of them was fifteen and the oldest was seventeen. There were two university students from Tehran, then Sahar and me. Besides us there was an older girl, who didn't talk or smile for days.

Information spread quickly. The prison we came from was an old prison in the middle of downtown Tehran, known as a place for torturing political prisoners during the Shah's regime. After the revolution, it was called Tohid, which means monotheism — another badly chosen name for a prison. Kachwie had tried to fool me by telling me he would take me to Ghasr, which means palace. It was only later that I learned Morad, the warden of the prison had intervened to save "the good girl" from execution.

I was now among the first group of women political prisoners in Qezel-Hesar, a prison that used to be for non-political prisoners, one hour away from western Tehran.

Tired from not sleeping but excited to be together, my fellow prisoners and I were busy talking when a small, skinny man of about forty dressed in army clothes called out to let us know he was about to enter. He came in with a big teapot, bread, and feta cheese. This gaunt man, known as the cook, left the breakfast in the vestibule just inside the cellblock. We drank our tea out of red plastic cups and finished the bread and cheese, as we were all very hungry.

At that point prison still seemed like a game or a temporary adventure that would end soon. Not knowing anything about the violence happening between the Mujahedin and the regime, we had no sense of being in serious danger.

Young and energetic, we laughed most of the time, full of naïve dreams. However, there were two girls who didn't share our easy-going attitude. One had eyes that spoke of fear, sadness, and panic. The other was the same girl who had cried as I had waited outside the doctor's office in the other prison. Later, with tears in her eyes, she confided in me and talked about her feelings of shame and guilt. She had signed a confession that she would no longer participate in any political activity.

I encouraged her to think of the future, not the past, and not to blame herself. It could happen to anybody who was afraid and didn't have much experience with fear, destruction, abuse, or unjust treatment.

Later, a large man of about forty, with a potbelly, toured our cellblock. He swaggered with long strides, which caused his thin, rather long brown hair to bounce. When he walked out, a bald spot on the back of his head shone under the light. He peered at us out of the corner of his green eyes as he walked impatiently, a mocking smile on his face. He screwed up his eyes at each prisoner as if he could read their character, secrets, and personalities. He appeared to file his assumptions in his mind for the future. He left the block without introducing himself or asking our names. Later we learned that he was the dreaded warden called Haji.

At noon, the cook brought two oval platters of mixed rice for our lunch. There were no plates to divide the food, but they handed out spoons. Separating ourselves into two groups we ate from the two dishes. The first spoonful was enough for the younger girls to quit eating. The rest of us stopped after the third spoonful. The food tasted horrible and had a strange odor.

"It's the camphor they add to the food in prisons to reduce the sexual desires among male prisoners," said a petite twenty-six-year-old medical university student.

The cook took back the food almost untouched. This continued for about fifteen days and he seemed not to care whether the food was eaten or not, but he tossed around a few nasty words each time he walked in.

After a few days, two women wearing black chadors over their army clothes came into the cellblock. The one with a large face and whitish tone of skin announced, "Warm water will be turned on for an hour." They then left us a few bars of soap before they went out. We didn't have towels or other clothes to change into, so the old gray manto I had received in the previous prison became a precious item. I lent it to the girl with frightened eyes to wear after her shower so she could wash her clothes.

In the middle of our shower time, Haji came in without warning. A girl screamed and ran to the bathroom. Two others who weren't dressed remained in the showers.

Except for Sahar we were all religious and believed in veiling our hair and wearing long sleeves and covering our bodies in the presence of men, even in the heat of summer.

"You need to knock before coming in because we may not be properly dressed." I said to Haji.

"You must always have your full hijab on," he replied and pushed me into a cell. He then quickly grabbed the iron chain that was hanging at the bar for the purpose of locking the door and began hitting me.

Sahar who was a witness yelled, "American hireling, don't beat her. Don't beat her, you betrayer."

Haji growled and turned on Sahar, shoved her into her cell, and lashed her on her shoulder and back. I screamed, "Don't beat her. She hasn't done anything wrong."

Haji continued going back and forth beating Sahar and me.

Sahar had taken a shower just a short while earlier, her brown hair curved around her delicate face. She had only a tank top and pants on, as she had washed her blouse in the shower. Her arms were crossed over her chest, clasping her bare upper body, and her chin was raised.

"Beat. Beat. Beat me, American hired hand." She cried, as if she were an actress playing the lead role in a play and would get a prize from the jury soon after this great performance.

After that incident, Haji saw Sahar and me as his enemies. Even though I hadn't called him names, he kept repeating, "You called me an American hired hand." Thereafter, whenever he wanted to punish a group of prisoners, he would include me, even if I hadn't been involved.

Sahar belonged to a pro Soviet Union leftist group who believed the revolution in Iran had been designed by America. They believed that the U.S. supported Khomeini and the Mullahs to prevent any possible communist takeover in Iran. But the Mujahedin organization that I volunteered for avoided attacking Khomeini directly, in order to buy some time to attract more people and to become stronger against the religious leader who still had absolute power.

About a week later, the two women guards in army clothes and chador came back and ordered Parva and Saba, seventeen and sixteen, to step out in full hijab, then took them away blindfolded. The following day the whitish-faced guard stood at the cellblock entrance, put her hands on her fat hips, and stated with mock joy, "I have news for you."

When we all stopped walking to hear her words, she continued maliciously, "Your friends are going to be executed in Evin. You will never see them again."

The cellblock turned cold and gray at once. How could it possibly be true? Was this the warden's trick to scare us? The young girls had simply sold political newspapers in their high school. That's all they had done.

Our days of sorrow and sadness passed slowly. Parva and Saba's high school friends no longer giggled. They walked in small steps with their heads down, whispering to each other. Like wildflowers picked from the field, they wilted, far from the green shore of the Caspian Sea, their homes and their mothers.

Crowded Prison Camps

(1981)

Soon fifty new prisoners were brought into our cellblock and the routine of our lives changed significantly. The young girls waited in the hall, most covered in loose Islamic mantos and scarves, and a few in normal outfits with no scarf. They looked apprehensive. From behind the bars, we must have looked inhuman and strange to them.

The cells were small, only slightly larger than the size of the three level bunks inside them. The doors with bars added an uneasy feeling to the dark old prison. The reflection of the florescent lights on the thin blue-green carpet in the hallway between the middle of the cells lent to the cold, harsh atmosphere. Here one really would feel the impact of the prison.

Like a petty tyrant, Haji had sole discretion of how to assign the cells. He considered the last two cells the worst. These were slightly narrower and located at the end of two rows of six cells at each side of the hallway. Sahar and I had occupied these two cells directly across from each other.

Haji stopped outside my cell, scratching his beard, looking pensive, as if he were solving a difficult problem. It didn't take long; soon his eyes glowed and he ordered me out and put me in Sahar's cell. He put five or six girls in each cell, and it seemed he didn't want the new prisoners influenced by two rebels. Now Sahar and I would create only one trouble-making cell. However, due to the lack of space, he added two new prisoners to our cell at the last moment.

We heard shocking news from the newcomers. The new president, Bani-Sadr, a liberal and a former supporter of Khomeini had opposed the hardliners in power. Demonstrations that had been going on to support him came under the attack from the Revolutionary Guards.

Using this opportunity, the Mujahedin had called for a massive demonstration on June 20, expecting to spark a general uprising.

On that day in June when I had smelled the burning rubber and heard the chanting voices, hundreds of thousand had marched in Tehran's streets against the regime in support of president Bani-Sadr.

Mujahedin members and their supporters equipped themselves with small bags of salt, pepper, box cutters or knives to join the protesters against the regime. The new prisoners had been arrested during or after those mass demonstrations.

It was hard for me to believe what I was hearing about the violence in the mass demonstrations. After I met Sohayla, a tall thoughtful woman I sensed that she was wise and trustworthy. I asked her, "Are you sure? Is it true? How come the demonstrators had knives? Sohayla, is this really true that our organization ordered its supporters to carry knives during the protest of June 20th?"

Sohayla hesitated and lowered her voice. Her bright blue eyes behind her thick glasses focused on the rest of the girls in the cell, "Well, our organization told us to use weapons in self-defense if the guards attacked us, so yes, I carried salt and pepper with me to throw in the guards' faces to give me a chance to escape."

It was hard to believe that in another public crisis, violence had prevailed.

During the time of the Shah, the Mujahedin were active in opposing the government's dictatorial policies. Their underground group used radical methods, to work to assassinate the Shah, his guards or American diplomats. Members of the Mujahedin were persecuted by the Shah's secret police SAVAK, either executed or imprisoned.

The prison survivors became folk heroes throughout the Revolution of 1979. This allowed them to expand their organizations after the revolution. The Mujahedin organization became more mainstream, embraced democracy, and forswore violence to achieve political power. I, like many others, had joined the Mujahedin when the victory of the revolution granted Iran a peaceful period.

I had no doubt in my mind about the members' good intentions. They were made up of well-educated Muslim human-rights activists. But the unity among the people lasted for too short a time, despite the fact that our purpose was to achieve an environment for open discussion, freedom and human rights.

The new regime's supporters attacked the intellectuals and activists for criticizing the new regime and selling pro-democracy newspapers on the street. But during the time I was outside the prison we never responded with violence. I wondered if the Mujahedin leaders had tried their best to handle such an exciting era of revolution. Considering that liberty was a new opportunity in Iran, had we thirsted for decades for one drop of freedom only to succumb to violence so easily? And let it end with such a dramatic change in tactics?

Alas, proud of their political strength and secure in their effective network, the Mujahedin leaders concentrated on one thing. They were eager to lead the people of Iran at any cost. They were full of themselves and we, the hundreds of thousands of excited followers were fools enough to readily respond to their commands.

On the other hand, the new Islamic regime was riding on fresh horses and was well on its way to establishing another dangerous dictatorship. This was the reality which spoke to me in a louder voice and I pushed the other thoughts to the back of my mind.

Bani-Sadr, the first president of Iran was impeached. He and the Mujahedin's first leader escaped to France before the fundamentalists could arrest them. Jails and prisons overflowed with people who had supported them and the opposition groups or had spoken out against the regime in support of liberty.

After about a week another group of prisoners arrived, and we learned a larger cellblock, called Public 4, was in use now across from ours. Haji lined up the prisoners in the main long hallway and asked them questions. One of the prisoners told us in detail how the prisoners who pretended they had no attachment or loyalty to their organizations ended up in the Public 4 cellblock. But any sign of relationship to opposition groups would influence Haji in his decisions.

In comparison to our Solitary cellblock, Public 4 was more comfortable, since the prisoners had access to a yard during the day. They could exercise in fresh air and hang their laundry outside. Thus, the "better girls," in Haji's judgment were placed there and the worst ones came to our cellblock.

Most of the higher ranked members of the Mujahedin manipulated Haji, covered up their true positions, pretended to be nonpolitical and ended up in Public 4. In two weeks, when more prisoners were transferred into our cellblock, Haji put about forty-five communist prisoners into two guardrooms that up to that point had remained empty.

One day as I lay on the bunk with my eyes closed in a rare moment of rest I suddenly heard the sound of women chattering. I opened my eyes and listened carefully. Walking out to see what was happening, I noticed a group of girls crowding around two newcomers. Searching through the throngs, I saw Parva. Next to her stood Saba.

Two months had passed since they had left us. Their high school friends and I were shocked to see them alive. I ran forward and pushed my way through to reach Parva and Saba. We all showered them with our kisses and hugged them tightly with joy and happiness.

But it soon became apparent that Parva and Saba weren't the effusive and happy girls that had left us. They now walked with fear in their eyes. I didn't know what had happen to them until Parva talked to me.

"They took us to court where the judge sentenced us to death. He told us if we spoke against our organization in front of a video camera, he would reduce our sentence to life in prison. Saba and I didn't know what to do. We had only a few days until our execution. We waited till the last day and finally decided to do the TV interview." Her eyes filled with tears, and she bent over clutching her stomach, racked with guilt.

These once dazzling young girls were ashamed and afraid to say what they had gone through to save their lives. I didn't blame her. I wanted her to forgive herself. However, I knew there were other prisoners who had expected the two girls to be executed and would not forgive them for doing the TV interview.

We all had the same dilemma. Giving in, even under the threat of execution, was considered an unforgivable crime. The prisoner would be condemned as a betrayer of the organization, the people, and their friends. It wasn't easy. We thought anyone undergoing torture should bear it and resist to the death. We were too naïve and young to understand the reality of human weaknesses. Nevertheless, I knew we shouldn't be hostile towards the prisoners who cracked. They needed our kindness. That was all I understood.

But under the constant pressure of unwritten rules, Parva and Saba became known as betrayers and were ostracized. Most girls didn't talk to them. I was Parva's only friend, and Saba had one of her high school friends to talk to. For a long time, it wasn't easy for them to live among us.

I learned later that these two who had made such a difficult decision were the most honest and the bravest of all. That man with the white hood in Tohid prison had gone to all the cells and asked the prisoners the same question, "Will you sign a paper and confess that you are a supporter of the Mujahedin?"

Seven out of ten girls had denied their sympathy towards the Mujahedin and didn't sign the paper. Parva and Saba were the only two who had signed their names to defend the movement against the regime.

It was obvious now that it must been Morad and no other who stopped the man with the hood from coming back to my cell. That was the only possibility. I must have had a backer, a powerful one, the warden of that prison, who hadn't allowed him to get my signature. He must have made an effort to save me from execution.

The plan to execute prisoners was the regime's response to the violence that had occurred outside. On June 28, about forty days after I was arrested, a devastating bomb exploded at the headquarters of the Islamic Republic Party, an organization that supported the regime. This explosion resulted in the death of Chief of Justice Beheshti, four ministers, twenty-seven members of parliament and other high-ranking officials who were meeting in that building.

A month later, on August 30, the terror campaign continued with the bombing of the office of the Prime Minister, killing both President Rajaei, and his Premier Bahonar. The building was completely destroyed.

The news reported that the Mujahedin had detonated the bomb in that building — one of the most important centers of the regime. The followers of the Mujahedin spread the news, feeling victorious and proud of their power. The non-violent political organization I had joined had changed into a military force. I still had no doubt about trusting the organization, but I couldn't feel happy about what was happening. I never thought killing and destruction were right, but had no real understanding of them either.

The thought of killing the opposition as the enemy was abstract for me. The general understanding among prisoners was that it was acceptable to kill the members of the regime, but this always troubled me.

For the government these assassinations created anger and frustration. They retaliated by taking revenge. The first act by Khomeini's government was to execute as many Mujahed prisoners as possible.

The public prosecutor and prison authorities had received Khomeini's permission to execute whoever confessed being a supporter or a member of the Mujahedin. The man in the white hood who was anxious to get my signature had been a courier of death. Parva and Saba, who honestly admitted their connection to the Mujahedin, had no idea that they were signing their own death sentences and would be transferred to Evin where executions took place.

I remembered then that right after the victory of our revolution I was walking down the street with a small piece of paper in my hand. I intended to throw it on the ground, but for the first time I sensed some strange love in my heart for Iran that was now a free country. I felt it was truly my home and I was responsible for taking care of it. I decided never to harm it in any way. I kept the paper in my hand until I arrived home.

Now, in less than three years, the whole country was about to collapse. The prisons' population had expanded dramatically with thousands of inmates who had expected to live in a democratic country. Some of the participants in the revolution for a free Iran were executed, some were shot in the streets. Many more young men were dying in the war with Iraq.

Three months after my arrest more and more prisoners were transferred to Qezel-Hesar. They had brought news about a great many executions in Evin. They had first thought that the terrible noises they heard were loads of iron posts being unloaded from construction trucks, but they soon realized that they were gunshots. They learned that each night the guards executed a group of prisoners, and at the end they shot each prisoner with one single bullet to make sure they were dead. Hardly a night passed without shooting noises.

Among the new prisoners, I saw Hamideh, one of the Mujahedin leaders I had hiked with during our group outings on Friday mornings. I hadn't seen her without a scarf before. Her short twisted hair covered her forehead and her pointed chin seemed narrower. Dark circles surrounded her eyes, indicating that something unusual had happened to her. It wasn't safe for us to show that we knew each other. With a signal from her, she and I went to the bathroom stall and I tearfully hugged her. After we calmed down we started to talk.

"What are those dark circles around your eyes and everybody else's who was transferred with you, Hamideh? Where have you been?"

"They starved us," she looked at the door to check if anyone was coming. "We were in Evin's new apartment buildings and most of the time we were hungry. We didn't get enough to eat."

"I'm so sorry."

"There were so many prisoners, and they had to place us inside Evin's compound, in some empty apartments, meant to be living quarters for the guards."

She looked around and hurriedly whispered, "I saw an astonishing picture of you in Evin." She smiled.

"Really? How come they have my picture? They never photographed me."

"Your parents must have brought the picture to find you in Evin. They're looking for you."

"Hamideh, I haven't given my name or any information to anyone."

"But you should. They already have your name in Evin. Your name was written under your picture when the warden searched for you among the prisoners. Next time when Haji comes in, talk to him and give him your name and address."

I was shocked. How could I possibly talk to Haji all of a sudden and give up the information I had protected for so long because of the organization's command?

"I can't do that," I said.

"You must do it. The organization's policy has changed."

Hamideh occupied a high rank among the supporters of our organization. I was supposed to do what she told me even if I felt hesitant to talk to Haji.

Once in a while, Haji came to our cellblock and rewarded some by transferring them to Public 4. He had already transferred Parva and Saba and their friends.

The next time when Haji came in, I told him my name, but didn't give him my right address. Giving my own address would be dangerous for my roommate, Sepideh, who used to be politically active.

One month before I was arrested, Sepideh married and moved out, but she still had the key to the apartment and kept her belongings there. Fortunately, Haji was busy dealing with too many prisoners and didn't reprimand me for withholding my name and address for so long.

One day Haji came in without notice. As usual, everybody in the hallway ran towards their cells to pick up some kind of covering except one girl who casually continued marching. Haji erupted in anger at her for remaining in the hallway without covering herself. The next day, Haji returned with a woman, completely covered in a black chador, her face veiled with a thin black cloth, hiding her identity. The cellblock was quiet with anxiety. Haji called out a name and the same girl came out again in her T-shirt without wearing a scarf or manto.

Haji read a decree aloud: "Fifty lashes, *Ta'zir*," a discretionary punishment for not wearing the hijab from the so-called Islamic Sharia Law.

Haji ordered the girl to lie on the floor. The woman in the black chador beat her on the back with a rubber hose while Haji's assistant counted the lashes. The girl jerked with each lash, but she never let out a single scream.

"Covering is mandatory for everyone." Haji declared angrily before leaving. You must put on a headscarf or chador anytime I walk in. This is a rule. Do you understand?"

For days, the girl who had been beaten had difficulty sleeping and moving because of the crisscross purple welts on her back. Her friends rubbed oil on her skin to stop it from cracking open.

Among my cellmates was a young schoolteacher with pink cheeks and a constant smile. She was an educated girl who taught at the school in the village where she grew up. Mina had been arrested in a demonstration in support of Bani-Sadr, the president. While in Karaj prison, she had received a one-year sentence from a Mullah judge in the quick hearing of an informal court.

Whenever Haji got a chance, he would come to our cell looking for Mina to humiliate her in front of everybody. His hatred for Mina was strange and unfounded. One of Haji's favorite ways of tormenting Mina was to tell her he had beaten Mina's younger brother in the men's cellblock. Haji repeatedly ridiculed Mina for her ethnic background and her accent even though she spoke perfect Farsi.

"A common villager!" Haji belittled her. "You see these other girls are from the city. Do you hear? What was a peasant like you doing in street demonstrations?"

Mina kept her patience. She looked at him, listened, and didn't say a word.

"Do you imagine I'll leave you alone?" Haji threatened her, "I'll send you to the top of the hills one day. You'll see."

The prison authorities executed political prisoners on the hills of Evin. Anyone sent to the hill was shot to death.

One early morning when all the girls in other cells were still asleep, Mina, Azadeh and I stood together in a row, did some calisthenics and then sang a revolutionary song. Sahar didn't participate because we were singing a Mujahedin song and she was a communist. That morning two new female guards unexpectedly walked in as we stood singing in low voices. They immediately left to come back with Haji. Haji called the three of us out.

"Come closer… you dreadful monafeghin…how dare you."

We walked down the hallway. All eyes were fixed on us.

"I'll show you. You sing songs together?"

After a moment of deadly silence, I said quietly, "We were simply singing, 'Death to America', unless you…"

Haji turned toward me and slapped me hard across the face.

"That's enough you damned girl. I'll show you what it means to call me an American hireling."

My face burned. I felt embarrassed and humiliated for being beaten in front of more than a hundred girls, but I didn't react.

Trembling with anger, Haji sent Mina, Azadeh, and me back to our cell and left, muttering and threatening to punish us. "If you think you can get away with this, you are mistaken."

A few days later, Haji came back and got Mina. Haji's hate for Mina made everyone fear for her. In less than a week, Mina was sent back to our cellblock looking much thinner. As soon as Mina walked back into our cell, we noticed that she appeared nervous. Her eyes flickered anxiously; her face had no color and her smile had disappeared.

Even though, Mina, Azadeh, Sahar, and I had become good friends it seemed Mina couldn't even see us. Azadeh and I searched Mina's face looking for an opportunity to talk to her. Hamideh, who was Mujahedin superior, quickly pulled her aside and we didn't get a chance to talk to her. An hour later, Mina was called and again taken away. We never learned what Hamideh had told Mina, but Haji had sent Mina for retrial and had sworn to give her a death sentence.

Mina never came back. Nobody said anything, and nobody cried aloud. Her death didn't hit me until three days later when I walked by cell number five. A thirty-five-year-old woman lay on her stomach on the bunk twirling her prayer beads. Gazing out from behind the bars, she looked deeply sad. I stopped. Her eyes fixed on my face.

"You should miss Mina the most. She was in your cell," she said.

"No," I replied.

She studied my face for a few seconds in confusion.

I returned to my cell, sat in the dark corner under the first level, and felt nauseous, with a pain in my belly. I couldn't believe Mina was gone and that I had tolerated her death so easily. It couldn't be normal. My easy acceptance of her death couldn't be normal.

In a few days, some close friends of Mina came to me to get some of her belongings as keepsakes. A voice in my head kept plaguing me. "She's gone. Look. She's not here anymore. Why don't you cry?"

I didn't cry for her until years later, when the numbness finally began to thaw.

Haji came back a week later. Standing outside our cell door, he turned to me hatefully, with triumph.

"It's your turn. You will be the next. I will send you to the top of the Hill soon. Do you hear me?"

He was as serious as when he had threatened Mina. I was Haji's next target.

I passed the next few days in a state of great uncertainty. Now I could understand Mina's feelings when she came back for an hour and couldn't look at any of us. Her eyes had seemed focused on an unknown place, disconnected from the reality around her, dealing with her emotions.

I had now become a guest in her unknown world. Facing death became real to me for the first time and the importance of life became a stark reality. Everything around me looked different. I saw how everybody else's life went on normally. Prisoners went about their daily lives the same way I used to. They swept the floor, ate their food, drank their tea, and talked to one another. But life had changed in my eyes. Each moment could be my last. But I wanted to live. Something inside my heart had changed and fear of death started to grow.

The moment was coming, whether I wanted it or not, whether I was ready or not. Yet, I couldn't share my feelings with anybody. My fear of death would only lower me in their eyes. Just as I had contemplated Mina's death, they would contemplate mine: a good friend and a cellmate who was gone.

The path of my life had come to this end and I had no other choice. This was what I had to believe so that I could pull myself together. I had to accept the reality the same way Mina had. She had left the world behind with all its beauties and possibilities to save her soul. In those moments, I put my sorrow into words and wrote a poem for her.

Mina, the white bird from Tankaman village
flew away among a flock of birds to the blue sky
who will ring the bell... now that you're gone
who warms up the classroom... in the cold winter
who will tell the children with broken pencils how to write
or teach the shy girls, seated on benches
when wind blows through their thin clothes
and snow melts in your remembrance
who will count the springs as they grow
when the dandelions arrive to spread the news
who wipes the tears on their pink cheeks
when the poet sings your story
from a cold prison on earth to eternal life in heaven

One day in September Haji suddenly came into the cellblock. As usual, we hurried back to our cells. He stood in the vestibule and announced, "When I call your name, step forward to get your prison sentence."

Prison sentence? I wondered how that could be possible. I had been in prison for four months but hadn't been in any court.

Haji couldn't resist taunting us, "Don't get too excited about the length of the time you are going to be my guest."

He then called out the names.

"Mitra Sabahi?"

Mitra stuck her head out of the cell, "I'm here," she said and ran out to receive her sentence.

Her friend rushed to her, "Let me see what you got? Four years," she whispered to another girl.

The news spread throughout the cellblock. "Mitra got four years."

"Zahra Badamchi?" Haji called out over the din.

"Here, Haji." she answered.

"Hurry up, you are my special guest." He mocked. "Life sentence."

We were shocked. "Why? Life sentence?"

"Shahin Zand-Irani."

Sahar gasped and jumped up, held onto the bars looking out with a surprised expression on her face. She turned to Azadeh and me and muttered, "Who? Shahin who?"

For a moment, Azadeh and I paused then looked at each other, trying not to laugh. Sahar's unusual reaction to that name revealed her real name. After she realized her secret might be out, she attempted to cover it up, but there was no need. We never discussed the incident with anybody and kept her secret.

Haji continued calling out about eighty names, but my name was not among them. Two weeks later, Haji walked down the hallway, stopping behind the bars of our cell and said. "The judge gave you a one-year sentence, hah, one year! But I objected and sent it back to Evin with my long report about you. I want the court to send you to the top of the hill, or not less than the life sentence you deserve."

I remained quiet. His words passed through the bars and hit the walls of the cell but had no effect on me this time.

Four months after my arrest my parents found me and came to Qezel prison with many other parents desperate to see their children. Haji didn't allow them a visit since it was the regime's policy to prevent prisoners from communicating with the outside. But they began to allow prisoners to write short letters twice a month.

Our parents brought packages containing towels, clothes, blankets, soap, shampoo, and money to buy rationed items such as jam or dates.

The day we received the goodies, new clothes, and things in plastic bags, the scent of perfumed soap, shampoo, and the aroma of chocolate filled the air. We relished wearing new clothes and divided our items among the cells to share them with those who hadn't received anything.

My parents had to ride seven hours by bus from Borujerd to Tehran just to bring me a package. Some of my discomfort was eased knowing they must be happy that they had finally found me.

After four months the guards were going to take us outside in the prison yard. Since our cellblock didn't have a yard, they sent us to Public 4 cellblock's yard to get fresh air. The Public 4 prisoners were sent back into their cells so there would be no contact between the two cellblocks' inmates as we passed through their vestibule to enter the yard.

When we stepped out into the yard and took off our blindfolds our eyes hurt from the brightness of the day. The mid autumn sun shed enormous light on the prison ground. The peaceful open sky contrasted with the old tall brick walls. On top of the walls, rows of barbed wire scratched the softness of the air. We walked in silence on the gravel and sat in the yard under the sun. Gradually the sound of our voices and laughter could be heard when a volleyball game began.

Several days after Haji visited our cellblock, a thin girl dressed in a bright chador went to him with her eyes downcast. She adopted a girlish tone with him and groveled, "Haji, I wanted to let you know I condemn the monafeghin."

She easily used the word monafeghin for the organization she belonged to just like the regime did, with no remorse, to assure Haji how sincerely she regretted her past. Haji nodded his head with pleasure, "Okay, gather your belongings. I'll take you to the Public 4."

How could this be? Especially that the thin girl was a higher ranked follower of the Mujahedin. Soon, Hamideh too cursed the Mujahedin and was also transferred to Public 4. Gradually new prisoners replaced the old ones except a few who remained in Solitary 4, in addition to those belonging to communist groups.

A few weeks later, three new guards in black chadors came in. My cellmates and I leaned back against the wall with our feet under the bunk. I was working on a needlepoint for one of my cellmates. Among the three women guards was Fattaneh, a short skinny woman with the raspy voice of a cigarette smoker. She wore a chador, but it didn't fit her demeanor. She seemed amazed to see so many young educated girls living in that place. She walked down the hallway with a sense of power and a happy expression on her face, acting sophisticated.

The younger, chubbier guard with crossed eyes and the tall overweight one with small eyes belonged to a different world. In contrast to Fattaneh, with her passionate voice and expressive eyes, they both had the appearance of simple provincial women.

As the three guards passed our cell, the woman with crossed eyes whispered to Fattaneh and she stepped back and paused. One of them nodded discreetly in my direction and talked to Fattaneh. After they toured our cellblock, they left us for the day.

When they took us to the yard in a few weeks, we occupied every corner of the yard actively for two hours playing ball games as if it were a high school tournament.

On our way back to the cellblock, Fattaneh, stopped me. She gazed at me in wonder and warmly chatted.

"What's your name?" she curiously asked, then smiled and gave me a compliment. I hurried to put my blindfold over my eyes and walked up the stairs to follow the others back to our cellblock.

When we got back to our cell, it was in a huge mess. The guards had come in and searched our belongings. They had taken away every piece of fabric and all the sewing needles. These precious tools had made their way into our cellblock with the prisoners transferred from Evin. The few books of Russian novelists and philosophers we had shared among ourselves were taken away, leaving those waiting for their turn disappointed.

When Haji came in, brimming with enthusiasm Fattaneh talked to him and pointed to me. Haji stared at me with doubt and distrust. He finally walked towards our cell and asked me to collect my things and go to Public 4. All my old friends had already been transferred there except Azadeh. Pleased with her adventurous position as a guard, Fattaneh had decided to do me a favor.

PART 8

Pretense

(1981)

W hen I entered Public 4, I couldn't believe how large it was. Five hundred young prisoners, each covered in a scarf and loose manto, were either behind bars or walking in the hallway. I followed Haji who walked in large steps ahead of me when suddenly I felt a sharp pain in my right arm.

I grabbed my arm and turned to see the girl who had pinched me, smiling and waving. The pain in my arm disappeared when I saw that it was Shela, who couldn't wait to express her delight upon seeing me and had to pinch me.

Shela was an educated and expressive twenty-eight-year-old girl who'd been on the same political team with me outside of the prison. Her long straight hair was covered with a blue cotton scarf and she wore a brown manto. I noticed that she had lost weight.

Haji took me all the way to the last cell, number thirteen. There were forty to fifty prisoners in a thirty by thirty foot cell. Parva, Saba, and their high school friends were in this cell.

Haji had just left me when I found Shela standing in tears waiting for me in her cell. It was an emotional moment for us to meet in here again. Shela had been arrested a month after me.

Prisoners in this cellblock looked relaxed and comfortable. The daily exposure to the sun, and the fresh air in the yard had made the cellblock bearable. On both sides of a large hallway, there were twenty-four cells. At the end of the hallway, there were showers and bathrooms.

This cellblock was often quiet, orderly and controlled. Most of the younger prisoners called each other fake funny names such as Carrot, Peach, and Cabinet. The more mature ones were called Aunt, Cousin, and Sister-in-law. Others were called Cat, Bunny, Chicken or other names that matched either bodily features or their personality. These were the prisoners who had been arrested and placed in Evin's newly built apartments and didn't give up their names for the first few weeks. These names lasted until Haji forbade us to use nicknames.

In the first week I was there, Hamideh asked me to move to cell twenty-one, which contained all the other teachers including Shela and Roya whom I had met during Friday hikes.

"Haji knows me very well and he might make a big deal out of my changing cells without his permission," I said.

"Among all these prisoners he won't even remember you. You must go," Hamideh insisted.

I had to follow the instructions of those who had been our superiors in the Mujahedin organization even now in prison. Hamideh really wanted me to move and I had to obey her. In this cellblock the higher-ranked prisoners from the Mujahedin organized the other prisoners. They had divided the prisoners into students, teachers and workers in different organizational groups, the same as outside the prison.

"We were so worried after your arrest and disappearance." Shela said to me, "No one knew what had happened to you. Your parents were looking and looking for a few months. I'm so happy to see that you're OK."

Shela had a masters degree in physics and came from an educated family. She was five years older than I was, and we met when she came to my apartment for a study group. Now, Shela, Roya, and I were assigned by Hamideh to study together as a team.

There were a few poetry books, a few novels and the Quran available. Since it was a common belief that it was hard to understand the Quran, we had never thought of studying the Quran together. We chose to read Rumi's poems and discussed his philosophy.

His poems fulfilled our desire for a fictional world. It's amazing that a poet from the 13th-century could be so popular in our time.

Roya was precise in learning each word and its root to understand the concept in the poem.

> listen to the reed as it sways alone
> hear him speak of the pain of separation
> I was cut from my reed-bed
> crying and grasping are women and men
> from the agony and pain
> in my sad song

Rumi

Outside in the prison yard, the gentle sunshine mingled with a cool breeze and softly brushed my skin. The prisoners paced the length of the yard in groups of two or three when I joined my friend Lily to stroll with her in the prison yard, as if in a garden with no surrounding walls. Women turned their heads and looked at my serene happy eyes, giving Lily a reason to say some of her daily flattering words.

"Your charm doubles when your spirit rises," said Lily. "Do you see how every one looks at you? Oh, Mehri you have a good-natured soul and you're beautiful."

I always felt buoyed by her praise. On the other hand, Roya nurtured my confidence in understanding literature and political discussions. Yet I was shy and didn't want to be noticed. I didn't see myself as beautiful as others suggested. But I was certainly attracted to the majesty of life, its mystery beyond my understanding. The greatness of creation had touched me many times and made me cry. Sometimes even death didn't seem like a dark and unknown place any more. I knew there was more to it than I could fathom.

In the seventh month of my imprisonment, everything was relatively calm. It was one of the most relaxed times for me in prison, even though some inmates couldn't stand the pressure of imprisonment.

One day a guard called me to the vestibule. I grabbed the nearest chador, one in a light blue floral pattern, to cover myself and hurried out. I slowed down when I saw Morad, the warden of the former prison, waiting for me in his jeans, white shirt, and sneakers. I stood two feet away from him. His amber eyes filled with curiosity.

"You look different…and how are you doing?" he said.

"Fine," I said in a muffled voice and kept my eyes cast down on the floor.

"Tell me more about yourself. What are you doing these days?" he asked softly.

Surely the scars on my face had faded and the bruises he had inflicted had disappeared. Standing shyly in front of him in a chador, I must have looked different from the rebellious girl he had known. Probably he didn't know that our organization had ordered us to pretend to accept the government's beliefs. Since I wasn't comfortable in pretending, I remained silent.

"Do you still sing?" he asked teasingly.

"No." I murmured and avoided eye contact.

He stood close to me looking into my face. I wanted to escape to my cell. Unable to break my silence, he left after a while.

Later, when Sahar transferred to Public 4, she told me Morad had first gone to Solitary 4 looking for me. He had asked her my name so he could find me. He had no idea what it was.

For a few months no one had visitors, just packages from our families. We could send letters to our parents when the authorities allowed it. Writing those short letters required some skill. We had to tell as much as possible in one-quarter of a page. We had to communicate things secretly, and we encouraged our family members to be patient and bear the situation with us.

The first visit with my parents was heart breaking. Several months had passed since I had taken the vacation trip with them. My mother, my father, and I were all crying. This was the way most visitations went. We met with our parents from behind a glass wall and talked by phone.

There were a few young girls in our cellblock who could not bear the pressure of being in prison. The most noticeable one cried and then laughed hysterically, a fifteen-year-old fighting madness. Prisoners believed she felt guilty because she gave in to the interrogators. No one talked to her, but all referenced her as "broken," a disturbing reaction.

She was not the first prisoner who'd been isolated, but she was the first one I'd seen who had buckled under pressure and drifted into insanity. Her childish, chubby cheeks of bright pink stay in my mind.

Her cell held all those individuals not involved with the organization's network within the prison. One day Sahar, who was in that cell, said to me, "I'm so worried. I don't feel safe in this cell. Would you ask your network leaders to change my cell? I'm afraid that the traitors in the cell will report me and cause me some difficulty with Haji. All five traitors are in this one cell."

The leaders of the Mujahedin organization didn't treat the other prisoners equitably. I knew it very well then, after they didn't take Sahar's request under consideration.

Having only one hour's worth of warm water for showering had created a problem. A crowd of young girls with towels and a change of clothes in plastic bags would run towards the showers all at once.

Soon Fattaneh, the guard, called everybody out into the cellblock's hallway. Prisoners assembled and sat on the floor as she announced, "I want to choose one of you to be in charge of the showers."

She was playing out her favorite role, that of a theatrical star. She searched our faces to find her chosen person. I had put my head down before hand, to avoid being noticed, until she called out, "You. From now on you will be in charge of the showers,"

I looked up to see whom she'd picked and saw her pointing at me, "What's your name again?"

"Mehri."

"Your last name?"

"Dadgar."

"Dadgar," she repeated.

"Get her permission before using the showers," she said while she was staring at me.

Fattaneh then rotated her torso around until her eyes settled right at Monir, who had just taken a shower that day. Her comely straight-shoulder-length hair puffed around her fair face and made her stand out from the crowd, and that caught Fattaneh's eye.

"What's your name?"

"Monir."

"Rise up, rise up."

Monir flushed and stood up.

"You will be in charge of food division," Fattaneh said. Then she dismissed the crowd, pleased with her selection ceremony; she thrust out her chest and strutted away as if she were a supermodel.

It was the norm for prisoners to be in charge of daily tasks and organize their ordinary affairs, but I disliked having been selected and having no say in the matter. After that, every day Fattaneh came in and screamed, "Daaaaadgaaaaaar."

Upon hearing my name all the girls, who associated me with the warm water, raced towards the showers. Those who were closer or fast runners jumped into the shower stalls. It was an embarrassing scene. The others had to wait for days, as the warm water ran out during the first rounds of showers.

After two days, I decided to take responsibility and solve the problem by going cell-to-cell, writing down names, and scheduling prisoners for their turn each day. Before my plan could establish a discipline and end the conflicts of shower time, Hamideh ordered me to stop my work.

"Why?" I asked.

"Because I said so. It's not your duty."

"But Hamideh, some don't get a chance to take a shower for days. I feel obligated to do something, plus, what's wrong with ending the chaos?"

"We'll decide who must do it," she said. "Do what I tell you to do."

I stopped scheduling the shower times, but Fattaneh, the guard, continued screaming my name everyday, and the girls with their towels and clothes in their hands continued to run towards the shower.

I would limit my showers to once a week, yet even then it was difficult to get in because I refused to run. An elegantly dressed, beautiful and kind woman called Sister-in-law made my showers possible by getting to a stall and saving me a spot.

Many nights, Fattaneh came to lead us in a group chanting prayer. In these traditional religious ceremonies, prisoners were supposed to feel a sense of redemption and embrace Islam. Voices merged when she asked everyone to sing with her softly and then cry out. The lights dimmed in the long hallway.

"She acts as if she's singing in a cabaret," one girl said mockingly to another. Several giggled in the darkness, pretending they were crying. Fattaneh beat her chest gently with her palm and enjoyed hearing the echo of her voice through a microphone. Her character and attitude became a subject of ridicule among the younger prisoners.

Days came and went in a normal routine until Hamideh sent her go-between to tell us to stop any kind of exercising or playing of sports in the yard. "No physical activity. You must participate in the ideology classes. All of you."

"Why can't we exercise when Haji hasn't forbidden it?" Roya objected without any success.

We gradually realized that the leaders' power in the cellblock was absolute and they were accustomed to it. They were also deeply convinced that the prisoners must follow their policy of pretending to be traitors. Hamideh and the other leaders refused to respond to any objections to their policy of giving in step by step.

Soon they came up with another plan. We were told to design and write a newspaper in favor of the regime as a prisoners' cultural activity. This policy would fulfill the organization's strategy of pretending that prisoners had converted and believed in the regime's legitimacy.

A few in our cell were assigned to write the articles and I was to draw the artwork, including a pencil drawing of Khomeini for an article about him. We accomplished our task despite our reluctance. Along with this process, we had to participate in all the ideology classes and group religious prayers organized by the prison authorities.

This was the Mujahedin's trick to fool the regime, convince the authorities that they had changed in favor of the Islamic regime and had become traitors, so they could be released.

Gradually my friends and I grew less enchanted with the Mujahedin leaders.

We understood that, under serious pressure, hiding one's belief might be necessary for saving lives, but since we were not under immediate threat, none of these orders made sense at all.

A few of us felt our leaders in the cellblock were giving in without thinking. It wasn't acceptable to us to play this dishonest game without our consent. However, the end justified the means for the Mujahedin organization leaders and many of their followers in the prison.

One of the prisoners, a tall athletic girl and a highly ranked follower of the Mujahedin, fooled Haji, pretending to be a turncoat and took charge of cellblock Public 4. Fattaneh and the other guards disappeared.

A young and simple Mullah was assigned to teach us weekly about Islam. Hundreds of young prisoners sat, forced to listen to him. The young Mullah would pull his short figure and his head up, standing on his tiptoes to get taller; his eyes stared down at the ground so as not to steal a look at the young faces. He was unaware that the girls were talking or reading books under their chadors, pretending to listen. Fresh jokes were made each time about the young man's dialect. His words brought a new tone and new vocabulary into the whole cellblock. His nonsensical religious lessons became entertainment.

As we giggled we didn't realize that we would be forced to

participate in a betrayal of all our values in a grotesque mockery of everything we had suffered.

In the next few days Haji entered unexpectedly and told the prisoners to put on their chadors and blindfolds. We had no idea what was going on until we heard we were being taken to Behesht-e-Zahra (which means Paradise of Zahra), a large and famous cemetery in southern Tehran, to march in support of the regime.

After the revolution, this large cemetery became an important part of the political advertising for the Islamic republic, as it was the resting place of the regime's men. Many important historical events, such as Khomeini's first speech, had taken place at this cemetery. Hundreds of martyrs of the revolution against the Shah, as well as thousands of victims of the Iran-Iraq war were buried there. Shamefully, Behesht-e-Zahra was also a group burial ground for hundreds of political prisoners executed during the past few months.

Prisoners gathered surreptitiously to discuss the situation. My friends and I thought it was a mistake to help the regime's propaganda machine and wondered what we should do. The Mujahedin leaders ordered everyone to go.

Before this event, prisoners considered that any support for the Islamic regime would be an abomination. Participating in an event for publicity, such as this, would confuse the public and erode their trust in political prisoners. Even though the Mujahedin leaders in the prison had ordered us to pretend and proclaim we had repented in favor of the regime, they used to say, "There is a line we shouldn't cross, no TV interviews in support of the regime and no information must be given to the enemy."

The prisoners were in prison sacrificing their lives in defense of freedom and the peoples' rights. Yet the leaders in Public 4 cellblock paid no attention to the actual course of events. They were leading us blindly. These decisions of the Mujahedin affected other political groups in prison as well.

Evidently the regime was using this policy of dissimulation to take advantage of the prisoners. In a battle like this, we could not win.

"I think this is crazy." Roya said and Shela agreed.

"Of course it is. They must be nuts to push the prisoners in the wrong direction to please Haji."

"I can't understand. Why should we go?"

"They're making us march in favor of this dictatorial regime," Shela said as she stood up, ready to walk into the hallway. "I can't believe this."

This was the result of the wrong-headed policy of systematically giving in to the regime. The pretext of agreeing with the regime had trapped the leaders into obeying the authorities' demands, which kept coming one after another. Now they didn't have the courage to refuse Haji's orders.

The prisoners' demonstration must have been tremendously important for the regime to risk taking 500 prisoners out in the streets. They probably expected a great payoff in the form of propaganda.

European countries had protested the tortures, executions, and human rights violations in Iran. This was an opportunity for the regime to show the world that prisons are universities and the regime is supported by students of ideological universities. This was repeatedly proclaimed by Lajevardi, the cruel warden of Evin.

My friends and I had no vote and no right to make decisions for ourselves, just as if we were slaves to our organization. With reluctance and remorse, we obeyed them and put on our chadors.

As I wondered how the guards would control so many of us, I thought there might be an opportunity to escape.

Under the control of hundreds of sharp-eyed guards, prisoners in black chadors boarded the buses that were to take us to the cemetery. Along the way, we were told to take off our blindfolds. Once at our destination, we stepped off the buses and walked in between rows of guards who formed walls on both sides.

We covered our faces as much as possible so we couldn't be recognized by our family and friends who might see us on TV, and would believe we really supported the regime. The regime's photographers and camera operators were recording the event.

I immediately lost my friends in the crowd and walked among the large group of prisoners who were almost running with their heads tucked down into their necks. None of us had the courage to stop this travesty. I looked up and saw people carrying coffins as burials were occurring in the distance. Large framed pictures of dead young men killed in the war were everywhere. Wandering old women in black chadors scattered over the graves. This was a land of death where many of our friends were buried without any signs or marble stones.

A group of bystanders watched us in silence. We stayed for only a short time, but even that small presence served the purpose of the regime.

The Revolutionary Guards guided us back to the buses. With hundreds of security guards creating a human chain around us, it was impossible to escape. Even an attempt could result in being shot right there or tortured later or executed.

When we returned to the prison, I lay on the third level of the bunk thinking. Hand in hand the Mujahedin policy and the regime's violation of our rights were now leading us. We had betrayed not only the people, but also ourselves. Among all these changes inside the prison, I wondered how Hussein was doing outside.

For the next days and weeks the routines of prison kept me going. We awoke for prayer, made our beds, ate our breakfast, then did chores. Walking, chatting and knitting, were customary in our calm and passive days. After lunch and prayer we continued with the same routine in the evening. We prayed again and went to bed around ten.

One day prisoners were asked to stand in line in front of their cells, for a group of five women, clothed in black chadors with covered faces, were about to come in with Haji. They were political prisoners turned into informants who looked down the line carefully at each prisoner's face. Afterward, Haji called a list of names and I was summoned to the office.

One of the young women stood beside a guard and asked me

questions in her disguised voice, her face completely covered.

I didn't recognize her voice and said nothing, but she confronted me with some information and revealed my status as a teacher, something the warden and Haji didn't know about me.

They sent me to the yard to join the other suspected prisoners who had been identified.

The sun was about to set behind the prison walls. Barbed wire edged the vast sky that was covered with countless clouds, which had turned deep scarlet. Our heads up, we praised the extraordinary beauty of the scene while we wondered what would happen to us.

Rumors spread, "Haji will send us to Evin for execution."

After a few minutes, I found Roya and joined her. We held hands, and I thought of Rumi's poem.

> inside me a hundred beings
> are putting their fingers to their lips and saying
> that's enough for now, Shhhhh
> silence is an ocean

After two hours in the yard, the guards took us into a large room and kept us there for long hours before they returned us to the cellblock.

Soon I learned that I would be sent to court the next day. I worried about how I would manage to speak without giving any information about my friends who were outside the prison. I didn't want to give them my address in Tehran for they would go after my roommate, Sepideh.

I asked Hamideh's go-between to tell her I needed help. I waited during the afternoon but no one showed up. During the night, Roya saw me distressed with the worries of my trial's outcome and helped me plan what to say in court, "Don't be worried; my roommate and I are both already in prison. Give them my address as the place of your study group and political meetings." She and I then reviewed the possible questions and came up with a simple story to tell.

My courtroom was stark with a mullah in a white turban, two chairs and a desk. His eyes downcast on the paper in front of him, he questioned me and made notes, but things went well. I protected the information that could have hurt others and returned to the cellblock happily to thank Roya.

Hamideh's go-between came up to me immediately to ask what had happened in court. I was aware of the game Hamideh was playing.

"Hamideh wants to know what's going on."

"Does it matter to her? Tell her whatever you like."

A look of dismay appeared on her face.

I was furious with the irresponsible ways of the organization, and this was my last connection with them. They never again contacted Roya, Shela, or me in this cellblock.

A blast was about to start in the prison, beginning when the regime went after the leaders of political groups and their key members with full force. The regime not only aimed to arrest and execute them, but also wished to break their heroic image among the prisoners. In February 1982, Moosa Khiabani, the second in command in the Mujahedin organization, and a group of members were trapped by the regimes' Revolutionary Guards. Twenty-three were killed by gunfire while they fought back the regimes' forces in their underground home. Television announced the news in the afternoon while prisoners watched it in disbelief and great sorrow. A recently released prisoner from our cellblock who acted as a traitor for Haji but was a high-ranking Mujahed was arrested again. It was said she was one of those who survived the violence in the team house.

Meanwhile, a dull young traitor who'd been isolated by prisoners reported that some prisoners in cell number 21 insulted her. This brought the fuming Haji into Public 4, to call the residents out. In the middle of his verbal attacks, he noticed I was among the eighteen girls standing in front of him.

"Curse you. Are you in this cell, too?" he yelled as his focus shifted to me. Haji then dismissed the rest of the girls and his anger mounted as he blamed me.

That same week, one of Haji's most trusted collaborator, Ezzat, was exposed as an infiltrator. Furious, Haji compiled a list of about ninety names including Roya, Shela and me, ordering all of us to gather our belongings to be separated from others. We were identified as resistant prisoners.

We were transferred to Cellblock 8, where we were packed into small cells to be treated in a way, Haji said, would make us "groan." In Cellblock 8 there wouldn't be any visitation or fresh air.

Ironically, Hamideh, an infiltrator who held a high rank in the Mujahedin organization, became Haji's trusted assistant.

PART 9

Leningrad

(1982)

It was almost at the beginning of my second year in prison. We walked into Cellblock 8, wearing chadors, carrying our blankets, clothes, and personal bags, not knowing that our new cellblock had become a colony of 200 resistant prisoners. There were far too many prisoners for the limited space. Haji divided us and sent each group into a small cell. I ended up in number seven, located at the end of the hallway among the thirty girls Haji believed to be the worst in the cellblock.

The other cells held about twenty-five prisoners. He ordered, Soraya, a political prisoner now on duty as a guard, to lock us inside the barred cells. I didn't know how and when this tall young engineer had started to work as a warden, but according to rumors she had a husband in the men's cellblock and they were divorced, now. They had been arrested for their political activities with a communist group.

Soraya, quiet, with a bitter expression on her fair-skinned face, did her duties robotically and showed no obvious sympathy towards other prisoners. She and her assistant, a slim short invisible girl, were housed in the vestibule to guard the prisoners.

There wasn't even enough space in the cell for us to sit down, but the girls in my cell handled it with a sense of humor and often laughed at our hard situation. We managed to comfort each other by sleeping in shifts and switching places. Ezzat, who had ended up in the cell across the hallway, teased us and said, "The worst and the best are in cell number seven, the most ill, the most beautiful, the tallest, the shortest are all collected in one place, cell number seven!"

For the next eight months that I was in Cellblock 8 whenever Haji came in for a visit, my cellmates would hide me behind them but Haji wouldn't leave without asking, "Where is she?" I had to thread my way through to come to the front, and announce, "I'm here."

He would then threaten me and leave.

For a few weeks, the doors were locked during the days and even at nights. Not only didn't we have room to sleep, but also during the day we were crammed together, sitting on the floor or on the only bunk in our cell.

Soraya and her assistant would open the doors for us to do our dawn prayers and eat breakfast. After breakfast at 8am, they locked the doors until noon for lunch and noon prayer. Since the wardens, the guards, and most prisoners were Shia Muslims we only prayed three times a day, and we were locked in again until dinner and our night prayers.

When the barred doors opened for one hour, two hundred girls wanted to use the bathrooms. The long line in front of the bathrooms created an impossible situation. We had to do our ablutions to prepare for our prayers, pray, eat, and organize things and this used up every minute. We rarely found time to walk in the hallway, wash our clothes, or spend time with our friends in the other cells.

Each day four prisoners took turns being the workers of the day. They divided the food in the fastest way possible and handed it to us as we sat on the floor around a narrow tablecloth we had made from stitching together the plastic bread bags. After food, the workers served us black tea in plastic cups with two sugar cubes, and then they washed all the dishes. When everybody went back to their cells and the doors were locked, the workers spread the used tealeaves on the carpet to prevent dust from rising while they swept the hallway.

We had no access to the bathrooms until a few hours later when Soraya unlocked the doors. At night there was not enough room to sleep except in a tough sitting position, so some took turns sleeping on one tier of the three-level bunk in our eleven by seven foot cell.

Lily and Marjan who had been politically active at the same high school were in the same cell with me. Marjan made us laugh with her funny stories, but Lily was sensitive, withdrawn and shy by nature. She sometimes sang passionately with her pleasing voice and stirred up deep emotions among the prisoners. Lily and I found that our taste in politics, literature, and philosophy were closely aligned. My friendship with Lily grew deeper while we lived in that cramped cell.

Roya, who was in cell number five, would run to me right after the doors opened so that we could walk and talk. This began to upset Lily who said to me one day, "You no longer have time to walk with me."

Sohayla, our cellmate sitting next to us, watched through her glasses with her pale blue eyes and naïve curiosity. She looked first at me then at Lily, and made a gesture as if she knew what was going on.

Sometimes I caught Lily looking at me with a smile. She would lean on her elbows, telling me that when she had first seen me she thought that I didn't look like a political prisoner. Then she wondered how I had survived in prison without being sexually abused. I told her about the man who was about to harm me during the first days after my arrest.

Shela was in another cell and I didn't see much of her, but we talked once in a while. Eventually, Haji realized that it was impossible to jam so many prisoners into such small quarters and allowed the doors to be opened during the night. As a result, we could sleep well now, but trying to get to the bathroom during the night became an adventure, as there was no empty space to step. Both the hallways and the cells were completely occupied with girls sleeping on their blankets on the floors.

We still didn't have any television sets and were prohibited from using the yard and getting fresh air. When the door opened at noon, most of our one-hour time allotment was wasted in the bathroom line. Looking for a solution, I made twelve sets of numbered cards and gave one to each cell to keep our space in the bathroom line so that only twelve prisoners waited in the line and thereby saved time for everyone else to do other things.

Being a worker was fun because it meant having the freedom to move outside the cellblock and do something when the rest of us were locked in. Four prisoners cleaned the cellblock all day, so our cellblock was always neat and organized. Each group of workers invented new ways to deal with our problems. They arranged our belongings, put everything in order, scrubbed the bathrooms and showers three times a day from their concrete floor to ceiling, so that they were sanitized and smelled good.

Once a week each prisoner had five minutes to bathe. Almost everyone wore her hair short because of the lack of warm water. My hair had grown long but my resistance to cut it short didn't last. I soon asked a hairstylist among the prisoners to cut my hair to adapt it to our cramped conditions. Some couldn't shower that fast so we always ran out of warm water for the last round. A friendly but firm high school student became the organizer of our shower time. Wearing her round glasses she stood at the shower door for two hours calling the names to go in or get out. It was hard work, but the eighteen-year-old did it well.

Once in a while our parents were allowed to bring packages containing towels, clothes, blankets, soap, shampoo, and money. Some parents found a way to sneak books in their packages to keep us busy for awhile. Lily always wanted to give me the best things she had.

"Look. Look Mehri." she exclaimed one of those times. "Isn't this a well designed pair of pants? I'm going to give them to you."

She pulled out a pair of dark blue, tailored pants from a bag her parents had just sent her.

"Well, I like them, but, no, Lily, thanks. Why don't you wear them yourself?"

"They look best on you. It seems as if they have been made for you. Please put them on, Mehri."

"They're lovely."

"Then go ahead, put them on," she said.

I covered myself with a sheet to change and put the pants on.

"Wow, Wow," repeated Lily with delight and searched for something more in her plastic bag.

"Here's the cotton blouse that goes well with them. It will fit you."

"I don't want them. You're going to give me all your new

clothes? No Lily."

"Oh, please," said Lily. "I prefer to see them on you." She insisted and insisted, so I put on the new blouse.

"You must take them," said Sohayla, encouraging me to accept the clothes from Lily.

What was the use of hurting Lily's feelings, I thought. We didn't have many precious things after all. For the next two years I wore that special outfit constantly for I had no other options.

Among the prisoners there was a famous novelist, Shahrnush Parsipur, a tall fit woman of thirty-four with large brown eyes, great self-confidence and high intelligence.

Parsipur was a well-traveled woman and her presence enriched our lives. She had started her literary career when she was sixteen, writing short stories and articles. When she was twenty-eight, she wrote her first novel. She was imprisoned for a few months under the Shah for protesting against the torture and execution of two journalist-poet activists by SAVAK, but later, she moved to France.

Her unique character, with an easy manner and high intelligence, attracted the prisoners. She was the royalty of the prison, even Haji treated her differently, with a certain dignity and reserve.

Shahrnush Parsipur was arrested for writing a letter to the Mujahedin's leader, advising him to let his followers remain at home and avoid a conflict with the violent regime. She was concerned that many of the Mujahedin's followers would be killed by the government. Her letter was discovered during a search of her house before she could mail it. For this offense, she spent four years in Tehran's prisons.

During the day when we were locked in our cells, we watched Shahrnush pacing the hallway for hours, but she couldn't talk with us because any communication between her and the other prisoners would incite Haji's ire.

She and her educated mother were located next to the vestibule in the hallway of the cellblock as if they were living on the street, their privacy violated daily by 200 pairs of eyes. Her mother, who was a kind and enthusiastic woman, had been arrested for having opposition newspapers stashed in the trunk of her son's car when the Revolutionary Guards stopped them. Khanoom Vala became the focus of our group, all eyes fixed on her elegant manner. She was pleased to give the young, inexperienced prisoners her attention and received much gratitude by each morning interpreting their dreams, which is an important part of Iranian culture.

Coming from the upper echelon of Iranian society the old mother and her intellectual daughter co-existed in a corner of a prison hallway with three other prisoners.

One day during free time, I noticed Shahrnush Parsipur drawing with pencil on a scrap of paper. I looked at her simple gesture sketch of a girl.

"Do you know how to draw?" she asked.

"A little," I said.

She passed her paper and pencil to me. "Then draw my portrait."

I sat on the floor and drew her face. While she posed, she studied me with her sharp eyes.

When her portrait was finished, she looked at it, then raised her eyebrows. "It's fantastic. This is exactly me. You're an artist."

With her compliment, soon I became busy drawing my cellmate's portraits. From a prisoner I didn't know I received a rare item in the cellblock, a new notebook, which I used to sketch many portraits.

I often stared at this mysterious character, Shahrnush Parsipur, and Lily would pinch me, "Don't stare, Mehri. It's not right."

Perhaps part of my fascination with this famous author was a subconscious connection that she created for me with the innocence of my former life.

In my teens I had discovered the wonder-world of writers and their stories. Closed doors opened suddenly to the outside world and I became more observant. I was curious about everything, but what I wanted to know about the most was the mystery of life.

I didn't have easy access to books, yet I dove into anything I could find to read, including a suitcase full of books belonging to my brother's friend.

My brother had brought that old suitcase home before leaving for his service in the army, not knowing I would discover the books of Mickey Spillane. The character, Mike Hammer, was one of my first introductions to the complex world outside of my family, my neighborhood and school. The other translated books don't remain in my memory except for the picture of a red haired woman with large blue eyes, called *Blue-Eyed Spy*.

Nevertheless, the first fictional story I ever read was in the fourth grade, *Three Bears*.

My fourth grade schoolteacher had left us alone with the excuse that teachers had to leave early. Fariba, the daughter of a rich army surgeon, sat next to me in the first row in her flawless school uniform, reading a story aloud to herself. Sophisticated as she looked, I couldn't do anything except be entranced. I must admit I had never seen a book other than our schoolbooks before.

I decided to wait for Fariba to finish so I could ask her where she had gotten that book.

There was no response for she was turning the pages, looking at the illustrations.

"The library," she replied at last.

"Library?" I asked.

"There," she pointed with her finger in the direction of the door. "At the principal's office."

I had never been in the principle's office, but I had seen a bitter woman from time to time fling the door open to walk into our classroom shouting, "Be quiet!"

Thinking of the books I could read overcame my reservations and I finally left our unattended classroom to go to the library. I entered through the open door into the principal's office with trembling steps.

Two respected teachers sat on chairs chatting with Mrs. Khandani who stood tall behind a large desk in her fashionable light blue suit.

"What is it?" she glared at me.

Mrs. Khandani's scary tone froze the words in my brain.

"What do you want?"

"…a book…" as I searched for the next word I saw a bookshelf with a glass door in the corner of the room and pointed to it, "from the library."

"Are you a member?"

"No." I swallowed my fear.

"So you can't get a book just because you are a student."

I stood wordless.

"You must give a book to the library to become a member. Then you can borrow books. That's how it works."

"All right." I left the principal's office, holding my breath. I went back to the classroom and sat on the front bench greatly relieved, playing with my fingers, thinking with pleasure of how I could buy a book.

Rain started before the school bell rang. I opened the new umbrella my father had brought me from a southern city in Iran and ran towards home. I was squeezing the umbrella's handle in my fist, looking at its pattern of blazing bright colors over my head and enjoying the most costly thing I had ever had.

Crossing the street, I noticed two girls were running after me really fast with their madly silly laughs, trying to get my umbrella. I ran faster towards the sidewalk, but in the middle of the street, suddenly, I lost control and before I could manage, my umbrella and schoolbooks spilled out around me on the wet pavement and I fell. A taxi screeched to a halt and the driver put his head out of his window cursing at the delay. He drove past me before I stood up and the girls, still laughing, ran away.

When I tried to stand up, my left knee burned with a stinging pain. I grabbed my wet books and gathered my umbrella and limped home before something more dreadful happened. I went to the bathroom to check my injured knee. It was bleeding, but it wasn't too bad. I washed my knee with water for I was afraid to tell my mother about what had happened.

All I was thinking of now was buying a book from a newsstand at the corner of Pahlavi Square, not far from our house. Two days later at the right time when the newsstand would be open, I headed up to be there.

I glanced at a colorful book with three bears in human clothes.

"How much is this one?" I asked the man inside the kiosk.

"*Three Bears*? Three rials."

My grandfather was my only source for coins. Every evening when he came home from his daily walk, his six youngest grandchildren appeared in front of him, each pulling a corner of his coat saying over and over, "Dashi, Dashi. Grandpa, Grandpa. Money! Money!" He quickly put his hands into his pockets and laughed kindly, as it had become his habit to make a ceremony of searching in every pocket of his coat until he came to the pocket where the coins were.

After dispensing coins to his other grandchildren, he found me standing at his side leaning against the wall my cheeks pink from shyness. As if it were the last coin in his pocket, he discovered a *dah-shahi* and held it in front of my eyes. "I found one. I found one," he joyfully exclaimed stroking my head and he put it in my fist.

Everyday I saved a coin or two. I counted my money a few times a day until I collected exactly three rials.

That afternoon I sat by the door in our living room writing out my homework and listening to my mother's footsteps until she disappeared into the kitchen. I walked out of the house holding my head up, with the hope that I would certainly soon become a member of my school library and read many books. A few men reading headlines around the newsstand blocked my way, but I looked between them to see *Three Bears* remaining in its place in the last row. I reached for the book that was going to be my first purchase on my own and the first storybook I have ever had. The bookseller from behind his stand looked at me and raised his eyebrows.

"Which one?" he asked.

"*Three Bears*," I said and raised my hand full of coins to rain them in his opened fist. He counted the money and gave me the book. I hurried home, hiding *Three Bears*, which was too much to show, under my shirt before I knocked on the door.

My sister appeared, trying to create a serious knot on her forehead, "Where have you been, Miss Mehri?"

"Outside." I replied.

Rolling her honey-colored eyes, she moved aside and ordered, "Get in now."

I closed the door and went to my quiet corner behind the large stack of guest comforters and folded mattresses to slowly pull out the book. I studied the details of the drawings of the bears in human clothes and kitchen aprons on the cover for a long time. I was afraid to open it since I didn't know if reading the library's book without Mrs. Khandani's permission was the right thing to do. I was worried that turning the pages would damage the book. At last my curiosity overwhelmed me and I could no longer resist opening the book, looking at its pictures and reading it cover to cover a few times. The bears lived in a jungle, made a delicious soup, and joyfully ate it together with the large spoons they had carved from wood.

The next morning I entered the office confidently and handed the book to Mrs. Khandani.

"Here is my gift to the library." I told her without fear.

She took the book and looked at it carefully.

"Very good," she said and pulled a key out of her drawer, opened the lock of the glass door, and pushed the book inside the rows of books.

"OK. You can go now," she ordered.

"I wanted…"

"What?"

"… to… borrow a book…"

She turned around looking at me over her glasses.

"Now? What lessons do you have now?"

"Art."

Her glittering eyes muted as if she became terribly unhappy and she roared, "Then you should go ahead and do your art. You must understand that library members can only, if they wish, borrow books at certain times such as during their gym class."

I left the office, waited and counted five more days as they passed slowly until I got out of my gym class to return to the library.

Kids were running around the yard playing together without any supervision. When at last I went to the principal's office with my chin low on my neck, Mrs. Khandani who now knew why I was there wailed, "Go back and play with the kids in the yard. This is not a good time for reading books."

I realized then I couldn't go back to the library, for she would never give me a book from the school library, but I very much liked the fact that I had read one of her library books, *Three Bears*.

Later with a little money I bought a wooden spoon when we went to the bazaar with my mother. After then I ate my food with the wooden spoon, which made it taste more delicious, even though my mother and my sister laughed at me.

The warden had recently arranged to sell a limited number of food items to prisoners. At a plastic tablecloth Shahrnush and her mother sat around cutting large fresh tomatoes. The image of the red tomato with yellow seeds and the juice running from it brought back a vivid childhood memory of the time I was a little girl.

My mother had sent me to buy some vegetables at a small grocery shop that carried fresh produce, roots and herbs. The shopkeeper stood between wooden boxes of fruit and vegetables, busy with a customer. Right in front of me was a box of tomatoes, some small, some large, some misshapen and some round and unblemished. I couldn't eat the raw tomatoes for my mother always served tomatoes cooked with other foods and I didn't have the money to purchase any. I told myself that some day when I grew up, I would take three rials to buy a kilo of fresh tomatoes and eat them all, raw.

Fresh fruits and vegetables were not available for us in Cellblock 8, but once every few months the prison store offered some items for sale. However there was a rule among the women political prisoners that we would not buy vegetables or fruit. It was considered a luxury that would spoil our revolutionary way of living.

I learned later that the men prisoners not only allowed themselves of this opportunity but also demanded additional rights.

My two passions in childhood, books and tomatoes, were strictly limited in prison. I didn't buy tomatoes, but I would read books whenever I had a chance.

In our small, crowded cell we acted like a bunch of high school friends sitting in tight groups creating funny plays and teaching each other English, Turkish, or the Lori dialect. It was our way of passing the time before the guards opened the door. With only a few books available, we had to wait a long time to get anything to read. During that time I fell in love with Hafez's poems.

I said happiness and joy
Passing time will destroy
Said Hafez, silence
Employ
Sorrows, too, will end my friend

One early morning before the sun was up, we heard that the doors would be left open. After being locked inside our cells for two months, this was a moment to cherish. We now had the freedom to use the bathroom, pace nonstop, read newspapers and wash clothes in the bathing stalls at will.

In the tradition of Shia Islam there are extra ceremonies and prayers. For the last few months on every Thursday evening, the guards had opened the door to the main hallway and called the prisoners to participate in one of these group supplications known as Kumayl prayer.

A man would sing into a microphone, imploring the saints to act as mediators to ask for God's forgiveness on behalf of the sinners. The crowd of male prisoners in front and women in the back rows, all sitting on the floor, would respond by repeating his lines.

Except for a few turncoats, no one wished to participate in those ceremonies or believed in the man's nonsense prayers to dead saints. Now, it became mandatory for Cellblock 8 inmates to participate in Kumayl prayer as well. At first, most prisoners in Cellblock 8 participated reluctantly, but over time fewer and fewer girls turned out for the event.

One day Sohayla rolled her blue eyes and said, "It's not fair. I'm tired of going to Thursday Kumayl prayers. Let's make a deal Mehri. Sometimes you or other girls go, and I won't."

"I truly cannot stand it. That's why I don't go."

She looked frustrated with my answer. So, I added, "Isn't this an individual decision, dear Sohayla? I don't like to pretend."

After a while Sohayla didn't go either. Ezzat, a higher ranked Mujahedin member in cellblock 4, and her circle of friends also stopped participating. After some months, not a single person in Cellblock 8 pretended to be a traitor and all stopped going to the prison ceremonies on Thursdays.

Since we were punished in this cellblock as the opponents of the regime, it made no sense to continue to pretend we'd changed our allegiance. Even some of those who had fooled Haji for months were exposed as double agents and decided not to participate in the charade.

Although there were twenty-five to thirty of us crammed into each tiny 11 by 7 foot cell, the days were ours. Our crowded cellblock became a place of creativity, art, and friendship. Inner happiness was our reward for our acceptance of our situation. Once a small group of us dared to dance together, not a conceivable move under Haji's oppressive order in the prison.

The eight months I spent in Cellblock 8 were one of the best times in my life. The healthy relationships and quality times we created for ourselves mitigated our physical hardships. Our closeness and contentment overcame the adversity. This established a sense of peace and vitality in Cellblock 8.

There were, however, a few exceptions.

Doctor, well read and philosophical, was in her mid-thirties. She wasn't a physician nor did she have a Ph.D., but wearing thick reading glasses made her a "Doctor" in prison. One day Doctor came to talk to me when I had scheduled a reading time with Lily. I promised to talk to her later, while I wondered why she wanted to talk to me. We hardly had talked before and weren't close friends.

Two days passed, and I became so busy that I forgot about what I had promised to Doctor. As we were sitting around the plastic tablecloth to eat lunch, I heard a heavenly soprano voice coming from the other side of the cellblock singing a revolutionary song, "I am a woman. I am a woman from the far land. I am a woman."

I held my breath. We knew singing a political song was absolutely forbidden. By looking around and noticing my cellmates' strange silence, I knew there was something wrong. What was happening?

It was Doctor. She continued singing for a few days on and off. Sometimes, she talked loudly and cursed Khomeini and his government; she was out of control. After Soraya reported her situation, the guards came and took her away. I felt guilty and regretted that I hadn't dropped my activities to talk to Doctor.

A communist girl who was a psychology student believed that Doctor had schizophrenia, a word I hadn't heard before. Doctor had lost her mind.

I sat in the corner of the vestibule where all the blankets were stacked on top of each other, pulled my knees up to my chest, and put my head on my arms. Tears flowed and I cried hard and loud.

"Shush," a voice came from across the vestibule.

"Is crying forbidden too?" I said and the whole cellblock became quiet. I objected, not to the girl who had hushed me, but to the regime. I was frustrated and sad about what had happened to Doctor and didn't want to take it passively; a woman had just lost her mind.

But the girl was right. I would only get myself into a scrape. My reaction wouldn't change the situation or restore Doctor's sanity. I went back to my cell and lay on the bunk with my face toward the wall. Lily stopped talking to me, thinking I was asleep.

Later, I didn't close my eyes to the situation of a short slim woman in her mid-thirties who looked deeply sad and walked alone with both hands in her pockets. Rarely did she talk to anyone. One day she covered her face with both hands and burst into tears, out of control. I felt her desperation but couldn't understand what was bothering her. I sensed she might simply be suffering from loneliness, not having any close friends. Or maybe she felt pressured by her family or terribly upset about being in prison. I didn't know if she could make it to the end with such unhappiness. Whatever the cause, she was devastated, I was certain.

Very soon, I asked her to sit as my model. She sat in silence for an hour and looked happier than I had ever seen her. Somehow, happiness surfaced from beneath her sad face, found its way through my pencil and brightened my lined notebook. She liked her portrait in my collection. A pale smile appeared on her face and lasted for a few days. With just a few wrinkles on her face, she was about to lose her youth behind the walls of prison.

Drawing my fellow inmates' portraits filled my time and my notebook. A playwright who had cut her long hair short into a boyish style sent her portrait to her family, probably my only drawing that survived the prison.

The cellblock became subject to repeated searches by the guards without warning. They hunted through the cells for hidden writing, books and art pieces. They opened our plastic bags of clothes and looked under the bunks.

One morning, the guards took us out to get fresh air in the yard. When we came back, we found our belongings spread all over the floor. The guards had come in our absence, searched the cellblock, and had taken away books, hand-made art pieces, and my sketchbook.

Once in a while, Ezzat, the Mujahedin leader who stopped going to the Kumayl prayers, walked into our cell to chat with me. Her husband, also a member of the Mujahedin, was executed after his arrest. Lying on the third level of the bunk, she talked about her regret of not having a child with her husband. I was quiet and listening until she stood up and said, "I can't believe how naive you are," and left. I guess she felt as if I didn't understand what she was trying to say and maybe I didn't.

Neither Lily nor Roya liked Ezzat. They both believed that Ezzat was dishonest and untrustworthy, yet I wasn't suspicious of her. Because my friends and I were not in their network anymore, we didn't know if she and her friends were still organizing the prisoners in the new cellblock.

One day when Soraya called everybody to put on our chadors and sit in the hallway at midday we wondered what was going on. We sat next to each other on the floor and saw Haji and a group of mullahs walk in. Haji introduced the chief editor of Etelaat, Tehran's most important daily newspaper. The chief editor said: "We were sent here to visit you and report on your condition. We have been assigned to come here to hear your stories, complaints, and suggestions."

Haji stood there next to him looking at the crowd. If anyone was going to tell the truth about the terrible living conditions in the prison, we knew she would face certain punishment. Our speaking out would anger Haji. Also, we were suspicious and believed that they had a plan. What if this was a trick to identify those who would speak against the regime?

The Mullah was in his mid fifties. He sat on a chair in the vestibule, seemingly ready to listen. Someone broke the heavy silence asking if we could have family visitors other than our parents. The mullah gave her a vague and non-committal answer. There were a few other such questions and answers. There were prisoners whose sentences had ended and yet they remained in prison. Someone asked if they would be released since the regime didn't allow any discharge.

The hallway was packed with prisoners. I, among a few others who had not been able to find black chadors, had covered myself with a white patterned sheet and stood at the back. A nurse named Shekar, which means Sugar in Farsi, stood next to me.

"Mehri. What should we do?" Shekar asked me.

I really didn't know what to tell her since after we settled in this cellblock Shela made it clear to me that it was a big responsibility to lead others.

"I don't know, Shekar. Do whatever you think is all right for you," I said.

I felt any wrong move could put my cellmates in another harsh situation and I couldn't play with others' lives. From what I knew, almost everyone believed that the regime didn't care about us nor would they improve our conditions, but we couldn't stay indifferent. It was my personal decision to speak out. I wanted to ask the visiting group to allow us to read books. That was the least I could do at that moment.

I raised my hand and with the mullah's permission I started to speak. Haji immediately turned to the mullah next to him and interrupted me.

"Please don't listen to her. If you want to know my opinion, this one is nothing but trouble. Her brother is one of the members of the Mujahedin."

"My God," I said in a low voice. "That's not true."

It was very dangerous for my brother, and his family, to be accused of being a member of the Mujahedin. The Islamic regime could easily execute him if they believed that.

"My brother has a family," I said loudly even though they didn't pay any attention to me.

"Mehri. What a defense!" Roya later laughed at me hysterically. "'My brother has a family'! So that means he cannot be political?"

I couldn't help laughing along with her. She was right. My reasoning was ridiculous. Some political activists had families, yet they stood up against the oppression.

Things were more or less the same for a while until Haji sent five experienced traitors to our cellblock as informers. Their duty was to watch us and report everything to Haji. With Haji backing them they had no fear.

The first day of their arrival, a tall, funny girl tied a stocking that looked like a tail on the back of each of them. They walked around unaware of the joke and were confused at why others were laughing. In a short time they became completely isolated. Each day, life became harder and harder for Haji's five traitors. On the third day, they sat together at the end of the cellblock in a circle like mice looking at a cat's paws, afraid of the inmates. I didn't participate in the game.

I didn't feel it was right to ridicule these spies and provide reasons for them to report us to Haji. On a personal level I felt it was unethical to tease them. They were just simple pawns.

The air in the cellblock became tense, like a warning of a tempest that was about to occur, but the prisoners who were involved couldn't see it.

The traitors left our cellblock after five days. We heard from prisoners who had overheard what Haji's spies had reported back to him: "Cellblock 8 isn't a prison. It is another Leningrad, a city in communist Russia."

Rumors spread that Haji was planning to send some of us to solitary cells in Gohar-Dasht, a newly built prison whose construction had begun during the time of the Shah. Gohar-Dasht now was going to be used for the first time by the Islamic Republic. The same night that we heard the news, we decided to learn Tap code from one of the prisoners who knew how to communicate by tapping on the wall. We knew we would need it to contact the prisoner in the next cell in Gohar-Dasht prison.

That night Lily looked nervous. With her hands behind her back, she was walking rapidly from corner to corner and up and down in the hallway. Was the thought of going to solitary unbearable for her? Was she made terribly anxious by the thought of separation? Perhaps it was a little bit of each. Realizing that her nervousness wouldn't help anything, she soon joined us.

Two days had passed when Haji came in and called out a list of names, those who must leave the cellblock immediately. No one else was to be out of their cells.

Roya, Shela, Shekar, and I were among the thirty-five called.

Lily's face had turned pale, her body shaking, doubtful if she would ever feel all right again.

"What is it? What's the matter?" I asked.

"I cannot believe we must say goodbye,"

Lily was in tears.

"Don't worry, Lily," I told her. "We'll see each other again."

I wanted to comfort her, but how could I guess about our future?

Lily's nervousness lowered for some moments. She pulled something from her pocket and put it in my palm. She had made a dark flat stone into a precious necklace. On one side, a small figure of a fetus was delicately carved. On the other side the word, "Journey" was imprinted. I was about to cry.

I turned to Marjan and I hugged her and I laughed instead of crying while she teased me and called me by my last name. Sohayla's bright blue eyes stared at me, I winked and put my head on her shoulder as if to say, "It's all right. Every thing will be OK."

Sohayla and I had been friends even when some doubted her devotion to the opposition movement. I respected her for her affectionate nature and independence in making decisions.

"God only knows how long it will be before we see each other again. Please be very careful, and take care," she said.

None of us could have guessed who would survive nor could any of us predict our destiny.

Marjan brought me my two blankets in a hurry. I took the older one, which reminded me of my father who had brought them for me. Lily gave me a plastic bag in which she had packed my belongings, including my toothbrush, towel, comb, and one extra set of clothes. Mohandes, the treasurer from my cell, gave me some money from the common box where we kept all the money our parents sent us.

We shared everything in Cellblock 8 in order to be equitable towards everyone. It was also the best way to manage our small space, keeping all the jackets and sandals piled on top of each other in two huge cardboard boxes.

My good-byes with my friends took time, as we were many in my cell. I finally hurried to the vestibule, the last one to get there. It was agonizing to leave my friends and memories behind and enter an unknown prison.

My friends weren't allowed to follow me to the end, and I couldn't find a matched pair of sandals inside the box next to the door. A girl from behind the bars, worried about my delay and yelled, "Hurry up, just pick something and go!"

I grabbed the first sandal in green that came into my hand and put it on. Then I grabbed a similar sandal in blue and stood undecided. The same girl behind the bars said, "It's all right. Just go!" I put it on and ran.

With the black chador that was a little too short for me, a pair of unmatched sandals, the blindfold, a plastic bag in my hand, and a blanket under my arm, I must have looked like a buffoon.

I walked out of Cellblock 8, where our schoolgirl camaraderie was effectively ended, towards an uncertain destiny.

I joined the others who stood in line not far from the door. A man checked our names and guided us along the main hallway to where the guards and prison vehicles were waiting for us. Our transportation didn't take long since Gohar-Dasht is also located in the west, outside of Tehran.

Everyone in the bus remained quiet.

After we arrived, the guards divided us up. I removed my blindfold inside a brand new solitary cell. The clean walls were painted as if new and the floor was nicely covered with tiles. A two by three foot window blocked with a thick inflexible blind barred my view, but allowed a few straight lines of the unreachable pale blue sky. A toilet and sink inside the eight by twelve foot cell made it convenient and even comfortable. A thick, solid radiator was installed next to the wall on one side, which made the air warm and pleasant in the cool fall. The room felt so empty, as if no inmate had ever been there. I put down my bag and blanket and looked up at the window. Through the top of the slightly open window sun-rays brightened the cell.

The sound of the squeaking cart moving on the floor repeated three times a day, in the morning, noon, and evening. The slow rhythmic banging of unlocking and closing the doors broke the sickening silence before a guard appeared at the door. He handed in a piece of bread with feta cheese or butter then poured tea into a red plastic cup from a huge teapot he carried on his cart every morning. I started my days with the dawn prayer and exercised before he arrived.

It wasn't long before I heard the first Tap code on the wall. I knelt down, listened to the number of taps four-three, two-three, one-five, three-one and one-one. I understood the word. It was Shela tapping in the next cell at my left. I answered slowly. We tapped to each other everyday and she told me the news she heard from the cell next to hers. Soon, I knew the names of all the prisoners in my row.

The smallest details we heard, guessed, or thought became so important that we passed them on. We soon became fast in both tapping on the wall with our fingers and decoding messages. If a prisoner knew that a guard was in the hallway, she would flush the toilet as a sign to stop the Tap code. The sound of many toilets flushing at the same time made the guards aware that it was our warning sign and they began walking without making any noise so that they could catch us Taping on the walls.

But Tap code was not only a way to communicate, it was also a way to kill the time in solitary. We learned that by lying on the floor, we would see the guards' shadows on the shiny tiles under the door while they walked down the hallway.

A month later a new group of prisoners transferred from Cellblock 8. Among them Lily and Marjan settled in Gohar-Dasht solitary cells, to suffer a notoriously long separation from others.

While I walked between the two corners of the cell in a fast pace, I spent an hour of my time brushing my teeth after each meal.

One day, a voice came from the other side of the hallway. I rested motionless on the floor to listen from under the door, "I am a woman. I am a woman from a far land. I am a woman," It was her voice. It was Doctor. She was here in one of these cells, but this was the last time I ever heard her voice. Many years later, when I lived in America, I learned that she still suffered from mental illness and lived in poverty in Iran.

When a melodious whistle playing Beethoven's Symphony Number 9 filled the hallway, I added the name of Broken-Tooth, to the list of the prisoners in Gohar-Dasht. Broken-Tooth was an attractive boyish communist from my homeland, Lorestan, who danced in a group of five with my friends and me in Cellblock 8. She expertly used her half-broken front tooth as a musical instrument.

In this new prison a middle aged, religious, female guard took us for a quick weekly shower one at a time. Every time she took me out of the cell to the shower, she put her arm around my shoulder and gently guided me, like a mother holding her daughter, with care and sweetness. She was the first woman guard who showed us respect. The other guard was a mean young girl.

It was some time during the first few weeks when one morning, the cell door opened. Haji along with Lajevardi, the prosecutor of Tehran, known as the Butcher of Evin, came in. Lajevardi was not tall, but his strongly built, muscled chest and wide shoulders held his head, with its short hair squeezing all the features of his face tightly together, producing a look of constant bitterness. His large eyes reflected nothing but cruelty from behind his thick glasses, framed in black, as he glared at me.

"Unless you give us the names of your organization's leaders in Cellblock 8 you will remain here until your hair turns as white as your teeth," he said confidently and pushed his glasses back into place.

"Her sister's husband is H.K., the senator, yet she is one of the most dedicated supporters of the monafeghin," Haji bent to inform the short prosecutor.

I stood there quietly in my black chador, never raising my eyes again until they left.

H.K., who had married my sister two years before the revolution, was our second cousin, a family oriented young man, born in a decent family. My mother had pressured him to grant her a favor and have me released through his connections in the government. He used to be a popular technician in a factory. The workers chose him as their senator for the parliament.

He came to Qezel prison once and told me that if I would write a few lines to confess I was wrong and promise never to stand up against the regime, he might be able to do something for me. I refused to do so, and this made my case even worse in Haji's mind, as he had known I was H.K.'s sister-in-law. At my mother's insistence, my sister's husband came to Gohar-Dasht to visit me again with the same advice, but I told him that I would never do what he wished.

Two months passed in solitary. The days became longer and more tiresome until my cell door banged opened after the several click-click sounds of unlocking doors and Shela walked in with her belongings.

I had only recently wished to have company, but surely I didn't expect to see Shela, my friend, walk in. We exercised together, and with warm water being available at the sink in our cell, we were able to wash up afterward. When one of us took a bath, the other turned her face towards the window to provide privacy for the other. We had to bathe carefully so as not to get caught by the guards who might open the small casement at the door to check on us.

Once, I put my cardboard sign under the door, requesting to go to see the doctor.

This was a way for prisoners to get out of their cells since there was no other chance. The guard took me out, guided me along a hallway, and left me in a room. The two doctors were political prisoners and visited the sick prisoners occasionally at the prison's health center.

"You may take off your blindfold and tell me what's wrong," the doctor employed a kind voice. I opened my eyes to see a man's pleasant smile.

"Doctor," I said. "I have two health problems: The first is twenty-eight small holes in my back and shoulders and the second is my occasional stomach aches."

The tall, thin doctor couldn't avoid laughing.

"How do you know you have exactly twenty-eight holes in your back but not thirty or twenty-seven?" he asked. "How were you able to count them?"

"My cellmate carefully counted them when she was washing my back."

He briefly checked my back.

"I don't see any holes," he said.

"The only real problem you have is your stomach ache."

He then asked me some more questions and said, "Your stomach ache is the result of bad nutrition." He gave me some pills while he went off into his hearty laugh again.

The girl in the cell on our left always took her weekly shower just after us. There were three stalls in the shower room and a wall that separated them from one another. Shela had an idea.

"Let's make a cake for her and leave it on top of the wall in the shower."

"A cake? Are you joking?"

"No, I'll show you."

She gently rubbed two sugar cubes together, making some powder to mix with butter and white bread to make a two by three inch layered cake. The cake looked so good and real. I loved the amazing things I learned from Shela and it was pleasant not to be alone.

But when Haji came to Gohar-Dasht to visit us, Shela picked a fight with him about Mrs. Farima, a prisoner who cooperated with Haji and was in charge of a large cellblock in Qezel. I felt uncomfortable with Shela's criticism of the woman. Her high energy and extreme enthusiasm clashed with my calm nature.

After a few similar incidents, I became exceedingly sensitive to everything Shela did, whether big or small. After three months of living together in a cell without a moment of privacy, it became unbearable for me to tolerate her strong presence. Reluctantly, I decided to ask the wardens to put me in another cell by myself.

At Gohar-Dasht, we had visitations twice a month. One day when they took Shela out of the cell to see her parents, I wrote a letter for her in the margins of a pro-regime magazine we had received twice. I wrote to say goodbye and explained I had lost my patience and needed to be alone. I had asked her to forgive me for leaving.

As I had planned, on the way back of my own visitation, I raised my hand, and the warden's assistant came close to me and asked what was wrong. I didn't want the other prisoners to hear my unusual request.

"May I speak to you in private," I said.

For a moment he said nothing then he pulled me out of the line.

"What's going on?" he whispered.

"I want to be alone in another cell," I said in a very low voice.

"Why?" he asked me loudly. "You must tell me your reason."

"I just want to be alone. That's all."

"No."

He returned me to the row of blindfolded girls waiting in the hallway, intending to ignore my request.

I thought of taking advantage of getting punished for breaking the rules, "I'm going to take off my blindfold right now."

I hoped this would make him accept my request, since being alone in a cell was a punishment. He pulled me aside again and commanded me to wait. He left in a hurry to get permission from his boss and came back breathless to take me to another cell.

After about two hours a guard brought me my belongings, including the magazine. When I opened it I could hardly believe that Shela had written two pages in it. We were so lucky that the guards didn't check the magazine before giving it to me. In response to my note, Shela philosophically analyzed the situation. She saw it as a result of the pressures of solitary confinement.

I remained in that cell for three more months, spending dull, long days alone. Gradually, I started to feel depressed and couldn't do my prayers or exercises. Most of the time, I slept for long hours and walked the rest of the day. My using Tap code with the people in the cells next to me became less and less interesting and all the news seemed small and repetitious. I remembered that two years before the revolution, I had read Dr. Shariati's experience of being in solitary confinement:

"No matter who you are, you become emptier and emptier and after six months, you lose all your ambition. That's how solitary will change you day by day."

It was my seventh month in solitary, and I had been in prison for two years.

In the last days of April 1983, a guard unlocked my door and told me to leave the cell with all my belongings. Going into the hallway, I heard other prisoners walking. Between the noises of plastic bags, the girls purposely coughed to relay their identity to their own friends. I recognized a long, deep, audible exhalation. She was Lily and I had no doubt Marjan was here among us, too.

It seemed we were heading towards another prison and my time in solitary was finally over. In a minibus, we were told to put our heads down and not look out from underneath our blindfolds. I sat beside a window and it was Roya who sat next to me. We held each other's hands under our black chadors.

"Where do you think they are taking us?" she whispered,

"I have no idea. What do you think?"

"Evin."

"Shhh... no talking," a female guard said.

We remained quiet for a while.

"Maybe they're going to execute us," I said quickly.

"Shhh...." The girls' hush made us quiet again.

It was a long time since I had felt the delight of riding in a car, hearing the traffic noise and feeling the life that was going on outside the prison. Apparently we arrived in the new place before noon and the mini bus door opened.

"All of you, get out and stand against the wall," a man's voice ordered.

We stepped out and I could see from beneath my blindfold that the minibus was next to a gray, concrete wall.

"Face the wall and remain quiet," the man said.

I faced the wall. In a few second the touch of the sun penetrated my chador, warming my back. Even though I couldn't see anything, at this moment, despite the circumstances, all I could feel was the joy of being outside in the warmth of the late April sun.

I couldn't guess that what lay just ahead of us would begin the harshest chapter of my imprisonment.

PART 10

The Unit / Vahed e Maskuni

(1983)

Roya A. and Mehri Dadgar," a man firmly commanded a response.

I nodded.

"Mehri Dadgar?" A man whispered in my ear.

I nodded again and stepped back right before he grabbed the side of my chador and pulled me inside a building. In the hallway he pulled me next to a metal chair.

"Sit," he said.

I sat. From beneath my blindfold, I saw a few sheets of large lined paper on the chair's handle. On the top, in red ink, was written, "Write down all the information you have about the organization's network inside Cellblock 8."

Now I knew we were under interrogation, and that man was an interrogator.

I grabbed the blue pen.

"I have no information," I wrote, and put down the pen.

The interrogator came back in a minute. He read my sentence and asked me to follow him.

"I will show you with whom you are dealing. You have no information? I'll show you if you have it or not." Walking with him, I discovered that he was of average height and weight and was probably in his thirties. He opened a door. We walked into a room.

"Look at her." I heard a voice from inside the room say, "Even her shoes are monafegh, one in blue one in green."

"Lie on the bed face down!" he commanded.

I climbed on the wooden bed and lay down on my stomach. I caught a glimpse of a tall, heavy, young man, dressed in black.

"Spread out your arms." He ordered. I obeyed while Azadeh's

voice about her romantic notion of torture echoed in my head. "Mehri, I'm so curious to know what torture is like."

"Look," the younger voice said mockingly. "How obedient this one is."

With one fast movement, he pulled my socks off my feet. He then tied my hands and feet with ropes, pushed a cloth in my mouth, and started to lash the bare soles of my feet with a heavy metal cable.

A sudden sharp pain moved like a flash from the soles of my feet all the way up to the deepest cells of my brain. Every lash of my feet created a fire that raced through my bones. In an instant the world changed in my eyes.

The men continue to beat me with the copper cable. The pain was so great that it felt like every cell in my body was joining together to cry. I heard an unknown scream come out of my mouth, muffled by the gag. Pain in every cell of my body was more than I could bear.

In a sudden moment I remembered something I had heard from a friend whose brother had been tortured during the Shah's time. "My brother had put up with the torture by repeating to himself: 'It will end. It will end. It will end soon.'"

I repeated those words in my head, "It will end. It will end. It will end soon," until the three interrogators stopped beating me.

Before the torture started, I didn't think much of it and thought I could take anything, but when they lashed my feet, the pain engulfed my body like a monster and threatened to overtake my soul.

Azadeh's abstraction of torture was as unreal as dreams. The concrete facts of torture were harsher than anything I could ever have imagined. But I had to remain loyal. I was clear that I wouldn't talk and that the torture would never change my beliefs. They would not get any information from me about anybody.

They untied my hands and feet and pulled me into the hallway. My feet had become so swollen that my sandals didn't fit anymore.

I noticed Shekar standing against the wall next to the door, her bare feet swollen. She was doing a slow stationary march. Shekar was a nurse and I was sure she knew what was best for relieving the pain. I started doing the same thing.

"Who allowed you to march?" the younger interrogator, Sameen, yelled at me. He grabbed my chador and pulled me back into the torture room. With the help of the middle-aged interrogator, Hamid, he tied me up to the bed and started to lash the soles of my feet again.

My screams seemed to come from miles away. With each strike, I screamed louder and louder. The ultimate reality of torture is pain beyond anything one can ever feel.

After untying my hands and feet they returned me to a room. I walked in pain into the room where from beneath my blindfold I secretly saw my friends in back chadors seated against the walls, their heads down. Sameen was whispering to the girls busy filling the pages with writing. They must have been asked the same question I had been asked. I wondered what they were writing on the interrogation papers.

A row of young women sitting with blindfolds writing hurriedly under the hysterical fear that had spread over the place drew nothing, but cruelty. Silence was broken only by screams of those in the torture room. The only thing I could do was to resist. I refused to write a word.

Then I realized that Sameen had left the room because the next thing I heard was a voice from the torture room.

"Brother. Brother Sameen. Please…I beg you…I will talk, Brother. Please don't beat me," the voice pleaded. I recognized it. It was Neema from Cellblock 8.

For the next few days, we sat blindfolded facing the wall in silence. At night we slept on the floor four feet apart and were not allowed to talk to each other.

The horror of the place was palpable. The constant presence of the three interrogators made the prison terrifying. The only respite I got was the look of kindness in the eyes of a tiny young turncoat whose duty was to take us to the restroom one by one.

My back began to hurt from sitting on the floor for days on end. Interrogators repeatedly walked into the room, handed out sheets of paper, collected the filled ones, read them, and came back with new questions. I could hear them talking to prisoners in low voices. The writing seemed to go on forever.

Sometimes, for no apparent reason, the interrogators made everybody stand up all day. It was agonizing to go through all this. I tried to remember a revolutionary song and started to sing it in a low voice to give courage to my friends to not give up in this unfair battle.

oh hear, our friends are singing
oh hear, our friends are singing
remember the bloody covenant
remember the bloody covenant

This made my fellow inmates uneasy. In one instant Shekar hushed me, shhhhhh………

I stopped singing honoring my friends' desire to avoid the consequences of breaking the law of that place. Day by day I waited hearing the footsteps across the room, the occasional noise of voices, including the spine-chilling screams and the slither of prisoner's sandals.

One day, a girl sitting next to Roya leaned over and spoke to her quietly.

Roya cautiously passed on the news to me.

"Mehri, Ezzat has broken."

When she was sure nobody was around she continued, "Ezzat told the interrogators that there was a network in Cellblock 8. She named you, Shela and me as the leaders of the rebels, the most dedicated to the resistance movement in prison. Ezzat represented herself and her followers as the moderate wing in the network."

I couldn't believe it. "Why? Why did she say that?"

"She broke and now works for them. She identified us as the source of resistance in Cellblock 8 to save herself."

I wasn't sure how reliable this information was. I had assumed there was not a network in Cellblock 8 or at least I wasn't aware of it. I decided not to believe what I had heard. Maybe this was a plot to trap us and make us confess.

Days passed slowly as we sat on the floor three feet apart, blindfolded. We were facing the wall, each with our small bag of belongings nearby.

The silence made it seem that no one was guarding us. A whisper started at the other side of the room. Someone called me. I turned. Looking beneath the blindfold, I saw Shela sitting next to Marjan and Shekar. Shela had pulled her blindfold off her eyes and looked back at me. Her eyes were filled with tears.

"It seems our destinies are joined," she said.

I smiled at her.

Lily, who sat on the other side, whispered to me, "Hello, Mehri, how are you?"

"Hello, Lily. I'm fine." I threw a small plastic bag towards her,

"Lily. Take it," I said and she caught it in the air.

"What's this?"

"The dried plums that you like…"

"Keep them for yourself."

"No, I don't need them."

Suddenly, everyone became quiet. Lily and I hadn't turned back to face the wall yet when I saw an interrogator had appeared in the room. He was slim and short, around twenty-eight in a casual black suit. He pulled Lily and me both out of the room and made us stand facing the wall at two ends of the hallway. He was pitiless Ashtari, the interrogator, his eyes two dark, cold spots inside deep sockets.

I knew he was going to punish both of us. My first thought was to protect Lily at least.

"What were you two talking about?" Ashtari's threatening voice hurt my ear.

"I said hello to Lily but she didn't reply," I said loudly so that Lily could hear me.

Ashtari went over to Lily. I couldn't hear what they said, but he took Lily back to the room and came back to take me to another place where he kicked me hard on my shins repeatedly. He ordered me to raise my hands and stand on one foot.

When it became unbearable to keep my balance on a tired leg, I switched to the other foot. He came back every once in awhile to check on me and kicked me through my chador to make sure I had only one foot on the ground.

Exhausted and disoriented I stood there all night. I had no idea how many hours I had been on one leg. Suddenly I felt a sharp pain. It was Ashtari kicking me viciously in my back. At some point I lost consciousness and had fallen to the floor asleep. It was early morning.

He cursed me and ordered me to stand up. I tried to stand up. He dragged me down the hallway by my chador. I lost my blindfold as a result. When he opened the door I saw the torture bed.

"No… my feet are injured," I tried to reason with him.

He continued dragging me and threw me onto the torture bed. I moaned. I thought I couldn't bear being tortured again. He left the room and closed the door. I pulled myself together. I was expecting him to come back at any moment.

Ten minutes or more passed. I felt better and savored every slowly passing second, living completely in the moment. Suddenly a ghostly whisper spread throughout the room. I looked around. There was no one there.

"Meeehhhrrrri. Meeehhhrrrri has broken. Mehri has broken… broken…broken…broken."

For a moment I was not quite sure whether I was awake or asleep. I examined myself and listened carefully without moving. It took me a minute to determine that the voice was not coming from inside of my own head.

"A warm and familiar voice; if I think better, might I know who is it?" I thought.

"No, no, I have not broken," I firmly said in a whisper and mocked the one who wanted to fool me. Her voice overlapped mine in the opposite direction. I was sure now. It passed through a door on the side, from an adjacent room. It was Ezzat who employed a dreamy voice repeating frequently, "Mehri has broken" to introduce this thought into my head.

I had no doubt that I wouldn't talk under torture, and I would never become a traitor. I was willing to die and would never give up any information. No way. Not while there was still breath in my body.

Ashtari flung the door open and came in with Hamid and Sameen.

My feet still had large blisters from the last torture, but they had no pity since they believed they were beating an enemy of God, and they were fighting for His cause. To them, it was a good deed to beat a monafegh. They believed they were defending Islam and they would use whatever force it took to establish the rules and laws of their own version of an Islamic regime.

We were oppressed either by the regime or by our own organization's leaders. A true believer would be ashamed of practices that prevent others from comprehending the true meaning of Islam. In the Quran, oppression is worse than murder, and life is sacred. Liberty is needed for all individuals to make real choices.

My greatest desire at that moment was to be who I wanted to be, a free thinker, a normal human being. I didn't want to harm anyone.

My reasons dissolved into the pain of the lashes. My screams filled my own ears and didn't allow me to think any longer. I listened to my voice as if it weren't my own. The moment they stopped, my screams changed into the cries of a girl for her mother. The sound of moaning drifted in the room. The interrogators untied my hands and ordered me to sit up. I pulled myself up and sat there rocking involuntarily from the pain.

It felt as if my lower legs had been cut off. Sharp pain collected in my knees. My legs were numb and my feet were soaked in blood. Crying out in my dialect, I couldn't stop calling for my mother. One of the interrogators placed a stack of newspaper under my feet to keep the blood from running all over the floor. The blood seeped rapidly into the newspapers.

How long was I on that bed? How many lashes had I taken? I had no idea. Later Roya told me that they had made her sit behind the door to listen to my screams. She had counted up to one hundred, but had lost track after that. The number of lashes, according to their own laws, was supposed to be under fifty.

Sameen collected the used newspapers and put another stack in their place when the door opened. A tall, good-looking man in a white uniform appeared. He froze in shock for a few moments. His eyes met mine as he gazed at me.

The sympathetic words that were reflected in his eyes touched my heart, and I understood that he was with me, that he cared about me, that he was so sorry to see me in pain and he appreciated my resistance against injustice, and if he could he would do anything to make me forget the pain. I stopped crying.

The man finally collected himself, looked around, and stepped into the room. He knelt on the floor beside the bed, opened his medical suitcase, and took out his supplies. He was a political prisoner. With his head down, he gently cleaned the blood from the soles of my feet. Then he sanitized them with swabs. The lashes had ripped the flesh off my feet and left holes in my soles. He wadded up pieces of gauze and filled the holes.

I can't remember what happened after that. When I woke up sometime later, I was in another room under a blanket. There was an IV connected to my hand. About ten other prisoners sat against the wall, blindfolded. I saw Haji by my side looking larger than before. His eyes cold, he stood there satisfied, watching me writhe in pain. My feet were in so much pain that I couldn't bear it and I cried.

"Do you want a shot of morphine?" he asked.

"No," I said and turned my face away from him. I didn't want him around nor could I trust him or believe he was trying to help me. I considered that what he could possibly be doing was turning me into a morphine addict. Yet, I didn't feel any hate towards him. For what I had learned years ago from the Quran about forgiving others hadn't cracked a bit in me. Mercy was a way to purify one's heart of hate.

Later, I was passing out from pain and could hardly recognize the one who bent over me, but I asked for painkillers.

"Please give me a shot, please…doctor. I can't stand the pain."

I don't remember anything after that until I woke up again.

Two years later, I heard that the doctor had been executed.

Looking in the doctor's eyes, I had seen an honorable soul, a man who couldn't abide by the rules of terror and torture, rules so against the teachings of the God in the Quran.

In the Unit, a secret place for torture, the interrogators pushed the prisoners to the edge of sanity. We were living in Hell, in Satan's Kingdom, far from God and His goodness. It was quite beyond our comprehension. Days would go by in such a strange way that made me aware of every second of it. I had to think of how to act, how to look, how to hold myself, what to say and what not to say in order to survive and avoid conflict.

I could see my friends losing hope little by little. Everyone suffered. The air was polluted with fear and constant anxiety. The truth seemed like a shattered glass. It was impossible to put those pieces back together.

The next morning, as I lay on the floor with the IV in my arm, the guards took all the other prisoners out of the room except for Neema who stood there without a blindfold. She was there to sweep the room with a broom in her hand. She swept and swept and came closer and closer. She struggled to make sure no one was watching.

"Mehri, please, you must write. Ezzat has told everything. You're resisting for nothing." She tried to convince me. "Please call Mrs. Farima tomorrow and ask her to talk to Brother Sameen to give you interrogation papers. Please listen to me."

She then continued to sweep the room. When she finished, Mrs. Farima, a traitor who used to be in charge of the cellblock 3, brought back the other prisoners to sit facing the wall, blindfolded. Neema put on her blindfold and seated herself among the other prisoners, crossing her legs. I didn't know if Neema was trustworthy and really had been making sure we were not watched, or if she was doing a favor for the interrogators. Why had they left her alone with me? Did they want her to talk to me? I didn't know.

Despite all my doubts, I wanted to believe that Neema had put herself in danger to help me. The next day, I called for Mrs. Farima and asked for paper.

"OK," she said and left to talk to Sameen, who stood just outside the room.

"Oh... is that right?" Sameen said. "Does she want to write? Well...well, I'll think about it."

I didn't have a blindfold on and could see Sameen rubbing his hands. He spoke loudly for everybody to hear, but pretended to be indifferent. This confirmed my suspicions about the scene with Neema.

"I don't want to write. I changed my mind about getting paper," I said loudly.

Sameen's face turned red and helpless, for his manipulation failed to make me confess. Suddenly, I felt glad that his approach hadn't tricked me, but I also truly didn't know what to write about. I didn't want to give information and couldn't make up lies and nonsensical stories.

Being straightforward suited me better. This set my mind at ease, at least for a few days.

One night, the two young turncoats assigned us places to sleep on the floor. The room was warm so we didn't need blankets and slept blindfolded wrapped in our black chadors. Roya slept close to me, her head only two feet away from mine. When the guards turned off the lights and no one was around, Roya reached for my hand and pressed it tightly, with warmth. Both Roya and I had been beaten and tortured. Not giving in made us feel closer than ever.

"I'm very happy," I whispered.

"Me too. The only thing I was afraid of was torture. No more do I fear that," she said; her voice wavered with sobbing from remembered pain.

That moment was one of the best moments of my life. I hadn't known that the price we had paid would reward us with feeling graced, belonging to a greater whole. I had no attachment to life anymore. None.

"I think they placed me next to you intentionally," Roya said. "I assume they want me to encourage you to start answering the interrogator's questions."

Our whispering in the dark ended without interruption and we slept, as we both were so tired.

I was severely tortured one more time, but this time they didn't bring the doctor. The wound on the sole of my right foot took five months to heal because I didn't receive adequate medical attention. Once a day for the first week, either Sameen or Mrs. Farima changed my bandages. After that, they did nothing.

I sat facing the wall with my blindfold on when Roya surreptitiously told me that the interrogators had forced everyone to write false testimony that corroborated what Ezzat had told them. The prisoners had drawn up an organization chart connecting their friends or cellmates to the fictional network Ezzat lied about.

The interrogators believed that Roya, Shela and I were the leaders of the organization. Strangely, they didn't ask about the network in Public 4 in which we had participated.

"We didn't have any organization in Cellblock 8. You know that, Roya."

"Yes, but the interrogators say whatever activities we have done will be considered as organizational networking. Even reading books, talking and walking together, making cards for the bathroom line and cutting our hair short. They want us to write down names and what we did every minute of the day."

What could one do in such unfair circumstances? The interrogators and the turncoats had already banished the truth by writing their own version of the story. There was no other way for me to avoid being tortured except to join the others and accept the allegations that I was a leader in that imaginary network. According to the law of the prison, the truth was a lie, and lies were the truth. Anyone who didn't comply stood out and was severely punished. That was the only way to survive.

That's how I was made to say that I was one of the leaders in Cellblock 8.

One day Mastooreh, the collaborator prisoner in charge, sat down next me and ordered me in a whispered voice to take off my chador,

"I want to see your hair." She then recorded the length of my hair to support the theory of the interrogators who were looking for the girls with short hair, a sign of membership in the prison resistance movement. In fact, prisoners cut their hair short to wash it quickly and easily because of the poor hygienic conditions.

"I'm puzzled," Mastooreh told me after she had examined everyone's hair. "The length of your hair doesn't match the others. You're the only one who has long hair."

In reality my short hair had grown long in the months of being in solitary and I had let it be.

In the morning, I woke up from a vivid dream. In my dream I was enjoying running in slow motion on a new street with plants and flowers on both sides. I passed a few people who were running as if it were a never-ending race. Then I alone arrived at a stunning garden that had a huge open gate. I paused, then entered and continued running. The park gradually became a town with streets and tall three-story houses built on hills, with no plants or flowers nearby.

As I continued running, I noticed that the city was completely deserted and quiet. I slowed down and gradually stopped. I looked around. With fear growing inside me, I looked for a hiding place and noticed a set of stairs. I climbed them and hid behind a jeep next to a door. I sat there and waited until a few people appeared on the street some hours later. It was early morning and people were heading towards work. I felt comfortable then to step out of my hiding place.

Another night I dreamed I was walking on a street. Many young boys and girls were building a big mansion from pastries. Suddenly the building collapsed and became a mound of mashed pastry. I tasted a handful of it. It was delicious. Then a group of girls in black chadors who were near the collapsed pastry building walked to the other side of the street, and I went with them.

At the intersection, I saw the nephew of a friend of mine who had green eyes, and used to have a crush on me. He was a follower of the Mujahedin, but in my dream he was wearing the uniform of the Basij, a government militia made up of young armed civilians. He was directing the pedestrians on the street.

As time passed, I realized the significance of these dreams, which seemed to foretell my future. Perhaps the later dream reflected the future down fall of the Mujahedin organization and my first dream came true many years later when I started to write all that happened to me in a city similar to the one in my dream.

The interrogators' questions were endless. They wanted to know the details of our acquaintances before being arrested. These questions were meant to identify the politically active people we knew. The interrogators wanted us to list them all with first and last names, addresses, occupations, and their political stances. The smallest bit of information could cause a friend or a family member to be arrested.

My fiancé, Hussein, was an active member of the Mujahedin organization and my uncle's oldest son and daughter were both politically active with one of the communist parties, Paykar. It was absolutely clear to me that I should not mention their names. I acted as if they had never been born. Nor did I mention any friends or neighbors who were connected to any political group.

When I had to answer the interrogators' questions, I only gave them a few useless first names, all of which they already knew anyway.

We sat on the floor against the wall all day every day, and were not allowed to talk or lie down. Two collaborator prisoners watched us closely so we couldn't exchange any information.

At the time I couldn't walk Mastooreh took me to take a shower. She wrapped my injured feet in plastic bags to keep my wounded soles dry. I dragged myself across the floor to the stall in a sitting position. Using the wall I pulled myself up and stood on my less injured foot, wobbling and struggling not to fall.

As I took off my shirt, my ribs stuck out like the bars of a xylophone and my skin looked like a sack on my skeleton. I took a shower, dried my body with my small towel, and put on a clean shirt. I limped away from the shower, put on my chador and my blindfold, and sat on the ground, waiting for Mastooreh to take me back. I decided not to think about my poor physical condition.

A few weeks later, I was in the shower again to wash my clothes. I put my dirty clothes in a plastic wash basin and sat down on the floor. Just as I started to wash my clothes, I heard a door open. I turned my head to see Roya walk in with a bag of clothes in her hand. How in the world was that possible? She was also shocked to see me alone. Someone closed the door behind her. She looked around in confusion to be sure no one was inside the three-stall shower room.

"Hello Mehri," she whispered.

I felt uneasy, thinking that someone was somewhere behind the door or window watching. It was impossible that they would allow Roya and me to have a private chat. I was certain this was a set up. But Roya didn't want to lose this opportunity and wanted to talk.

"How are you?" She asked.

Her voice was soft. My heartbeats ran faster. I didn't say a word. I didn't even look at her or smile back. I didn't know what she was thinking. I watched her from the corner of my eye and I saw her smile dry up and her happy face turn to disappointment.

I clearly had in my mind an occasion, not long before this, when the interrogators had taken us outside into a tiny adjoining yard, without blindfolds for the first time.

We were sitting opposite each other in our black chadors around the perimeter of the yard. For the first time in weeks we were able to see each other. Roya her back against the wall, looked across at me and smiled. Even though she tried to hide her smile by pulling her chador over her mouth, Ashtari, the interrogator saw her smiling at me.

He motioned for her to stand up and walk toward him. He then beat the palms of her hands mercilessly with a metal cable. Roya bent forward, twisting in pain. She shrieked with each blow, her eyebrows tightened and her smile disappeared. By the time she walked back to her place, her tired face looked even thinner. My heart broke for her.

With this memory fresh in my mind, I didn't dare talk to Roya until Mastooreh walked in and took me back to sit among the others, blindfolded, face to the wall.

I knew all too well they watched even our slightest gestures. The interrogators and collaborators as our guards were looking for any signs of communication to punish us severely. I had decided not to play a role in their game and avoid any foolish movement.

Ashtari took five of us to a small windowless room with an iron door to spend almost a week in nearly complete silence. There was a small bathroom in the room so we didn't ever get to leave the cell. Inside the room we didn't wear blindfolds or chadors and could walk around but didn't dare talk to each other. We feared that the interrogators might seize that opportunity to question us about our conversation. No one knew who might break under torture or who might have already been broken.

I always assumed that the rooms were wired. Was there a specific purpose for putting us together in this cell? Periodically, Ashtari would burst into the room, look at us, and leave without saying a word. To guard against his sudden entries we kept our chadors in our hands ready to put them on in an instant.

Ashtari then took us to a large room where all the windows were covered with newspapers. To our surprise a group of prisoners with cold eyes, none of whom we had been aware of before, were living there. It was our fifth month in the Unit. It seemed as if we were now released to some extent to live as a group.

On our first day in this large room, I stood in line to use the bathroom. There were four girls ahead of me. One of them was the higher ranked girl in Solitary 4 who two years ago had cursed the Mujahedin, called them monafeghin so that Haji would transfer her to Public 4. Her right foot was wrapped in a white bandage. She couldn't walk properly.

I volunteered and helped her walk to the bathroom, she thanked me and I got back in line.

When I returned to the room, I stood beside a slightly open window thinking about this overwhelming and terrible situation. As I turned to walk away from the window, I saw Ezzat standing right behind me. She used to have many friends. But everyone knew now that not only had she cooperated with the interrogators but also that she had made up a story about a network in Cellblock 8, causing many of us to be tortured for what we hadn't done.

She unhesitating looked into my face. Tears filled my eyes.

"Why, Ezzat, just tell me why?" I asked her.

She paused for a second and then without saying a word, began to cry. I felt that her tears were real and that she was truly sorry. She said nothing and disappeared quickly. I also noticed that the injured girl in the bathroom had disappeared just as quickly. I didn't see either of them again for about a year.

Where did they go? Why were they there for such a short time? At that time, I didn't know the girl I helped in the bathroom line wasn't truly injured. She had a fake bandage on her foot and was sent to this room as a spy to determine who felt sympathy for someone being tortured. Ezzat was also there to report on prisoners. Mastooreh, the collaborator in charge, told me these things some months later.

A short while later I found Neema, who had tried to persuade me to write while I was resisting. She lay in a small room by herself, gasping for air. It was terrifying. She couldn't move and tears were streaming from her large green eyes. I sat next to her and tried to understand what she was saying but couldn't because her voice was weak.

"What's wrong?" I asked her. "Do you need help? Should I call someone?"

"No.....I am fine b u t...l i s t e n," she said and put her hand on her chest.

"Is it your heart?"

"No......N o.....l i s... t e n,"

"I'm listening."

"Believe me I don't want anything, but to see the downfall of this cruel regime. I am telling you this regime is the worst. It is out of the question for me to believe otherwise."

I noticed the expression on her face changed when she started to curse the interrogators and the regime and she could speak more clearly.

I told her again that I wanted to call somebody to help her but she insisted that she was fine. It was difficult for me to figure out if she was playing a role for the interrogators or was actually ill. I thought it was crazy to curse the regime, and I tried to stop her.

"I... k n o w...what I'm... saying," she said.

Closing her tearful eyes and trying to catch her breath, she went on talking. Through all of this, I had a disturbing feeling that she might have been acting, yet I didn't leave her side. She grew worse and worse, as she kept crying. Finally, she couldn't speak and only mumbled, rough sounds breaking from her throat. Two girls from the new group of sixteen that we met here walked into the room. They stared at me rudely as if I were their enemy and deserved to be torn apart. I sat there and comforted Neema until she stopped crying.

It slowly dawned on me that this group in the large salon were all traitors, cooperating with the interrogators. For them there was no shame in betraying their cellmates. I never fully understood why they were there or what their exact orders from the interrogators were, but without a doubt, they had no hesitation to put their hands on our backs to push us down to the bottom of the darkest abyss.

I constantly reminded myself that this was a hellish place, that its fire might burn all humanity and turn everyone into traitors. I must not give any information to anyone under any circumstances.

In the large room where everyone had no hope of escaping from this secret prison they brought us a TV, to watch "The Great Escape," starring Steve McQueen. We lay on the floor and watched prisoners escaping from prison with the rapt intention of a sweet dream. It was only at the end that I noticed the collaborators' eyes were on us and they would report in detail who had watched the movie.

Even with this constant surveillance I hung my long hair at both sides like the ears of a rabbit, walking in my dark blue pants and the colorful shirt Lily had given me. I enjoyed being in this room for I was able to move around and see my friends. Nevertheless, our stay there was temporary and lasted just one week.

It was the September of 1983 when the interrogators isolated us again from seeing anyone, we were blindfolded day and night. No light, no sound, and no human interaction. Besides my past five months of suffering from torture and persecution, this too, was one of my severest punishments.

No one from the outside world, not even our families, knew where we were.

At that time I did not know that this cellblock was divided into spaces as small as graves and I didn't know what to expect. Unable to stir, we faced controls that were much more stringent. For three days straight, I stood up, face to the wall, as Ashtari had ordered. With my right hand, I held my chador under my chin and tried to keep my balance while my life before prison ran through my mind like a movie.

There was nothing in my prior life to make me sad or feel ashamed. I hadn't done anything wrong. Only then, when I thought of my parents and Hussein did I realize that every bit of my time and energy had gone into surviving the interrogation and torture, so that I hadn't had even a moment to think about them. A feeling of regret grew in my heart. How were my parents doing? Where was Hussein? Would I ever see them again?

I wished I had spent more time with my father and asked questions about his childhood.

My father was the son of a wealthy family, all lawyers, judges or businessmen. From an early age he was on his own, for both his father and mother died when he was a child. According to his father's will, his uncle, who was a judge, took over his inheritance to hand it to him when he grew up enough to take care of his wealth. All I knew was that my father never received his inheritance nor did he get a chance for an education. My father even took care of his three sisters. Why? I never knew the story. I didn't even know my grandparents' names.

I wished I had paid more attention to my mother.

Then, as if I could see a different world other than the one I was in, I entered into a daydream. I was sitting next to my father with a pen and paper.

"Agha joon," I said, "what was my grandpa's name, your father's name? Who was your mother? Whom did you lose first? You were young when they died. How old were you exactly? Do you remember them? How did you feel?"

My father stared into space recalling the past and began to talk about his life.

Then I thought of my mother, who had always wanted to see the Caspian Sea in the north of Iran. Lamenting deeply, I imagined that I had taken her to Ramsar Beach where we could walk along the sandy shore, between the green side of the Alborz Mountains and the blue sea,

"Maman." I said, "Hold my hand. Don't be afraid. Let's go in the water together."

We laughed and ran into the water and looked at the sun reflecting on the waves.

"It's been a long time since I've laughed," I said to my mother.

Then I took her with me on one of my regular Friday hikes to the north of Tehran. The perfume of the wild flowers along the path made her light headed, but she carried on. Another day we explored the Bazaar and breathed in the aromas of baked goods and new fabrics. I bought my mother the clothes she liked.

My heart was full of love for her. Looking at her, I noticed how she blushed, her cheeks a bright pink. I sensed her joy for life so strongly that I couldn't help smiling. I was about to tell her how grateful I was for her care for the family when I was interrupted. She immediately vanished from my mind. I could no longer see my mother. I heard Ashtari's voice, filled with hate, whispering into my ear as he drew himself very close. His bad breath made my stomach turn.

"How are you doing?" he asked.

It was the month of Ramadan. All the prisoners and interrogators were fasting. I was hungry and Ashtari's empty stomach rumbled.

"Wonderful," I replied.

"You're so strange," he said through his teeth, and left.

That day, he ordered Soraya to allow me to sit. I sat blindfolded in a thick silence for seventeen hours every day. I was seated in the same spot every morning until 11 at night. I became so sick with a stomachache that I couldn't continue fasting and received small portions of soup, lentils, or rice three times a day after my daily prayers.

Soraya was there all the time, watching over us in complete silence. Her chador rustled when she bent down to leave a plate of food beside me on the blanket. Her soft milky hand would reach out to take the empty dish away after I left the plate cleaned of food at my side. In her quick departure, the billow of her chador gave me an instant of coolness in the humid heat.

One morning, Abraham, in his plodding and careless way of walking, almost stepped on my chador while I sat on my blanket on the floor. I knew that I would feel worse if I didn't keep some bit of dignity and say something. I wanted him to know that my space, a four foot long old blanket, still belonged to me.

"Please don't walk with your shoes on the blanket. I pray and live on here," I said to express my feelings of being disrespected.

He paused for a second, then replied in a steady sharp voice, "Were you dumb and unable to say something earlier?"

I had heard Abraham's voice before while I was under interrogation.

"Well, well, the famous Miss Dadgar they talk about is you?" he had asked and tapped his pen on my head. "The Brothers say you are the worst. A hopeless one. Every one of them believes you will never come back to Islam!"

Each interrogator had specific prisoners to interrogate. Abraham was in the Graves to check on his assigned prisoners and push them towards repentance. Suddenly he squatted beside me in a submissive attitude.

"Which part of Iran are you from?" he asked.

I answered and when he asked specific questions about my dialect, he realized he, too, was born and raised in the same part of Iran. This discovery pleased him to the extent that he continued talking with me respectfully, "You knew I was an interrogator, but you weren't afraid to tell me not to walk on your blanket."

When he squatted down to sit and engage me in a conversation,

I momentarily wished I had said nothing about his walking on my blanket.

He then asked questions about my sister's spouse, the senator, wanting to know what I thought of him. Surely, he knew H.K. was my relative and he must have been an acquaintance of my sister's husband himself.

H.K. was my second cousin and I had many good memories of him. He was humble, kind and perfectly happy at home. He was not at all the same as most Iranian men; he liked cooking and gardening and worked around the house. If he had become entirely different from what he used to be before, or disgraceful to his people as a senator, I had no idea.

"I think he's an honest man," I said.

Abraham leaned toward me. He has his face close to mine so he could whisper, "Mehri, I believe you are a person who'd never break under physical punishment. You need to accept and understand matters logically. I think a person like you is worthy of repentance and joining Islam. I don't care about the others. You are the one who has values and I want you to return to us."

His comments made me uneasy. I had close to nothing in common with him. I hoped he wouldn't want to talk to me again, but my fate was otherwise. After Abraham had taken over my case I was never beaten again, for Abraham was determined to convert me in a different way.

In an early morning the silence was broken by a speaker for the regime who talked on the radio about freedom. After many days of sitting in silence, I was eager to hear a voice other than my own in my head.

"Splendid freedom, expression of feelings and ideas, satisfaction ... the result..."

The words flew gently in the air, breaking the silence and warmed me, filling the tiring long moments with thoughts. "Oh my God, they believe in what I believe. I must have been blind, not to see this important fact about the regime's men and their philosophy."

Then I felt guilty for not appreciating their values. I concluded, "It was all my fault to oppose them. It was me who was wrong."

Ashtari, the cruelest interrogator, came in and stood close to me. His silence, which would raise fear in whomever might be around, brought an immediate thought to my mind, "How foolish. If they believe in freedom why then I am here for selling newspapers? I barely escaped his torture alive." In that moment I became aware that something was happening to me. But what was it? I thought about it, and then it clicked. I had almost been ready to accept anything they would feed my mind. How could I have become that stupid and accept their idiotic world? How had that happened? I didn't know anything about brainwashing then, but years later I understood how their method worked.

"It is not what one says, but what one does that shows his beliefs, and these are evil doers." This is what I promised myself to always remember.

I noticed that Sameen the interrogator walked into the room next to where I sat. He was in the vestibule talking to someone. I recognized it was Marjan on the other side of the wall I was sitting against. After Sameen left, I tapped carefully on the wall, keeping my hands covered with my chador. I put my forehead on the wall to hide my knocking the Tap codes. I knew she had heard the talk on the radio as well.

"Marjan this is Mehri," I said.

She tapped back immediately.

"Marjan, don't forget," I tapped, "these men are the torturers and this government is a dictatorship."

"I won't ever forget that," she replied.

I stopped tapping, knowing that it was too risky. Ashtari always walked around silently to catch us breaking a rule.

Abraham preached to me whenever he came in to convince me that the regime was godly and righteous.

"Mehri," he said. "Your real name is Fatemeh. The prophet's daughter was called Fatemeh. You know, your family is different.

You have come from a good family that has always been religious."

I was blindfolded and couldn't see Abraham's face, but I could almost imagine him with tears in his eyes when he talked about Fatemeh, Muhammad's daughter. He sounded so passionate and spoke with a great deal of respect when he said her name and associated me with her.

In fact my mother wasn't a religious person at all and I wasn't either until I started to read about religion at the age of nineteen. But Abraham had made up his own story, imagining me as his ideal Islamic woman, something he probably wished for all the women in the world.

I couldn't tell Abraham that when I was born my mother decided to name me Mehri, but when my father went to get the birth certificate he forgot my name.

"I'm sorry," he had told the man who wrote certificates. "I should go back home. I have forgotten the name my wife wants to give our daughter."

"Don't worry." The man laughed. "There are many names that you can choose," and he started to recite all the names he could think of.

My father and the clerk picked the name "Fatemeh" for me. My father came back home to face my mother, who was so disappointed that she yelled at him. My family called me Mehri until I was about four years old when my older brothers began teasing me by calling me "Fatemeh."

They sang a song about Fatemeh, an ugly girl with crooked eyes who was killed and cooked in a big pot. I cried so hard, not wanting to be called Fatemeh. I was as young as four but I knew Fatemeh was an old-fashioned name, belonging to poor or old women. It was at school when I realized Fatemeh was my given name, and I had to live with the image of an ugly head in the cooking pot.

Abraham was devoted to corrupt Islamic beliefs, which he thought were honest and good. He wasn't aware of being a member of a cruel, blind system. When he fired my resistance like a match to gunpowder, I had to bite down on my words and remind myself that this wasn't the place to tell Abraham what I thought of the men in power who were determined to wipe us off the face of the earth.

"This is ridiculous," I told myself. "Why does he exaggerate so much? What is he gaining from complimenting me?" I finally felt distraught and exhausted. I wished he would leave me alone to bear the long hours of sitting in one corner by myself.

I had been in the "Grave" for two months. My knees, back and shoulders hurt constantly. I felt my flesh melt into a curse of torment. Sometimes I punched the wall in front of me with my fists just to release my pain and frustration.

Abraham's persistence wore my patience thin, and I felt like I was going mad. A vague fear and uneasiness filled my mind. I began to see that I might not be able to bear the physical and mental isolation any longer. I felt I was close to the breaking point. I tried to convince myself to bear it bravely, but everything told me I was near the end. The war between my tired body and my desire to be truthful was about to end in favor of the flesh. A cloud of self-doubt was destroying my certainty, and now the battle seemed physically impossible. The desire to carry on was no longer enough.

There was only one thing that I thought might preserve my dignity and sanity: suicide.

I had never thought of suicide before. I became aware that I had already lost the war in this graveyard. I was exhausted. Now I wanted to die to end my suffering. I thought of rolling my chador like a rope to hang myself from the bars at night. I hoped the traitor guard would fall asleep.

As I was preparing to take my life, a battle of fear raged in me. Thinking of my foolishness, my face became wet with sweat. I never wanted to die. Never like this. I put my forehead on the wall and cried. How could I take my own life?

In a new morning, heavy footsteps and the voice of a man yelling alerted me that something unusual had happened. Despite my blindfold and restrictions, I couldn't resist turning my head slowly, with great caution.

My breath almost stopped in my throat. I saw Sameen running and dragging on the floor a bloody body covered in a chador. The woman's head was twisted to one side. Sameen bent over the body, grabbed the victim's legs, and pulled her back towards the door.

He saw me looking and yelled, "Don't look, you cursed fool."

As Sameen left the cellblock, Soraya ran behind him and closed the door.

I stayed still, horrified by the fact that someone had in truth committed suicide. Thousands of thoughts flooded my mind. Who was she? How did she do it? Would she live through it? If she survived, what would they do to her?

Now I took a quick survey of the place. There was no one here. Where were the others?

I took my hand out of my chador, braced myself against the wall and slowly turned around again. I recognized the empty cellblock as the same model as Cellblock 8. We were somewhere in Qezel-Hesar prison.

Two days passed. Ashtari came in at night and asked me to follow him. He stopped, opened a door, and told me to take off my blindfold.

I found myself with Ashtari and a three-year-old boy in a very small yard with tall brick walls. The boy didn't pay any attention to me as he sat on the steps playing with his toy car. It was surreal. Ashtari stood there looking at his son without saying a word. For the first time, he didn't look like a demon. He was a father.

I looked up across the night sky and saw the moon was out in the middle of many sparkling stars. A cool breeze was blowing. I took a deep breath to take in the fresh air. How splendid nature was, and how light and carefree the boy was. How fast time passed before he took me back to sit blindfolded in front of the wall. I hadn't seen the stunning night sky for more than two years. Ironically, I had lived in too many dark days, instead.

The next time Abraham came in, he asked me if I accepted the regime. His voice seemed impatient, tired and perhaps this was my final choice. I wanted to say, "No," but I found it impossible. I had to get out. I was no longer able to carry on. "I have questions," I said by way of compromising, a cold dread running in my veins. He knew that my response was a diplomatic surrender, but it was the end of it for both of us. The next day, Abraham took me out of the "Grave".

He returned me to the same large open room where all the windows were covered with newspapers and all the prisoners sat next to each other around the room creating a rectangle in black fabric. Fourteen of them were my friends, sixteen were the traitors, four collaborating women in charge, and four interrogators stood at opposite sides.

The first face that drew my attention was Roya's. Her natural good temper had been buried under suffering. Her eyes were cold and distant, tiredness in her face. When she saw me, she looked down.

The interrogators called out each prisoner's name one by one. The prisoner had to condemn the Mujahedin organization and confess that she had been wrong in following the 'monafeghin' group. She had to say that she was repentant and returned to the Islamic regime. Roya, Marjan, Lily, Shela, and the rest were called.

All in turn, they condemned the Mujahedin organization. Their confessions meant nothing except to show the cruelty of the prison authorities. The only way out of the "Grave" was to forsake one's beliefs. Even death was not an option.

Listening to the false confessions of my prison-mates was heart breaking. We lived in a world where the judges insisted on hearing lies. Everyone had been called except for me. An interrogator spoke as if the show was over. I wondered why they hadn't called my name.

My mind started to work quickly and for a brief moment nothing made sense. An instinct, stronger than reason, told me that I had to do what the others had done. I suspected the interrogators had a plan for me. I felt that something strange was going on. Without even asking for permission, "I also wanted," I said loudly, "to say that I have questioned our organization…"

The interrogators looked surprised.

"…In one of the organization's demonstrations," I continued, "with thousands of participants, a fight broke out between the organization and the Islamic regime loyalists. In the scuffle, one of our women lost her headscarf but she didn't care enough to retrieve it. I don't think that was right."

I felt relieved after I criticized the organization to prevent myself from getting caught in any of the interrogators' schemes. What I said was the only thing I could think of. A girl's hair showing was not important to me, but it was important for me to break my silence and talk.

Ashtari, with newly shaved head, spoke again. His breathing hissed as he surveyed the room. He preached confidently about his trip to Mecca, where the pilgrim must abstain from arguments, bad language and killing wild animals throughout Hajj. Ashtari was ready for bloodshed. "When I went to Saudi Arabia for Hajj," he said, "I saw the greatness of Islam and the Islamic Republic of Iran. And you, monafeghin, are nothing except the enemy of our sacred system. If I had a machine gun in my hand right now, I would execute you all at once."

Ashtari had addressed *all* of us with the same threat. He included the terrified traitors who were sitting among us in the room. Like a devoted Nazi, the energy and belief behind his words made his small figure seem bigger. Unpredictable as a hungry beast, he was ready to kill the repentant prisoners as he would kill the rest of us; we were all the same to him—worthless enemies.

Abraham called me to another room after the meeting to criticize me.

"Who told you to talk?" he said incredulously. "I wanted the resistant prisoners to come to you and show their real political views so we could identify them."

I had been right. They wanted my friends to see me as a hero so that they would confide in me. I was glad that I had trusted my intuition. It would have been terrible to be part of a plan against my friends.

Delighted that my talking ruined the interrogators' plan, I decided that the interrogators would never be truthful. For the most part depending on my intuition was my only weapon in staying alert.

The interrogators finally called an end to the session and let all the prisoners be together in one place. I walked around the large room, until I got a chance to speak to Marjan who'd been out of the "Grave" weeks earlier than I. I wanted her not to mention our Tap coding in the "Grave" with others, at all.

"I promise," she said.

"And Marjan, do you know who committed suicide?"

"Yes, she was Donna. As you see she is not here."

"Oh, my. How did that happen?"

"The guard found her in the bathroom stall. Donna's clothes and sandals were soaked with blood. Soraya noticed her broken glasses, on the floor and realized what she had done, so she hurried to call for Sameen."

"Did...did Donna... survive?"

"I don't know. I better go now, Mehri."

I looked around and saw Lily's eyes were filled with delight by some thoughts or emotions and I assumed something must be going on with her. Once I had seen Lily walk across the room after Hamid, her interrogator, talked to her. Lily fluttered out of the room with a bright light in her eyes and a strange smile on her face. I heard her interrogator talk to Lily in a soft voice and Lily listened to him attentively and replied in a feminine tone.

I was not quite certain what was going on, but I guessed that Lily was emotionally involved with Hamid. She, with her ingenuous emotions, hadn't surprised me.

I lay on the floor next to the wall thinking, my hands crossed under my head. Lily came closer, stopped, and sat next to me.

"Mehri," she exclaimed turning her back to the others

"Yes, Lily," I said.

As usual, she began to talk as if life were a romantic novel and the reality of the Unit could never change her fantasies. I used to like this quality in her.

"Mehri, he may ask me to marry him."

"Who?"

"Hamid, my interrogator."

I became speechless.

"And if he does, I will say, 'Yes.'"

"But think Lily," I said in a very low voice. "Are you crazy? Do you know what you are talking about? If there is any nonsense ever, it is what is in your mind."

I saw the struggle in her face and her excitement disappeared. I understood why she wanted to marry him, as I knew her well. It was her romantic solution to escape the awful reality, but I could never approve of something like that.

"When I get out of the prison, I will kill him," she said with a phony voice trying to get my attention.

"What?" It wasn't possible that she meant what she was saying. Her good-natured soul had been savaged by circumstances, putting her in the position of thinking of a murder. I knew she was not telling the truth and she knew that she would never do that, never.

"Don't ever say that again, Lily. Have you lost your mind?"

Tears filled my eyes. My own frustrations about not being able to continue standing for the truth against the lies surfaced, and I wanted to talk about my feelings.

"Listen, Lily, I'm also suffering so much. I feel…I feel like a jerk."

"Yes, Mehri, you are a jerk," Lily yelled at me. "You are a real jerk."

I didn't expect to hear Lily repeat my own self-humiliation. I needed her to be my friend and to comfort me. How could she say that? Maybe she was more frustrated than I was.

Yet, what had I really done? Nothing. I felt guilty for letting my exhaustion keep me from standing up to the interrogators.

From that time on, the terror of the place seemed even greater. I decided that I could no longer share my feelings with anyone. Lily, my closest friend who had admired me for speaking the truth, had turned against me.

Seven months had passed since we were transferred from the solitary confinement of Gohar-Dasht to the more brutal treatment in the Unit. We were now incarcerated under the control of three male interrogators and twenty traitors, four of them in charge of the Unit.

The young, kindhearted traitor who had always treated me nicely had been transferred out during my first month here. Mrs. Farima appeared again to help Soraya, the tall woman with delicate features. Soraya retained her feminine elegance along with a bitter expression on her face that showed her constant dislike of what she was doing.

Mrs. Farima, who had expected to be pardoned and leave the prison quickly, was truly upset. She was now locked up in the Unit to guard the prisoners whom she saw as the cause of her confinement. To seek revenge she insulted the prisoners and invented negative reports about them. It was impossible to spend a day without her abuse.

The interrogators were determined to keep the outside world from knowing what was happening in the Unit. They chose two trusted collaborators to help them. This was bad luck for the transferred traitors who lost their former privileges in the normal cellblocks. Now, in this austere setting, they had to be on duty day and night and live along with the rest of us in a tense situation, punctuated by pain and misery.

Like the prisoners, the traitors descended into a black hole, cut off from their families. Beside the four collaborators in charge, the other thirty-one prisoners in the Unit were divided into two groups. About half were the prisoners who struggled to keep their secrets, since they believed that giving them up would destroy their dignity and jeopardize others. This group only gave worthless information to the interrogators.

The second group who lived with us were not tortured. They

cared only about themselves and were brazen in their disregard for the other prisoners and falsely accused them of various petty crimes, hoping to please the interrogators.

My friends and I were under tremendous pressure and didn't dare to even engage in simple activities like talking, reading, or walking. When we had to walk down the hallway, we looked down so as not to be accused of having eye contact with others, and we didn't touch books or magazines to avoid being accused of being interested in learning.

Nothing could be said without fear of the collaborators interpreting it wrongly as exchanging information, yet all this couldn't prevent the collaborators from inventing false accusations. Among them, Mrs. Farima, who wasn't considered a real political prisoner or a human-rights activist, was the worst. She was in prison because she had been a Shah supporter. One day when she hurried to the food pot to take the best part of the food as usual, Soraya protested, "Do you know what they make of you doing this?"

She looked at us, trying to preserve some dignity, and continued, "They will complain to the Brothers. It will be embarrassing for us then."

When I saw Mrs. Farima become angry, I tried to defuse the situation, "I don't think it matters at all. We won't complain."

Food was the least concern for the prisoners who were under constant interrogation. In fact we wished the traitors would have more entertainment so they would leave us alone.

We had a poor diet for eight months. Our cellmate Shekar was ill, and after a few months of living in the Unit, her health grew worse. Even though she was an experienced nurse herself, her knowledge was not of any help. She couldn't hold any food down without vomiting.

She had learned to live with her illness and no longer complained, but her health was steadily declining. Her face was pale and gaunt and her hands shook. There was nothing that could be done to improve her diet in a place where we hardly ever had fresh fruit or vegetables. During the past eight months in the Unit we only received fresh tomatoes twice and we had to pay for them.

PART 11

Evil's World

(1983)

During all this time we had no visitors, until a day the interrogators announced we were going to have family visits. I impatiently looked forward to seeing my mother and my father. During these months of fear and terror none of our parents knew where we were. It would be a great relief for them to visit us, even if only for five minutes. I could not wait until the next day to see them.

The night before the visits, I dreamed of hugging and kissing my mother. Yet when the visiting time came, I was the only one without visitors. In contrast to my joyful dream, I was left alone in the dark, like an uprooted plant beside an unknown road. It was strange and pathetic. My parents hadn't received a call and didn't know they could visit me. Sameen carelessly said they didn't have my parents' contact information but would call them for the next time.

That day came a few weeks later.

I was standing behind the glass wall waiting for my parents. Suddenly the door opened and a crowd of old men and women entered, looking confused. They searched the faces of the girls standing in a row who all looked similar to each other. We stood in black chadors behind the glass windows. Some of the parents were running and some were walking. A few went to the wrong windows, then looked to the next station, staring for a few seconds, then left in a hurry to get to the other window.

Among them, I saw my father. I started to cry. His hair was whiter and his face was thinner since the last time I had seen him. His back was bent as he searched for me among the prisoners. It was painful not being able to run to him. I wanted to hug and kiss him as much as I wished. My mother followed, weeping.

I wiped my tears, not wanting them to see my sadness and grief. My mother recognized me. She stopped, stared again, and rushed towards my cubicle. My father walked faster to join my mother. They both stood on the other side of the glass, their eyes filled with tears, unable to talk. Anguish had closed my throat and tears fell down my cheeks.

My poor mother. She looked so weak and distressed. She finally grabbed the phone.

"Maman jan," I said. "Oh, I have missed you so much. Thank you for coming this long way. Please don't cry, Maman jan, please, look Maman. I'm fine. I'm perfectly fine. I love you. I love you. What's up? Please talk to me. How's everybody? My sisters? How are my bothers? Everybody? Maman, please talk to me. Don't cry."

My mom gave the phone to my father who was wiping his tears with his handkerchief.

"Hello, Hello my dear Agha jan. How are you?" I said.

"How am I, my dear? We've been dying every day to get a bit of news from you, my darling. We were so worried about you, checking all the prisons to ask about you. Thank God, you're fine. Thank God, but not having any news about you for eight months killed us."

"Mehri, my dear daughter." My mother now held the phone. She was smiling.

"Mother. How are you, Mamani?"

"I'm happy that you're fine. Just happy now. Tell me how are you? Do you need anything I can bring for you next time? Tell me if you want anything. Please Mehri take care of yourself. We can't bear not hearing from you. Please Darling, you be careful."

Maman jan, I'm fine. How's everybody? Maman, how's everyone?

"Fine. Fine. Everybody is ..."

Her lips moved but I couldn't hear her. The transmission was cut off and visiting time was over. We were ordered to step back from the windows. I watched the ease vanish from their faces. My mother hit her chest with her fist; tears covered her sad face. My father covered his wet eyes with his handkerchief. I waved and waited until my parents disappeared behind the door. I put on my blindfold and walked with the other girls in the opposite direction, remembering my mother in mid-age, laughing long and hard.

Before my teen-age years, the happiest times were our regular family gatherings. These gatherings were a time for eating, running around with my cousins, inventing games and discovering new hiding places with the neighborhood kids.

On Fridays, my sister and I followed our mother to join my uncle, my aunt and their kids in my grandfather's yard for a barbecue; most of the time it was kabob. Our time together felt effortless in each other's warm presence from morning to late afternoon.

On one of those hot summer days in my grandfather's home, my cousins were playing in the yard framed by fruit trees and roses. Everyone was frenetic from running around and jumping up and down.

My grandfather had already prepared for the barbecue. The center of the black coals had turned to red in the fire, ready for skewers wrapped with the ground meat. He squatted next to the fire on a small stool, with his knees open to the sides and pulled a handful of skewers close to him. The ground lamb had been mashed and marinated with salt, spices and onion the day before.

My mother, my aunt and my grandmother sat together, chatting and laughing while they prepared the rice and filled a basket with a mixture of fresh raw herbs—basil, mint, green onion, leek, and small red radishes.

The smell of the barbecue meat carried over the yard with the cloud of smoke rising up above the coals in the barbecue pit. "Bring the bread, dear," my grandfather called to my mother.

My mother stood up, got the packs of fresh Sangak bread and handed them to my grandfather so he could put the Koobideh Kabob into the folds of the bread. The smell of the smoky kabobs made me hungry. I turned towards my mother hoping she would let me have an early taste of the kabob, and I saw my mother's shoulder shaking from a hard, silent laugh. Turning her head up, she had closed her eyes. Then with great difficulty she signaled my aunt discreetly.

"Come on hurry up, Mali."

My mother whispered something in my aunt's ear and they broke off with a loud laugh. I saw my mother looked towards my grandfather who sat beside the fire holding the skewer with one hand and sticking the ground meat onto it with the other.

Grandpa noticed his daughters' laughter was unusually long and loud and looked over at them. He saw my mother had almost fallen down, holding her sides with laughter. Grandpa suspected something and caught them looking at his pajama-type pants. He saw his pants had a big hole in the center.

He held his breath and his brows went up. He was in serious trouble since he hadn't worn underwear and his hands were greasy. He kept his eyes straight ahead, showed no panic and deftly moved his hands from skewering meat to refitting himself back inside his pants. My dignified Grandpa pretended nothing had happened and calmly continued sticking the ground meat around the skewer.

"Yuckhhh, I won't eat that food," My aunt said with a giggle, then she laughed at grandfather's deft move.

My mother winked and said, "Let us eat from the ones he cooked before the accident," and laughed like a teen-age girl—so much that her stomach hurt again.

Hungry kids gathered around the tablecloth that had been spread out on the ground and eagerly ate the kabobs. They didn't know why my mother and aunt were laughing. My grandfather washed his hands and joined his family of three children and ten grandchildren to eat his own homemade kabobs with relish.

After lunch my cousin, Farid, tuned his accordion and called Shirin and me to stand in a row with his own sister, who was my age, to practice a group dance he had choreographed. He raised his voice to lead us in harmony, "Dim da dam da dam dim da da dam."

Farid was a thin, tall, talented boy and a natural leader, three years older than me. After we danced he called the boys to join us to play *dabelna*, an Iranian version of bingo while our parents chatted together and took their afternoon naps.

These family gatherings ended when I turned thirteen and entered high school.

No one in the Unit caused as many problems or complained about the prisoners as much as Mrs. Farima. Looking for a way to calm her down, I thought of something. I cautiously asked Mrs. Farima if she would like to take art lessons from me.

"Before my arrest, I was a painter for several years."

She looked at me in disbelief and put me to the test.

"Here is my brother's photo. Can you draw his portrait?"

"No problem."

I couldn't imagine anyone having a family photo in prison, but she had it. I drew him with pencil on a sheet of paper Mrs. Farima provided; but I wanted to have her doing painting.

"If my parents could get permission, they would bring the supplies we need, so I could teach you how to paint."

The next time my parents came to the prison door, they gave my paints and brushes to the guards and I started to teach Mrs. Farima. With the regime's traditional approach towards art and creativity, I could only teach through painting a portrait of Khomeini. I arranged my canvas against a wall and began the work.

However my attempt to keep Mrs. Farima busy was not successful. Not only did she have no experience or talent, she also didn't have the patience for painting. She was consumed in whole with the desire to be released from prison in the third year of her confinement.

At the end I had to work on the painting by myself, thinking no one would object to me painting Khomeini's portrait. As I was sketching the portrait, I heard one of the collaborators ask another, "What's she doing?"

"Painting," said the other.

"Painting what?"

"... Imam," said the girl with bitter scorn.

After Sameen saw it, and asked why I had painted the Imam the way I had, I looked at it as if I were looking at it for the first time. In my painting, Khomeini's eyes were cold with no sign of kindness, knotting eyebrows in his long face. I tried to change it a few times, but the spirit in the painting must have emerged from my subconscious, showing my disappointment with the regimes' leader. He remained angry, looking at the viewer.

Under the restraints of the Unit, we could do nothing more than live moment by moment, anticipating the next crisis. Sometimes, I sat on the floor and put my head on my knees, stealing glances at my friends, feeling how everyone suffered and tried to avoid conflict with the collaborators.

In those harsh days, one of them discovered a lentil-size hole in the layers of newspapers that were put up to blind the windows to the small yard, and reported this to the interrogators immediately. They called us out one at the time to find out who had made that hole. The investigation went on night and day for over a week.

Another day a collaborator announced that one spoonful of her milk powder had been stolen by one of us. She wanted to find a victim, an object for the interrogators' wrath, and to be rewarded with their mercy.

Sameen threatened the thief with severe punishment. He believed stealing from the collaborators, was a declaration of war against the regime.

Fear appeared on the faces of the accused prisoners. I was certain there was no thief. No one was stupid enough to do such a thing in our situation, but since the interrogators were always searching for traces of resistance, nobody dared to object or say anything.

The entire staff continued to look for the thief, while flying accusations exhausted the prisoners. I wasn't accused only because Abraham favored me. One day, Abraham called me for interrogation and asked me about the thief. I wrote: "Certainly two prisoners couldn't be thieves." One of the accused was Roya whom I knew never would steal food. The other was Shela who was not brave enough to do so.

I had to say it in such a way that Abraham would not know that I was defending two friends of mine who were under suspicion and endured constant pressure from the traitors.

Sadly Shela, who ignored Mrs. Farima's antagonism, had become her target. Shela complimented Mrs. Farima often in an attempt to mollify her, but Mrs. Farima, her face red with pent-up anger continued to put Shela down indirectly. The tension mounted to the point that I was afraid that something terrible might happen to Shela. I wondered, was it her way of dealing with her fear that she ignored trouble?

One day Mrs. Farima and Soraya called a meeting, requiring all of us to participate. It was strange that they asked everyone to talk, when we had no right to talk about anything. This meeting must have been arranged by the interrogators to check out our states of mind.

In this exceptional opportunity something was drawing me to speak the truth and talk from my heart. I knew that in a few minutes, all eyes would be on me, and yet in that moment, I was determined.

Soraya was on duty to write down every word and report it to the interrogators. The meeting started with Mrs. Farima. Full of hate and anger she railed on and on about those who groveled. She blamed a monafegh, a hypocrite, among the inmates who was trying to deceive her.

I began talking about the hypocrisy that Mrs. Farima had condemned.

"One of the obvious means of recognizing a monafegh is to look at the person's intention. Hypocrisy is toxic. There is more to being human than just to trick each other."

I was perfectly frank and at the same time considered my listeners ready to address our common problem. I felt it was necessary to be lighthearted to survive in those dark days. I cited religious quotes to argue that hypocrisy harms everyone. I talked generally to help my friends who needed encouragement and motivation to bear the hard situation.

Mrs. Farima spoke again to blame her target, who made her so upset. She was uneasy and couldn't resist saying, "She thinks I don't know what she's doing. A monafegh whose behavior I just can't stand." Mrs. Farima said the last words to end the meeting. Everyone remained quiet except Shela who put on a fake smile.

"Oh, Mrs. Farima," she said, "I think you're right. That's too bad. I think you should announce who she is. Why don't you tell us her name? Please, Mrs. Farima, tell her name."

Shela was talking as if there was no way that she was the one, and this made Mrs. Farima irritated and speechless.

Everyone worried. Shela made the situation even more tense.

A voice screamed in my head. "Shut up, Shela. You know she's talking about you." In an instant, I felt I had to do something to help her. I stood up, walked towards Shela and slapped her on the side of her face. Shela jumped in shock.

"Why did you hit me?" she cried out.

"Because I'm your friend. Why don't you take a vow of silence for a while? Why do you think you need to talk all the time?"

No one knew what to do. The meeting was over, yet no one had moved. I sat first, then got up and went to the next room. I would never have imagined Shela as unaware as she seemed and I had to wake her up. At that moment, I couldn't explain to Shela why I had struck her and what was going on around her. Shela was sobbing as she followed me to the other room.

"Not everybody is a hero like you," tears were raining over her face. "Can't you understand that some people might be weak?"

I had hurt my friend in a wild attempt to save her. Her anger towards me was just, and I couldn't have expected otherwise. She was revealing her true feelings, honest and brave, against me. I felt relieved, even though I knew she might never forgive me. Yet I was left with a question in my mind: did I do the right thing?

Soon, the interrogators heard the news about my slapping Shela. I expected to be punished. I had preached to others to be truthful and to avoid hypocrisy. I had told Shela that I was her friend and advised her to be quiet.

We all waited like the grains of sand sitting on windy hills wait for another storm to raise them up, twist them in the air and smash them down to the ground. Apparently the interrogators, who did not like Shela, were pleased that one prisoner had struck another and they didn't punish me. We knew this couldn't be anything near to the end of our pressure, but at least this clash released the dreadful tension between Shela and Mrs. Farima.

A week after the meeting, when Shela was still quiet and thoughtful, the traitors found another suspect. This time they picked on Sara, a quiet, charming girl who walked around so gently, like a fearful deer. She had soft eyes with perfectly rounded eyebrows, as if they imitated the new moon.

The interrogators came into the narrow room and called everyone.

"Come here, you idiot. Sit. Fool, monafegh."

Sameen put a chair into the middle of the room for Sara and made us all sit on the floor around her. She was rendered helpless by the overwhelming force of the three interrogators. They started ridiculing Sara, who sat on the edge of the chair holding her head down. Sameen sat excitedly, looking with feverish eyes straight ahead at Sara.

"Who was your damned sister's spouse?" Sameen asked Sara.

Since Sara remained silent, Sameen answered his own question, "A monafegh."

He laughed out loud with the other two interrogators, Ashtari and Abraham. It seemed like Sara was about to faint.

"Do you know why he was arrested?" Sameen asked.

Sara said nothing.

"Wasn't he the one who influenced you? Don't cover up. Speak."

Sara was still silent.

He continued in a louder voice, "It's all right." He's not a problem anymore…

"He's damned dead now. But you?"

Sara's face contorted, as if in pain. Sameen looked around the room at the prisoners,

"Look at her. Here she is, a real monafegh," he yelled. Then he turned to Sara again.

"Can't you stop being a fraud? No, you can't. I know you can't with your sick mind."

I knew that Sara cared for her sister's spouse and loved him so dearly as a family member, and a human-rights activist. His execution hurt Sara deeply. The room was quite warm, and Sara, under the black chador, was close to passing out. She sat silent, pale, and motionless. The anguish had turned her lips blue. She finally lost consciousness and fell off the chair.

From mid spring to summer and into the fall we lived in the Unit under horrendous conditions with no hope for any change. I was living inside an endless darkness, as if I had never known anything else. The darkness in the Unit was my whole world and I lived in it with acceptance. The longer I lived there, the more real this world looked. I became weaker and weaker and that was what the interrogators wanted. They were determined to break us down until we had no feelings towards any other human beings.

Friendliness, gentleness, and compassion were considered as signs of resistance. Prisoners showing these qualities were the ones taken to the interrogation room and blamed for fictional infractions like petty theft.

Suddenly one day, the three interrogators appeared in the Unit. We ran to put on our chadors and form a black rectangle around the room with only a bit of our faces showing. The interrogators sent for Ava and me to meet them in the other room.

Ava was one of the young collaborators. Her light green eyes shone often with a pleasant laughter, setting her apart from the rest. The interrogators sat on the floor in the narrow room by themselves when Ava and I entered. Following Ashtari's pointing finger we located ourselves in front of them and put our heads down waiting to hear why we'd been called.

"Mrs. Farima and Soraya have been transferred." Sameen said.

"Wonderful." I repeated twice in my mind, thinking this great news would make my friends as happy as I was, but why I should be there with Ava? I questioned and some of my happiness fled from my heart, for Sameen's voice was soft and gentle and I must be the first to hear the news. Why?

"We have decided you should replace them and be in charge of the Unit along with Mastooreh and Setareh."

Like being hit with a hammer on my head, I thought, "Me? This is horrible. Replacing Farima, a kingship lover who abused the prisoners, reported them, accused them, and hated them? Replacing Soraya who'd been known as a turncoat, a warden of Cellblock 8? The one who locked up the prisoners inside the cells for months? Haji's slave-driver? Are you crazy? Are you asking me to be a guard? A guard? Me? No way. I would never be a guard." I repeated these in my own head.

Disoriented, I regretted that I had foolishly encouraged Abraham to transfer Mrs. Farima and Soraya. What I had done to save my friends and myself from Mrs. Farima had now ensnared me. "What's Mrs. Farima's crime that she is locked up with us in here?" I had asked Abraham, hoping he would show kindness and free Farima so that we would be free from her abuse. I was not at all thinking of promoting myself to such a position and wearing the disgraceful hat of a prison guard. How could I think of such a nightmare when I had wished for the abusive guards to leave, just to make our life a bit easier?

I had wanted to trim an eyebrow, but blinded the eye as it says in a Persian expression. I had dug a hole for others, but fell into it myself. Chosen for the most dishonorable position was even worse than falling into a hole or blinding an eye. I searched in my head desperately for a way out. "What should I do now?"

I looked at Ava. Her face had brightened with gladness, pleased and feeling blessed for being chosen. She was ready to co-operate as a guard, a position which she might have wished for, for she made a greater effort than the rest to comply with the interrogators' rules in the Unit. She was only seventeen-years-old, seven years younger than I. The three men watched my face for any possible reaction. In spite of the blood that ran into my face, I tried to keep my calm demeanor and choose the right words, and not be seen as torn apart.

I had no doubt that my position at this moment was impossible, but I chose my sharpest arrow, pulled it hard and released it all at once, to persuade the interrogators that they shouldn't choose me.

"You have been betrayed by infiltrator prisoners in the past," I said. "Why would you trust me? I am not in agreement with you."

"This is what we all have decided," Abraham said.

"No." I straightened my words, "There are many who want the position. Why don't you choose one of the sixteen Repentant sisters? I'm sorry. I cannot accept your offer."

"We are not asking for your opinion." Ashtari pressed his teeth together, "You have no choice."

I felt a cold sweat on my back. Eight months of being in the Unit had passed and I hadn't cooperated with the interrogators at all. Never. Yet they had chosen me to be in charge of the prisoners along with three traitors? Why? Why me?

Abraham must have persuaded Ashtari and Sameen to go along with his wish and choose me. He must have told them they should invest in changing me, the worst one, as they believed I was. He even must have thought he'd done me a favor.

Ashtari asked Ava and me to follow them to the other room, as if it was all over. From this room to the other, was there any hope for me?

Twenty-nine prisoners, about half of them collaborators were sitting on the floor all in black, Mastooreh and Setareh stood guard. All looked down so that their eyes wouldn't meet the men's.

"Mehri and Ava will be in charge of the Unit to help Mastooreh and Setareh," Ashtari said. "You must listen to them and follow the rules."

I was so embarrassed. What would Roya, Lily and others think of me? Would they ever believe that I was forced into this position? That I had refused their offer to guard my own friends who'd been tortured for resisting? No. They would not know if I wouldn't tell them now. I must tell them right now how I feel. I have to tell my friends. The show is not completely over yet. I have to speak out.

"I already have told the Brothers that I cannot accept this position," I said. "I think one of the sixteen Repentant Sisters should take charge of this place."

No one said a word.

"Please say something…" I asked.

Silence.

The air was still. No one said anything and no head moved to look up. I was beating a dead horse. They saw, too, that there would be no choice for me or for them.

"In this case," I paused and looked for the right words, "I must announce starting from now, I have no friends. I will treat all of you the same."

I was warning my friends not to act naively, thinking of me as a friend. I had to protect them before my job as a guard began. I was certain there would be tremendous pressure on me to report the prisoners.

During the two days between hearing of my selection as a guard and the time Ashtari came back, I experienced the worst time in my life. I felt deeply miserable and consumed with despair. Every muscle in my face was quivering with nervous tension and pain constantly moved from one side to the other. My face felt so tight and crooked that I feared it would explode. Every now and then, my whole body shivered as I thought about my situation. My figure grew thinner and smaller in my skin, by just thinking of cooperating with the brutal regime.

I decided to keep myself busy, for I knew otherwise I would lose my mind, but what could I do? The only thing I could do was to become a simple worker, without taking any sides or betraying anyone. I had to forget who I was and become another person, someone who had been hired to work as a warden, a good warden. I convinced myself that I could remain human as long as I did not deceive anyone, neither the prisoners, nor the interrogators. I decided to just take care of tasks without being a spy. Everything should be straightforward. At least, there would be less lying and deceit.

When I woke up in the morning, after two bad nights sleep, the first thing that came to my mind was my disastrous situation. The night before I thought I could avoid collaborating through serving the prisoners but now I felt hopeless. I couldn't ignore the fact that there was a great deal of wickedness in prison. I knew the path that lay ahead of me was nothing but disgrace. As I contemplated my dilemma, I decided to paint. I worked on Khomeini's portrait to avoid being asked to report the prisoners. Ashtari returned after a short absence.

"What's the news?" he asked me.

"Nothing. Everything is okay…"

He frowned and was dismayed. I felt drained, for I knew his expectations. I wished that he would walk away and that I would never see him again.

He walked away, but the following week, he came to me with the same exact question as before.

"I did some cultural activities," I said.

"What? What did you do?"

"I continued to work on the portrait of Imam Khomeini."

"Your cultural activity doesn't do any good for me. I'm not interested in cultural things."

I hoped my painting would convince the interrogators that I was cooperating with them, but they didn't care.

During the short days of winter, it felt as if the sun disappeared forever, and my hopes died away in the barren, cold season. I was so mired in the situation that I had almost become a different being. I was so down that I didn't even think of asking God for help. Hope leads people to God, and I was completely hopeless. I felt I had to live in disgrace and hide my thoughts and emotions inside of me from then on. It was an unfair battle. Neither the interrogators nor the prisoners should know of my suffering. I had become incapable of talking to others. I had no choice but to accept the situation.

For the first time a new group of prisoners transferred into the Unit. To our astonishment, they were all those of higher ranks in the Public 4 network. Ezzat, Hamideh, and the girl who had pretended her foot was injured earlier were among them. Suddenly the atmosphere became more tense. Where had they been? Why were they here now?

They walked, laughed, and talked to each other freely. This was in a sharp contrast to us, who were afraid to even look at each other.

Ashtari came in with a calm expression on his face. He talked to me privately.

"I want you to treat the new prisoners humanely."

I couldn't believe my ears. But he was serious.

"All right," I said, casually. I couldn't let him see that I was relieved that he didn't command us to harass them.

From the three rooms in the Unit, the four of us in charge occupied one room and the rest of the girls lived in the other two. We all shared the two bathrooms.

After Ashtari left, I went into the middle room and found Ava, my compatriot, cursing the newcomers to prove that she was genuinely on the side of the regime. Now I had an excuse to talk to Ava and tell her to treat the prisoners kindly. I found her in the hallway. No one was around. It was hard to bring up the subject.

"Ava," I finally said, "Brother Ashtari wants us to treat the new prisoners humanely. That's what he told me…"

I hadn't even finished my sentence when Ava separated herself from me and ran towards the room where Mastooreh and Setareh were resting. I followed her in a hurry.

"Mehri is trying to deceive me." I heard her say to the other two collaborators in charge.

I realized that they would not believe me even if I tried to explain myself. The two traitors looked at me with distrust.

There was something strange about the high ranked members of Mujahedin who had just arrived that I couldn't understand. Hamideh walked confidently, with no hesitation, to face Roya, Shela and me. Had she forgotten how they shunned us in Public 4?

"You haven't forgotten me?" she asked when she walked towards me, acting as if she hadn't been at fault, leading the prisoners to side with the Islamic regime. I had never seen her act so friendly, using her charming smile. I wanted to forget my negative feelings toward her. I walked with her into the small hallway. Regardless of what had happened in the past, we still were on the same side. She and I were both prisoners.

"No, I haven't forgotten you," I said, tears filling my eyes.

The day after, Abraham came in. Everyone put on their chadors. He called me into the hallway.

"Mehri," he said. "I've heard that you cried while talking with Hamideh. Are you still emotional?" he asked accusingly.

I clutched my chador tightly under my chin. I was puzzled. Who might have reported me? It took only a few seconds for Hamideh and me to walk down the small hallway. No one was there and we separated quickly. Did Hamideh report this? If not, who else could have done it?

"She's a manipulator," said Abraham, referring to Hamideh, as he tried to persuade me I shouldn't trust Hamideh. I listened but refrained from engaging in a discussion.

"Hamideh is a complicated person. You won't believe it, but she was even trying to seduce me. Open your eyes, Mehri."

Only after the higher ranked prisoners were taken away, and the rest of the prisoners were severely punished, did I learn that the higher ranked prisoners had been there as spies to report on their fellow inmates. Hamideh and her friends were there to find out who was still resisting. They had reported everything to the interrogators. Yet with all the occurrences that had taken place here, this was not a surprise.

This incident occupied my mind. There must be some of them who didn't wish to betray others. Did they have a way out? I knew even one cruel person among them was enough to cause trouble for the prisoners of the Unit.

After hearing the news, Lily's patience was exhausted. She sank on the third level of the bunk, rocked to the right and left saying, "I can't believe this. I can't. I'm going crazy. What's going on? This is all unbearable. These were our leaders. And now…how dare… they spy on us? I can't understand. No. I can't make sense of this."

Lily was so out of control that she didn't fear being reported.

No one tried to comfort her. She mumbled all morning in a sad voice until she wilted on the bunk and slept where she was.

After the higher ranked prisoners left, the Unit remained with its permanent inhabitants, thirty-three prisoners, more than half of them collaborators. The interrogators confined the accused prisoners in the narrow room that had a bathroom and a shower. Prisoners were not allowed to walk out of that room.

The days of punishment continued. I kept myself busy doing most of the physical labor assigned to the guards in charge. I divided the food, swept the rooms, and the hallway. None of the other three girls in charge liked to work. When it was their turn to do the tasks, they did them grudgingly, cursing the resistant prisoners.

I didn't know why the fourteen prisoners were put in the narrow room and I didn't see them for a few days. After a snowy, cold night, I was called in the morning to give the prisoners in the narrow room a broom. I opened the door and saw them sitting there without chadors. Their washed clothes hung on a rope stretched from one end of the room to the other. There were plastic plates under the clothes to collect the drips. They all sat alone, distancing themselves from their cellmates.

Some had put their heads down on their knees to avoid any eye contact. I wasn't allowed to go inside the room. I dropped the broom they needed inside the room and immediately closed the door.

Ashtari entered the hallway. I came face to face with him. Before he had a chance to say anything, I asked for his permission to take the prisoners' wet clothes to the small yard to hang them up. He agreed and I was thrilled. He left after visiting the prisoners. I opened the door to their room, stuck my head in, and asked them to collect the wet clothes and give them to me. I hid my happiness from everyone, so as not to be reported for showing affection for my fellow inmates.

The small yard and the rope had been covered with snow. The cold fresh air, and the sun light softly brushed my face. It was my first time entering the yard after months. I stood in the snow. The brightness of the snow under the sun was immense. A nostalgic moment took me back to the time I was a student. My sister and I walked on untouched snow to go to high school in the mornings. Stepping out of the warm house in the cold was not easy, yet I liked the crisp air. The breeze touched my face and my eyes burned from the stinging cold.

Covered with my black chador from head to toe I was in total contrast against the white in the yard. My fingers turned red and ached after I hung the first cloth, so I blew on them, warming them with my breath. I put the clothes up one by one until I finished the load. I didn't want to go back inside. At the time, I wished I could stay there until the early afternoon sun disappeared and watch the water dripping from the clothes turn into icicles in the evening.

When the clothes were dry after two days, I collected them, returned them to the room and asked for more.

A few weeks later, Sameen walked in. His black shirt could hardly cover his big belly.

"Why is Mehri the only one hanging the clothes in the yard?" he asked the three traitor guards, "Why aren't you helping?"

Someone must have reported this. Anything small could be a subject for someone's report. After Sameen left, the three guards competed greedily to hang the prisoners' clothes in the yard.

Gradually, by the beginning of the spring, the snow melted and the sun warmed the earth for another new year.

The interrogators announced that we were going to have visitations. When I walked into a small room with Setareh, Mastooreh and Ava, I was astounded to see my family. Even my brother Shareef, who was four years older than I, was there. I had not seen him in three years. My mother hugged me and wouldn't let go. As she kissed me repeatedly, I heard voices crying and laughing.

I tried to smile, but tears filled my eyes. I hugged my father and held his thin, shaking hand in mine.

"Mehri, do they torture you?" my brother asked me, wiping his tears.

I wondered what to say. I looked around to check who was watching us. Setareh, Mastooreh and Ava, were busy with their own families. I saw my oil painting of Khomeini hung on the wall of the main visitation room.

"Look." I said, pointing at the portrait. "I painted that."

"Really?" he raised his eyebrows.

My mother was examining the all-the-way-down-to-my-chest headscarf that I wore underneath my black chador, and I could see that she was uneasy.

"Mehri, my darling, please don't you ever report your friends," she whispered in my ear. "Please don't, my dear."

I felt humiliated. It was known that collaborators wore a stricter hijab than the rest of the prisoners. I wore a strict hijab, and I was among the ones who had private visitations. My mother was worried.

"No Mother, I won't."

"I'm glad to hear that," she said. Her words had touched me. I felt embarrassed, yet I wanted them to know the real me. It was up to them to understand what was going on in the prison.

The interrogations started again. During my day shift I saw Roya, who was sitting among the rest of the prisoners, raise her hand. I knew it was still dangerous for us to talk to each other, but I was a guard. I went up to her. She was sitting on the floor, peering out from under her blindfold writing answers to the interrogators' questions. I kneeled down next to her. She showed me a paper she had filled and asked my opinion about a false chart she had been forced to draw. She wanted to know if my chart matched hers. I hadn't opened my mouth yet when Ashtari appeared in the room and walked towards us in a hurry.

"What were you telling her?" A severe expression settled on Ashtari's face.

"Nothing."

"But you were talking to her."

I rose and faced him.

"Well, yes, she raised her hand and I had to ask her what she needed."

"What did she need?"

"I don't know."

He sat next to Roya and asked her questions. I walked away and couldn't hear them. Then he got up and left. I sighed in relief. Roya had fooled him.

Because of Ashtari's presence, the slightest details, every word, every gesture, and expression was important. I always needed to pay attention to what was going on and then decide what I could do.

When spring arrived, a major change took place at the Unit. At the time, I didn't know that five of the prisoners had signed a paper, confessing they were followers of the Mujahedin.

My experience with such confessions was that they would be followed by a superficial trial and the death sentence. This new situation made me to think of three years ago, at the beginning of my imprisonment, in 1981. The political prisoners who showed sympathy for the Mujahedin, the paramilitary organization, were sentenced to death. They would be executed unless they repented and confessed in front of a video camera. But this situation was much worse. The prisoners didn't have a choice to repent.

In the last week, the interrogators kept the prisoners up all night until the dawn prayer before sunrise. After the dawn prayer, they allowed the prisoners to sleep. When the prisoners had fallen into a deep sleep, the interrogators would kick them with their shoes to wake them up. The prisoners had to stand up all day and night.

All this happened behind the closed door in the narrow room. Ashtari wanted to get their confessions in any cost. He continued to punish the prisoners by keeping them on their feet and preventing them from sleeping day and night to get confessions. Five out of fourteen prisoners signed confessions to end their suffering. Shela, Sara and Donna were among them.

Donna, who had slit her wrists in the "Grave" with her broken glasses had survived to sign a confession, another attempt to escape from a miserable life.

Ashtari had promised he would stop punishing those who would confess. After five days and five nights, these five prisoners couldn't bear the sleep deprivation anymore and had confessed they were supporters of the Mujahedin. They were then sent to another room to sit down during the day and sleep at night. Whenever I entered the room to give them their share of food, I found them sitting quietly next to each other in a corner on the only blanket in the room, wearing their chadors.

Donna couldn't eat any food except toasted bread and sugar cubes. I saved her the toasted parts of the lavash bread, the main part of our daily diet, before dividing them. I also gave her a few extra sugar cubes. A week later, sitting among the other four prisoners, Donna refused to take her share.

"No thanks. I don't want any toast or sugar cubes," she said.

"Why?" I asked.

"Sister Setareh doesn't want me to take the bread and sugar cubes from you." Setareh was one of the collaborators in charge, working on the other shift. There was no way she could know what I was doing unless…I looked at their faces. Shela's eyes were unusually tense, as if she were trying to hide something. She might have been the one…? But there was no way I could know who had reported to Setareh. I tried to solve the matter by explaining.

"The extra sugar cubes I've been giving you are my share that I don't use, so it's all right for you to take them," I said.

I continued serving Donna the bread and extra sugar cubes until Setareh once again objected and Donna refused the sugar and bread. Setareh looked for any opportunity to report her fellow prisoners and could pressure only Donna. She didn't dare to report me to the interrogators for fear of Abraham who favored me.

I felt desperate not being able to help, even in my small ways, because of the cruelty of the twenty-three-year-old traitor in charge. I couldn't fight her, for I didn't want to be reported to Ashtari, who was against me. I had to be careful.

Finally, Setareh and Mastooreh were transferred away from the Unit, but four upstart collaborators from among the ones in the Unit replaced them to work, control and abuse the prisoners.

All the prisoners including the turncoats were moved to a new room, which I had never seen before.

Another room adjacent to this room was occupied by three prisoners who were collaborating with the interrogators by reading the interrogation papers. They helped the interrogators to find out detailed information. If they had been cooperating since the beginning of the Unit, this was the first time we saw them.

At this time thirty new arrivals from other prisons arrived to answer the interrogator's questions. Their bruised faces showed they had been beaten severely.

PART 12

Madness and Betrayal

(1983)

I was called into a room. When I entered, the three interrogators were sitting at the edge of their chairs waiting. This couldn't be a routine call, I thought. But what can it be?

Ashtari held a picture in front of my face.

"Do you know her?" he asked firmly.

I was terrified. It was my cousin, Farzaneh. The interrogators had asked me about my relatives many times over and over and I had never told them anything about Farzaneh. Now the interrogator had evidence against me for withholding information. I strived to overcome my terror and not to react. I thought that they must have known a great deal about us or they wouldn't show me her photo.

"She is my cousin," I said, looking at Ashtrai's face. My eyes were burning; my head was spinning. Was Farzaneh in prison? What had she told them? What did they know about her and me and the rest of our family? Did they know about Hussein, my fiancé?

I decided not to mention Hussein at all and protect Farzaneh by carefully downplaying her role in protesting the regime.

"She used to be a Paykar follower a long time ago at the beginning of the revolution, but I lost touch with her after I moved to Tehran, so I don't know what she was doing."

I remembered that my mother had told me secretly that Farzaneh's elder brother, who was also a communist activist, had left the country. I was certain he was out of reach.

"She was only influenced by her brother," I said. "She was not that active."

Their gaze weighed on me. They probably didn't believe me. I didn't know what they would do next, but Abraham with a frown, lapsed into silence and with a nod of his head dismissed me.

The new comers had to spend countless hours sitting in a corner. Each day I would see prisoners with a black eye or bruised face or hands. All knew perfectly well to be quiet and no one even dared to think of objecting.

About three years had passed since that May afternoon when I was knocking on doors with Kati. I was twenty-two then and now I was twenty-five. I had been in four prisons and had survived various types of treachery and torture, but now I had no moments of rest to think about the past or the future. I was exhausted from the struggle to maintain my integrity. I was not aware of how I was losing myself little by little.

It was the beginning of the second summer in the Unit. That day I could take a brief rest on the bunk.

"Brother Sameen has called you," Hanna said with a twisted smile as she entered the room. "He's waiting in the small room."

I jumped off the bunk, put on my chador and went to the room. I knocked on the door.

"Come in," Sameen said.

I went in. On the right there was a bed. A girl lay on it on her stomach. She was covered with a chador. During the past two months, this room had been filled with new prisoners. I had served them food and water when the interrogators allowed. The prisoners sat around, faces to walls, writing their answers to the interrogators' questions. I hadn't seen a torture bed since the time I had been tortured. Standing in the middle of the room, Sameen pointed at the girl.

"Do you know what she says?" he asked me.

The girl raised her head with difficulty. I couldn't see her face but when she cried out, I recognized her voice. She was Badri, a thin, tall girl from a city in southern Iran.

"Brother Sameen, please, let me explain," she urged.

"Foolish, nonsense," Sameen said, turning to me. "After more than a year of interrogation, she still says there wasn't any organizational network in Cellblock 8!"

"But listen brother Sameen, please let me speak, I mean..." Badri said.

"Tie her to the bed," Sameen said to me, and put a pair of handcuffs in my hands.

I tried to say something, but my voice was trapped in my throat. My mind stopped working and the handcuffs felt cold and heavy. I went towards the bed, bent over, and reached Badri with my shaking, clumsy hands. I was terrified by the fear of what would happen next.

I had never touched handcuffs before and I couldn't get them to work. Sameen saw my frustration. He pulled the cuffs from me to show me how to secure them, but I failed again so he handcuffed Badri himself.

I moved towards the door to leave, but Sameen put his finger on his lips, asking me to be quiet and not to move. He looked at me sternly with a cruel commanding expression in his eyes and gave me a thick steel cable. He wanted me to lash Badri. Staring at him in disbelief, I remained shocked in my place.

Seeing the cold, powerful expression on Sameen's face, I had the sinking feeling that I didn't have the will to say no and confront his threats. I was stuck in the moment. Thoughts flew in my head. I was one of those in charge of the Unit, and it was impossible for me to say no. If it had been months earlier, I could have refused him and taken my punishment. Now, after being in charge for six months, Sameen could accuse me of being an infiltrator. I hadn't given them any names or information. What if they beat me to the point that I would break? These thoughts filled me with fear.

Neither resistance nor escape was possible. My position of being a guard for the past six months was the greatest burden I had borne. The interrogators would make it catastrophic for me, and maybe for all of us, if I resisted.

I had never thought this would happen to me. I was completely incapable of thinking beyond the present moment to resist his command. By making the prisoners participate in the torture, they could tell who was a resistant prisoner and who was truly a collaborator. In my heart, I admired Badri's devotion for telling the truth after a year of hardship, but I was trapped with terror.

The immediate answer was on the torture bed. Badri was going to be tortured anyway. My lashes would be weaker and less painful for Badri than Sameen's strong hands. I was going to favor her with less painful lashes. These were my rushed perceptions.

Sameen had put his finger on his lips so I wouldn't say anything and Badri wouldn't know it was me beating her. Sameen made it easier for me to put the shame aside and follow his command. I made up my mind.

I reached to take the copper cable. The cable weighed a ton in my hand. Sameen gestured for me to start. I turned towards Badri's bare feet. I felt disconnected from myself and everything around me. I was a stranger. I closed my eyes and raised my hand. The cable came down on her soles and she screamed. One...two... three... I lashed.

I opened my eyes and saw Sameen give me a malicious, triumphant smile. He reached his hand to take the cable from me. I immediately left the room.

Instead of going back to the prisoners' room, I waited behind the door. Shame was drowning me. I kept trying to convince myself that I had to do it. I didn't have a choice, and I had lashed Badri only three times.

Ashtari was coming towards the torture room, and he saw me in a strange mood.

"What's going on?" he asked with an amused, wicked shine in his eyes. I made no reply but gave him an agreeable, stupid smile and left hurriedly.

That night I slept badly, waking up repeatedly, unable to get the horror of what I had done out of my mind. I didn't understand why I was picked to be in charge of the Unit and why I was picked to beat Badri. The next morning I had to go back to work.

When I was six years old, I was living with my parents in a small town where my father had his shoe shop. It was my first day attending school. In our unattended classroom, kids were busy at their places. I bent over a notebook making marks with a pencil. Suddenly a well dressed woman with short hair entered. She stood at the door and looked at us then pointed at me.

"You, come here."

Tearing myself apart from the tall bench, I saw another girl rising up so I sat back.

"No, no, you come here." She pointed to me.

"Me?" I asked with doubt.

"Yes, yes, you."

I followed the teacher, entering another classroom. The students were sitting there, all quiet.

Turning my face away from them, I glanced up at the teacher in confusion, wanting to know why I was there. She squeezed her eyes together and shook her head with suppressed anger.

"These are fourth grade students, the lazy ones, who don't know how to study their lessons. They should learn from you, little girl. Tell them, 'learn from me you lazy girls.'"

I didn't know what was going on and stood quiet, embarrassed to talk.

"Yes, yes, go ahead and say it."

Blood ran through my face and burned it with heat.

"Learn from me …"

"You lazy girls," the teacher said and I repeated after her, in a very low voice.

I wanted to escape from that teacher who made me repeat the sentence over and over again and yelled at the girls, "See, if you don't study I'll take you back to sit in first grade. She is younger than you, but you lazy girls must learn from her. Understand?"

Turning to me the teacher dismissed me and opened the door to let me leave.

Before going back home we lined up around the yard where the principal stood to talk to us. All of the sudden, the students hushed when he asked, "Whose bag is this? It was left by the tank?"

No answer.

I gradually recognized the brown leather bag with a yellow zipper and two locks in front. It was mine. I had drunk some water earlier and left it by the tank. The bag in the principal's hand was mine.

As he asked again, I was afraid to speak up.

"I promise I won't do anything to you, just come and get your bag, whoever you are." The principal said looking around at all the faces.

I stepped forward and walked slowly towards the center where he stood, my bag hanging from his hand.

"Is it yours?"

"Yes," I nodded, looking in his eyes.

"Why did you forget your bag?" he asked with dismay and unexpectedly slapped me hard on my face.

I wanted to cry from the pain of slapping, but didn't. The pain subsided against the tide of shame of being beaten in front of the students, including the fourth graders.

My early experiences acquainted me with humiliation, but my beating Badri took me to an evil place. It made me a betrayer and a torturer.

For a while, I tolerated Hanna, the traitor. She had been following me for three months. She stalked me like a hunter with a bow.

"I want to tell you something." She had told me one day in her thick voice,

"When you were sleeping beside me, you looked so pretty that I wanted to kiss you."

For lack of enough room we had to share the bed bunks. Since she had told me what was in her mind, I'd been careful not to sleep close to her.

After the interrogators dismissed Mastooreh and Setareh, Hanna became one of the guards, so it became more difficult to avoid her as she was bold. She was twenty-six years old, 5'6" tall, with big bones. Her unremarkable face rested on a short, thick neck and her straight hair was always covered under a long black scarf.

The second summer had come to the Unit. Hanna and I were on duty while the blindfolded prisoners sat against the wall, quiet. The interrogators were not around. Towards the end of the day when everyone was supposed to remain silent, I stepped briefly into the adjacent bathroom to wash my hands. I was about to leave when the door opened. I turned around. It was Hanna.

"Mehri," she whispered after closing the door. She moved closer, looked into my eyes, and embraced me.

I stepped back and said, "No."

Ignoring my refusal, she continued embracing me tighter and put her lips on mine. Hanna was taller and stronger than I was. I couldn't push her away or say a word. Someone could hear us and report it. To be caught in another woman's arms could cause me serious trouble. I could be executed or imprisoned for life. I knew, too, that my natural reserve in talking about such circumstances would make it impossible to defend myself.

I was trembling in her arms thinking of her as a stupid worthless woman who is abusing her position as a guard. I didn't know how long she was going to continue; disgusted by her lips and teeth, I tried to pull away for she was pursuing her uncontrolled desire in exchange for my morality and spirit. What she was doing was harmful, ruining and wicked.

At the very moment that I was thinking how sick she must be, I observed a sudden change in my body. I felt one with her need and suddenly became conscious of a strange desire to let her hold me. I felt the warmth of her arms and a physical pleasure from being kissed. Hanna sensed that I had stopped resisting. I finally made another effort and broke free from her embrace and left the bathroom in a hurry. The prisoners in the adjacent room were quiet. Probably no one knew what had just happened; it was a very strange incident that made me feel ashamed of myself.

Two days later, Hanna found me alone again.

"Mehri." she whispered passionately in my ear and collapsed in my arms. Among all my confusing feelings, I wanted to let her embrace me; I couldn't help myself. Even though I didn't like this woman, I wanted to forget who I was and let her hold me. I was selling my body like a slut to get something I needed. It was not just a physical impulse, but a way to escape the suffering. I wanted to forget the past, Badri and everything else and let it all go, even for just a few moments.

Hanna was a nonpolitical, simple-minded woman from a northern town.

"My father never showed me any affection," she told me. "Maybe that's why I'm always looking for love and attention."

I felt increasingly uncomfortable during our next two encounters until I spoke firmly to Hanna.

"I'm ashamed," I said to her. "I don't want this to happen again. Do you understand? This is sickening me. I can't do this."

The excitement vanished from Hanna's eyes,

"Yes, I know," she said. "I feel the same. I, too, don't want this to happen again."

I had trouble believing her.

I was on duty when a new prisoner said with difficulty that she needed to see a doctor, putting her hand on her throat. I rushed to Sameen who asked me to bring her to another room, where he looked at the girl.

"What is wrong with you?" Sameen asked her angrily.

The girl stood there with no sign of choking.

"She looks OK now, but she told me she was sick," I said. There was a tone of meanness in my voice to please Sameen who was upset. As soon as I said it, I lowered myself, siding with an interrogator against another prisoner.

I was invaded by the inhumanity of men in power. My sense of empathy was vanishing bit by bit. Maybe not all at once, but without much effort sooner or later I would be like the subject of the famous poem by Saadi, a poet of early thirteen century.

all the humans are just one family
since they have been created from the same being
when the calamity of time afflicts one member
the rest won't remain at peace
o, you who have no sympathy for those in misery,
unjust it would be to call you a "human being"

In the hallway, I ran into Haji, who didn't seem to approve of my position as a guard in the Unit.

"Where are you heading in such a hurry?" he asked me, looking straight into my eyes. "What are you doing?"

I stopped, but didn't respond to him. I hadn't seen him since the time I was paralyzed in bed rocking from pain.

"Aren't you like a condemned work horse that runs and runs with closed eyes and doesn't know where she's heading?" he smiled mockingly, shaking his head. "Both times, when you were a monafeghin sympathizer and even now, you are nothing more than that, a work horse. Poor thing. I feel sorry for you."

His head moved to his left and right and his mouth opened and closed. I couldn't hear him anymore. My own head rocked and shook inside. I felt I was drowning, deeper and deeper each minute with nothing to hold onto. My hiding place in the darkness had suddenly become an illusion. Haji who lashed my flesh with a chain in the past, struck my fearful soul with his cursed, cold words. Whatever I had become, it was me, feeling like a murderer who was handcuffed by her own gang leader.

Haji tore the dark veil that had blinded me. I saw the hell of my own world. I saw what I had become. Truly a "dead" person. It didn't matter who had done it, Haji, Ashtari, Abraham or me. "Dead" is "dead."

I sat on top of the steps to the small yard, covered my face with my black chador and cried. My voice became louder, and louder, and gradually changed into hysterical laughter. I cried and laughed. Not far from madness, I was now in the shoes of the sixteen-year-old girl I had heard laughing and crying three years earlier.

I don't know how long it took for me to be aware of the solid presence of two collaborator guards staring at me. I stood up, walked past them and went to the bathroom. I washed my face and cried quietly.

I finally went back to the room to lie on a bunk bed. I stayed there all afternoon and overnight. The next day Abraham, who must have heard about my hysterical laughter called for me and offered advice without asking me questions.

"Don't give others a reason to talk about you, Mehri," he said. "They have reported you because you don't curse the prisoners," he continued. "The Repentant Sisters believe you're still resisting and that you are against the regime. Don't give them reasons to prove themselves right."

Abraham didn't seem to know that Sameen had made me beat Badri. That I had to mourn for my soul, that didn't belong to this secret hell of wolves and foxes. That I lived in confusion and shame and that I wished everything would disappear all at once and I could be alone. Just be alone.

Before summer turned into fall, the fourteen months of subhuman conditions, interrogation, and my position as a guard ended all at once. The second-in-command to Khomeini, Hossein Ali Montazeri had learned from some prisoners' families about the "Graves" in Qezel-Hesar prison.

Montazeri sent his committee to Qezel-Hesar and discovered the coffin-like cubicles that Haji built to hold the young communist prisoners for nine months. The committee documented the "Graves" that were under Haji's control.

This forced the prison officials to close down the secret Unit before Montazeri's investigators discovered the Unit. We were finally going to be transferred back to a cellblock where our friends and former inmates were.

In 1984, Lajevardi, the Chief Prosecutor of Tehran and the warden of Evin prison was temporarily removed from his post. Lajevardi announced in the media that the prisoners volunteered to confess in front of video camera that they had been wrong in their political beliefs and now were defending the Islamic Republic.

Inside the prison the prisoners knew that Lajevardi, was responsible for the torture and execution of political prisoners and that this systematic torture forced prisoners to confess. Under Lajevardi's supervision the number of executions were in the thousands.

In the summer of the same year we passed the long hallway of Section 3 in Qezel-Hesar prison to enter Cellblock 8, the former famous Leningrad.

Entering Cellblock 8 didn't make the inmates of the Unit think their lives would change. For none of us knew about Montazeri's group and what had brought us back. We were going to continue living with the same terror as in the Unit.

We were going to be called traitors, the broken ones and repentants by our former cellmates and other prisoners. For the first time I felt the ugliness of the layer of the long scarf underneath the black chador over my head, the known uniform of broken prisoners. Who would believe I had been forced into a position as a guard? How could I explain the violence and the terror that made me to put my hand into the hand of the Devil and work for the destructive Satanic regime?

Under the load of shame, there was an imminent dread tangled with happiness. I had not given up my information and I was certain I must continue to keep it secret.

PART 13

Back to Leningrad

(1984)

When we arrived at the door of Cellblock 8, I wanted to hold onto my blindfold so as not to see my cellmates' faces.

Life in Cellblock 8 hadn't changed since we left for solitary two years earlier, except for prayer rugs that didn't exist before. Prisoners performed long prayers and sat on their rugs afterwards to read the scripture of the Quran. There was a reflection of light in their eyes, a comfort in their slow walking. Their piety contrasted with who we had become. Bruised all over with the lashes of injustice, we arrived to disturb their serenity.

The collaborators from the Unit were now mixed with the rest of the prisoners. Cellblock 8 was now the playground for them in which to battle and prove their loyalty. They were here to ruin and damage others until they were forgiven and released.

Faces of the inhabitants of Cellblock 8 ached from disbelief. Some stood apart from all of us. Some others were ready to seek revenge on us, the women in black for whom they shed tears during the last two years. We were no longer their friends, but their enemies.

The gang of real traitors walked around, cursing the other prisoners. At the beginning, I tried to distract them from tormenting other prisoners by entertaining them and laughing with them, but I couldn't bear being part of their group and started to avoid them after two days.

I chose to lie on the third level of the bunk in my cell and read from Khomeini's book of sharia laws. Reading that book would automatically label me as a broken prisoner, preventing my former inmates from getting close to me or sharing their information. It also made me safe from the traitors who looked for excuses to write reports.

This was my way of being left alone, avoiding any new interrogation and at the same time having time to think.

I had accepted the shame of being seen as a Repentant, but there were rumors about me. Some hadn't believed that I was broken. One of the prisoners in the Unit had told others I couldn't be broken since she had seen me serving the prisoners with compassion and Abraham had told Roya in the last day, "We know Mehri is not broken."

Hanna was still around and checked on me here and there, but I thought she couldn't be a threat with so many people around. Once in the small shower stall, a young girl and I had turned our backs towards one another washing, as was the norm in prison, when Hanna entered, her eyes full of lust.

The young girl pulled herself away to open space, her face an inch away from the wall. I pointed to Hanna to leave me alone, concerned about the young innocent girl who was uneasy. She pointed for only one kiss. I hesitantly bushed a quick kiss over Hanna's wet lips, but she didn't leave the stall as she had promised. Ashamed by what just happened I left the shower quickly.

I thought constantly about how I ought to behave. I wanted to retain my status as a Repentant to avoid being reported. Yet, I wanted to avoid the role of a traitor or reporting others.

I would have liked to talk to my cellmates, but I was no longer free to communicate with them. I greeted one cellmate when no one was around, but she received me coldly as if she never knew me.

On the third day, I was called, in full covering, along with the collaborators from the Unit to the main chamber outside the cellblock. I sat alone at a small table. Someone I couldn't see placed a question in front of me asking for reports about the prisoners in Cellblock 8.

Besides the interrogation, this was the first time ever I'd been asked to write a report on my fellow inmates. Worse still were the months I had to be a guard, yet what to write? When would they leave me alone?

I didn't need to think much for I knew I wouldn't speak against my fellow inmates, but what could I say?

"There is no political activity; no one really does anything. Most prisoners walk either alone or two by two."

There was a tall girl whose father was a senator from a famous family. She was in the spotlight for that reason. She took the brunt of the traitors' verbal attacks and was an easy target for their reports.

I had no doubt that she had already been named as a resistant prisoner. For my part I had to dim her role, "Bahar, for example, walks all day with her friend."

Of course, everybody in the cellblock, including the guards, saw that Bahar walked with her friend, all day, every day.

One day, fear conquered me. There was evidence that I had not revealed my information. For the first time I shared a prisoner's real name with Hanna, and she immediately reported it to Haji. After being in prison for three years, that girl had to admit her real identity.

I felt terrible about what I had done. What was I thinking? I feared that one of this prisoner's friends would talk and tell everybody I had betrayed them. Thank God it was a rather calm and easy period in Qezel prison, and Haji didn't punish the girl for using a fake name.

I was dreadfully frustrated. The Cellblock 8, where I had experienced moments of growth in humanity with my fellow inmates and experienced one of the best times of my life, now posed frigid and dusky.

One of my former cellmates, who spent two months in the Unit, came to me, wanting to talk. She, like many others, had come back from Europe after the revolution to live in her liberated native country. I had always liked her gentleness and wisdom.

One day during the sleep deprivation punishment in the Unit when I was on duty, she was so tired that she fell asleep on the bare floor. I didn't want Ashtari to see her sleeping.

"Oh, wake up," I called to her.

She woke up. "I think you really need to stand up," I whispered in her ear.

"You know I wasn't asleep, but I need to sleep now," she kept on saying this over and over again while she tried to go back to sleep. I looked around. No one was coming, so I knelt next to her and asked her again to stand up, but she didn't.

"You know I have to sleep now," she said, her face terribly pale. "I must go to bed. You know I have to sleep now. This is sleeping time. Brother Ashtari has told me to sleep."

She was exhausted and disoriented. She was confusing her wishes with reality. What could I do for her? Nothing. I didn't want her to get beaten. She had a child and a husband waiting for her outside the prison.

Now that the nightmare of the Unit had passed and we both were in Cellblock 8, she wanted to talk. I walked down the hallway with her calmly.

"You know," she said, "I want to come back to Islam and repent, but I'd like to do it with understanding."

She strove in vain to make me say something good about the regime. I remained silent, hoping that this fine young woman would realize that there was no place to go back to. There was no logic. No understanding. I hadn't returned to the regime's Islam by logic or choice. I hadn't repented at all. I was trapped in that hell by force. I left her in complete silence without uttering a word.

Next day when the guards took us outside for fresh air, Lily came up to me to say, "Hello." We were glad to be together. Neither one of us felt like talking and we both knew why. We walked in silence for about half an hour.

Afterwards, Hanna accosted me with an anger I had never seen from her before.

"Mehri." she said threateningly. "What were you talking about with Lily?"

"Nothing."

"But I saw..."

"Yes, we just walked together."

"How romantic!" she said.

"Calm yourself, Hanna. This is only your fantasy, not Lily's, not mine," I said and walked away from her.

I'd been in Cellblock 8 for two weeks when Haji transferred me to cellblock 7. It seemed as if he had hatched a plot to make me an example for the rest of the prisoners. Haji was to show how their system broke the prisoners. If I had difficulty facing a group of my former cellmates in the new cellblock, it also was a relief to get away from Hanna.

I didn't wear the large black scarf under my chador anymore and when I arrived, I took off my chador immediately. Dressed in my gray cotton shirt over my flowered skirt, I didn't look like a collaborator. The prisoners who knew me ran in excitement to lavish me with kisses and embraces, wanting to know where I'd been. I hugged them promptly and went to my assigned cell with my personal items and blanket, in order to show I had no further interest in talking. I couldn't be myself as long as there was a chance of being interrogated. I had to continue living with reservation and accept the shame as its exchange.

The prisoners in this cellblock were diverse in ethnicity. Many tall Kurdish young women in bright patterned long skirts had given cellblock 7 a new look. They walked straight, held their heads up, and talked aloud, differing from the political prisoners' secrecy. They had been arrested in cities close to the border of Iraq where the Iran-Iraq war was forced on the people.

The next day I strolled in the prison yard. The sun was up, shining gently over the bushes in a garden, planted by the former male inhabitants. I eagerly breathed the fresh air, my eyes wide open to the beauty and color of dark purple, pink and white geraniums waving in the breeze. The laughter of young girls was a shadow of joy in the small prison yard.

The temperature had dropped, making for a cool summer. Prisoners sat in groups, relaxing in the sun and talking to each other. A girl of about twenty with long straight hair and a wise, deep gaze approached me to discover all that had happened to me before my arrival. I knelt in silence looking towards the garden, touching the flowers and hiding my eyes from hers, just trying to smile as if I was practicing kindness. I wasn't able to tell her anything.

"Behind your eyes...there is a secret...I can tell you have a secret." She said during these days after the Unit, trying to reach me beyond my mask.

It was a bad omen that four days later Hanna was transferred to my cellblock and began to follow me everywhere. The next morning, around the little pool of running water in the yard, where prisoners were washing their clothes, a girl with a soft voice moved closer and closer after I had walked away from Hanna. She lowered her voice and told me, "The prisoners talk about you, please be careful," her eyes on Hanna who was not far from us.

I gasped for breath and held my tears. When the girl finished washing her clothes and left, I knotted my eyebrows together and cried out in a low tone to Hanna, "Leave me in peace, for God's sake. Would you?" Then I rushed away breathless to avoid her, but my response made no difference to her. The same night she excused herself, due to the lack of space, and slept next to me on the hallway floor where prisoners crushed next to each other.

I woke up in the middle of the night feeling Hanna's arms around my waist pulling me under her blanket. Rejecting her hands, I pulled myself into a sitting position, tears running down my face with a loud cry. I saw the blurry faces of the sleeping young girls awaking one by one looking up in the dark. Embarrassed to face my former cellmates I wished to escape from everybody and everything to a solitary cell, to be left alone.

In the early morning, I raced towards the office of the young collaborator in charge of the cellblock. I requested to be transferred to a solitary cell, voluntarily.

"Well, you are a prisoner. You know...you can't change your place in prison, or request things, but why a solitary cell? I believe you have a reason." She said.

"I just won't go back to the cellblock unless you do something."

"Then you must write your request down and explain why."

She handed me a few sheets of interrogation paper, and promised me that she would hand them over to my interrogator.

It was impossible to openly explain my reasons to Abraham; I mentioned that Hanna annoyed me. The next day, I was called to the office. While I was still waiting, Hanna came in without permission, red-faced and frustrated, she cried and said that I shouldn't leave.

I remained seated on the chair at the other side of the room and didn't look up or talk. I was determined to leave that place even when, as a result, I was transferred back to the terrifying prison of Evin.

Evin was used as a confinement center for the prisoners awaiting their trial and also as a regular political prison for many. Most prisoners would be transferred to the huge prisons of Qezel-Hesar or Ghohar-Dasht after they received their sentence in Evin's unofficial courts. Evin also served as a work place for interrogators and other investigative branches. For this reason, the most prominent prisoners were kept there.

The young traitor, Lida, from the Unit, was transferred with me. I assumed Abraham, who was now back in Evin, sent her to watch over me. The next morning, I was called and taken to Abraham. Strangely, he didn't ask me any questions about Hanna, but I understood I would be watched closely.

PART 14

Evin

(1985)

Evin's cellblocks, different from those of other prisons, concealed their cruelty in layers. The guards in charge were not prisoners but were women who served in the formal religious military group, the Army of the Guardians of the Islamic Revolution. The turncoats were not obvious and loud, as if persecution spoke in quiet, whispering tones.

Lida and I entered into a two-story building with a small courtyard, surrounded by tall brick walls. The long L-shaped hallway had seven rooms, three bathrooms and three showers with concrete walls. The larger cells contained about forty-to-fifty prisoners.

More than 200 prisoners upstairs and 200 downstairs were kept separated each from the other. The yard was shared by the two cellblocks in shifts when the prisoners would use it for fresh air hours.

Lida and I were in two different cells in the downstairs cellblock 4. Lida, as young as sixteen, had found it difficult to fit in with the old collaborators of Evin. She panicked in the crowded cellblock when others wouldn't recognize her, a young stranger. In the Unit, Sameen provided support to the young girl to fight against the resistant prisoners, but in Evin the lack of security had discomforted Lida. I also had no place to hide.

I was looking for a way to escape from the pain of dishonor. In spite of the terror of my past, I was full of the most unhesitating desire to live intelligently and with goodness.

I knew I couldn't go on if I didn't pull myself back together. Self-pity was not going to help me now that I was just out of the Unit for three weeks.

As I arrived, I overheard the conversation of two sisters who used to be inmates of Qezel-Hesar prison.

"Are you serious?"

"Yes, that's her. That's Mehri."

"She can't be!"

The older sister, turning towards me, continued. "But Mehri's eyes?"

She stepped forward to get closer to me.

As she drew near her voice changed from wonder to sympathy. "Oh my God. I didn't recognize you, Mehri." she shouted. "You have changed a lot. Is this really you?"

"Yes, it's me," I said, "but I don't remember, have we met before?"

She laughed and changed her tone to tell a girl sitting next to me, "We were in the same cellblock in Qezel for a while." Then she turned to me, "Well, it was crowded so you might not have noticed me, but I couldn't miss you."

I didn't know what to say, especially since I didn't want her to ask me why I had changed. The other sister called her and I used the moment to walk away.

For a month I was in despair, with horrible memories of the Unit. Sometimes I felt that I hadn't been executed just to show how weak I could become. I had to survive to see my own misery. But why?

Sometimes crazy ideas came to my mind. I wanted to ask Ashtari if I could go back to recreate my time in the Unit. I wanted a chance to do better. I imagined playing an amicable role. I would talk to my interrogators without fear and tell them it wasn't right to torture and isolate us for our beliefs. I would make them believe I didn't hate them. The interrogators would become kind and understanding men and happiness would replace terror.

Whenever I recalled the past, I couldn't forgive myself. How did I become what I had become? Why didn't I refuse Sameen when he told me to torture Badri? My answer was always the same, "It was impossible to say no."

Why? Why? Why? It was impossible to say, "No?" I asked myself, looking at the faces of the prisoners laughing, walking and talking.

I was aware I had done wrong. I suffered, for I was ashamed of protecting myself at the cost of harming Badri. I wished to be able to redo the past, but how?

I went on thinking, in the Unit I wasn't able to imagine what might happen to me in the long term, but I could see it now. I had lived without having a chance to see anything else beyond the Unit. I was trapped in each moment, filled with the terror of the place. I was drawn into that graveyard and couldn't think.

Now I stood on the edge, struggling mentally and emotionally. I couldn't bear being with myself any longer. Everything about the Unit looked unreal. It was as if I had woken up from such a horrible nightmare that even life in Evin looked normal.

As it happens in concentration camps, the inmates of the Unit had lost much of their beliefs and trust. As for myself, I had lost my identity as a truthful person.

When the symptoms of depression kept growing, I became certain of the urgent need to change my way of thinking. I found in the deepest part of my heart that I had an uncompromising wish to resist injustice. This gave me a vague feeling of hope.

In Evin also, the collaborators put great pressure on the prisoners. I wanted to resist their persecution and the regime's constant demands to give in. I wanted to feel revived. I wanted to gain some confidence. I decided to object to the injustice in my small territory, with my own body, in my own mind. That was the only way to improve myself.

I started a hunger strike without announcing it. I avoided doing things that would attract others' attention. I left the room and went to the hallway when my cellmates were eating and I returned when they had finished. Among forty prisoners in the cell no one noticed that I wasn't eating, and I didn't have a close friend to watch what I was doing in the cell.

But young Lida was in my way. I declined eating something with her with an excuse. After sunset, she appeared again to find that I hadn't eaten some dates that were treats in prison since prisoners had to buy them. She came back to check on me later and saw me avoiding food. For three days, I had two cups of tea and no food. On the afternoon of the third day she stared at my pale face and said, "Oh my God! Sister Mehri!"

I saw in her eyes that she suspected my hunger strike, for I had refused to eat a few times, a few items. I was called for interrogation.

It was Abraham. He asked me what I was doing. I had no energy or will to talk to him. He didn't pressure me to confess what I was up to, but I knew he had a report from Lida about my hunger strike. The same day I was transferred to a less crowded cellblock with fewer traitors.

Once I found a new space, I decided to break my fast to celebrate. If the hell I lived through had turned me into a dead stone, I was about to soften that stone with life.

It was some time later that I noticed that in the dimly lit corner of the room an extremely attractive young woman looked straight ahead, as if at a movie screen. Her large brown eyes, empty and lost, stared at one point; her raised eyebrows two thin crescents. Weeks came and went without her moving from her spot. One day I sat close to her.

"Mam," I said, "do you need any help?... With… anything?"

She was as motionless as a statue.

"There's no hope for her," a girl whispered into my ear.

I looked up.

"She needs to take a shower," the girl continued, "but she won't. She doesn't respond to anyone. We have tried. She doesn't care. Her poor family. You know, she has a husband and two children."

I could tell now that she was the source of the bad odor in the room. No one could bear to sit close to her.

"Dear…" I said leaning closer to her, "Please think of your family, if you won't think of yourself. What would they do if you harm yourself? You need to take a shower. I will help you if you want."

Not the blink an eye. Her eyes, not mysterious nor deep, were far from here, so far away, lost in nowhere.

Many days passed. She sat against the wall, not moving. And then, one day, she came to me, looked into my eyes and with a pleasant smile offered me a pair of her new socks.

"I would like to give you these to wear."

"Thank you so much," I said in shock, "please keep them for yourself. You may need them."

I hadn't finished my sentence when she went back to her corner to sit down and look straight ahead. "Should I have taken her gift?" I asked myself.

I went over to apologize.

"I want to thank you," I said. "You know I didn't want to take your new pair of socks because I thought you might need them. Please don't be sad."

It was as if she had turned into a statue again. She neither talked nor looked at me. A few days later when the warm water was turned on, I saw her sitting in the corner of the hallway, next to the shower door. I became so happy and stayed around talking to her, but she didn't respond. I encouraged her to take a shower. For four hours, she didn't turn her eyes and stared ahead while prisoners went in and out of the shower.

"Please, go on, go. I can help you…if you want. You need to take a shower. You may get sick. Please go on. Believe me, it's easy."

The shower time was over, but she remained in the hallway, sitting next to the door to the shower room. The warm water was turned off at 8 a.m. and wouldn't be available until the next week at dawn. The young, pretty woman sat there until late at night.

The next morning when it was still dark, she once more took up her post at the shower entrance. This went on for several days. The poor young woman had lost the will to live. That's why everybody had quit on her.

Finally, she returned to the cell, sat in the corner, and stared at the wall without taking a shower.

I stood back to view the new comers walking towards their assigned cells. I repeated, "Oh, God, oh God" when I saw the girl I had scorned in the presence of Sameen, the interrogator, in the Unit when she had ask for a doctor. I knew living in peace would be too hard for me unless I make it up. I walked towards her. "Oh, sister, I'd..." She didn't hear me. I waited until after she settled.

At that moment I felt no words could describe my remorse, but I explained it was necessary to talk to her. Perhaps she had expected this moment and seemed prepared to accept my request. She came to my cell where most prisoners sat in small groups talking to each other. I gave my space to her to sit comfortably and I sat against her facing towards the wall, not wanting other prisoners to see my face. As I started to talk, I couldn't avoid crying.

"I wanted... to ask for your forgiveness," I said. "Please forgive me for what I did to you."

"I forgave you then, right away," she said convincingly. I cried harder. "How could I've done it?"

Years later when Lily and I were out of prison, she told me that Hamid, her interrogator, had told her, "Do you think we let Mehri leave the Unit as a hero?"

It was then that I understood that the interrogators had sown the seeds to destroy me.

Now, two months after we got out of the Unit, I had the perspective to see what truly happened to me. I had aimed to resist the violence and injustice, counting on my own limited physical strength and my own limited mind. I hadn't had the guidance to survive the harsh battle between good and evil. I had forgotten that without God it was impossible. Hardship brought me fear and fear brought me to my knees. The horrendous result was my walking in the shoes of a guard, pretending everything was all right when it was a place I had to keep my feelings and thoughts hidden from everybody.

When I was nineteen, in search of the meaning of life, I became passionate about God and the teachings of the Quran, but my political activities separated me from the teachings of the Quran. Events followed one after the other in the chaotic kingdom of Satan. When evil took over Iran, there couldn't be any triumph for me or others. With empty-hands and no guidance we were facing Satan's dark hearted soldiers.

One day in the most bitter moment of my loneliness, I was looking at the top of the hills beyond the tall walls of Evin when I felt someone staring at me. Slightly to my left there was a young woman in her manto and scarf, a smile on her face. I smiled back which made her walk straight towards me to praise the beauty of the sunset. She chatted with enthusiasm and high energy, her light brown eyes alight.

Before I met Seena in the prison yard that evening, I had seen her lecture on closed circuit TV in the Unit. She was one of Haji's prisoners who came out of his Graves transformed into a devoted Repentant to the regime. She had cried and confessed that she was wrong and now was faithful to Islam.

I thought of her as a rare free thinker who had truly realized that theories of atheism and materialism were not convincing in addressing the great complexity of creation or the mystery of the human's mind and faith.

"I grew up believing in the principles of morality and of my grandma's religion," she said, "but later on I became a staunch believer in communism. My father is a rich man. Well, I called him bourgeois since he is a factory owner. I never lacked money. However, when I got into the university, I made my own choices.

"During my studies, I turned to what seemed to me freedom from historical constraint. I became a communist and later on, joined the Sahand Party and lived in a team house. I was one of the theorists in my group."

Looking at her scarf, I wondered why she insisted on always

covering her hair even if no man was around in the women's cellblock.

"I'm now a religious person," she continued, "and have returned to the Islamic Republic and Imam Khomeini."

I thought I must not forget that suffering was twisted into her life in prison.

"Do you think punishment contributed to your changing?" I asked her cautiously, not using the word torture. In my response, she paused for a moment.

"Yes, I believe it did," she said.

I knew quite well what torture could do to people and she was educated and brought up in a high-class family. Yet I didn't understand why she didn't hesitate even a bit. Why was she so proud of turning her back on her beliefs and so eager to advertise the regime's ideology? It even appeared that she was comfortable about swinging from one extreme to another. I also couldn't understand how a young woman of such great intellect could fail to see that the regime was fanatical. How could she devote herself to the men who had executed so many of the young generation, including Seena's own husband.

Despite all of this, I admired Seena for her strong belief in God. When I became a political activist, I had forgotten the necessity of remembering God in my daily life. Just believing in His existence didn't do me any good.

Seena seemed different from the others in her openness and sincerity. She was the only repentant prisoner I knew who used her time for serious reading and religious practices with a constant smile. When she spoke, unlike the rest of the Repentants, she wasn't boring, nor did she look depressed. It seemed as if she were falling in love with some new discovery or new theory everyday. I was amazed by her enthusiasm for life in every single moment.

Even though the authorities considered her a real repentant, I had realized that she wasn't an informer. This made it possible for me to talk to her again.

I needed to understand why she was the way she was and why things came so easily to her. My two years of being prevented from communication with other prisoners ended by talking to Seena on a regular basis.

Seena was a confident young woman with an extraordinary ability to lead. Whatever she did, she did it with intensity and passion. Whether she was an extreme communist or a devout Muslim she was able to convince people to accept her opinion and follow her. Of all the people in the cellblock, she was the one who had no fear of talking to other prisoners openly. It wasn't only because Haji, the warden, had confirmed her repentance, which immunized her from any accusations. I believe she couldn't live otherwise. Her mind was set to direct others and in the prison she became a religious leader.

I was thirsty for deep discussions on philosophical subjects, and Seena became the source of my spiritual nourishment for a few months. I was most captivated when she talked about God. I started to regain my lost confidence. Even though daily prayers were forced on all the prisoners, I did them willingly.

"You must thank God for everything He has granted you and pray to Him for anything else you are thinking of. In Him, we may find peace, consolation, and love," Seena kept telling me.

Even though she didn't go a lot more beyond what religion was generally understood to be, I began to feel changes. I wrote two pages of lyrical prose and showed them to Seena. She liked my writing and became excited, as I expected.

One day Seena invited some of us to listen to Khomeini's speech on TV, and she with two of her acolytes came to my cell. We sat quietly, backs to the wall, put our heads on our knees, fascinated with his pious manner and speech. My cellmates, who had absolutely no interest in him, went about their normal business in the cell and ignored us.

After a few months of Iran's revolution, I had separated myself from Khomeini and opposed his regime because they had established totalitarian rule. It was always hard to judge Khomeini. As infamous as he was among the intellectuals he appeared as a humble person and a believer. Whether he was a man of God or a murderer, I didn't have an answer. My understanding of right and wrong became confused when it came to him. How could a man of God, whom many worshiped for his spiritual ascendancy, let all this cruelty happens under his leadership? Killing so many innocent young people alone was a major crime of a leader which I couldn't deny.

One night after many years of having regular prison dinners, the meal was going to be something unusual. We were going to have cutlets for dinner, a kind of Iranian hamburger. This became important news. Joy and silliness spread throughout the cellblock. Some girls jokingly announced the dinner news loudly and laughed cheerfully about the cutlets that hadn't yet been served.

Seena wrote a few pages in response to the prisoners' reaction to cutlets. It was a well-written criticism of the prisoners' excitement. I enjoyed reading her writing and responded with another essay. This time I chose to read my poetic prose to one of the popular communist girls in my room. After I finished reading it, she raised her thick eyebrows and turned to me, "Mehri," she said with a stern expression on her face. "What do you think we live in? This is a prison and we are prisoners. Don't you ever think that we are free to choose what to do or what to say."

I blushed, for I knew she was right. Evin was not a place to explore literature or knowledge. I didn't try to reply, for I myself didn't know why I denied the happiness found in the simple things in life. I was aware that God not only allows joy, but He also promises perfect happiness in this world for those who follow the laws of His harmonious kingdom.

The spiritual world was a way to forget the ugly face of my time in the Unit and my life in prison. By being spiritual, I was better able to bear the harsh reality of prison.

The collaborators of Evin hadn't in any way accepted Seena as one of them and Seena attempted to reach out to the important members of the Repentant group in her room. Her efforts to join the collaborators and her extreme religious practices made me avoid going to her as often. I wanted no part of the traitors.

But Seena was satisfied with her way and herself. Almost every day she fasted, made additional prayers, and covered her head with a scarf from morning to night. She was instinctively, by her nature, convinced that she was always right. Her past life was wrong only because it had passed.

I saw her less and less until one day one of Seena's cellmates came in a hurry and called me to their room, cell number six.

It was after lunch. About thirty-five prisoners sat around in the cell, next to each other stretching out their legs. The steam of hot tea rose from red plastic cups in their hands.

Seena was on the floor rolling from one corner to the other end. The prisoners' eyes turned to me and my eyes turned to the girl who had called me.

"What's going on?" I murmured.

"She did this a few times last week. I thought she might listen to you if you talk to her."

I sat next to Seena.

"Seena, it's me. Mehri," I said, bending over her.

She was making strange sounds and sentences.

"Let me fly."

"Listen, Seena. Everybody is watching you. For God's sake, they may think you're going crazy. It's not good for you."

"But I can't be. I'm truly enjoying it," she said as if she were drunk.

"Seena, listen. Even the most religious, those closest to God from the beginning of Islam never did things like this."

She was completely indifferent to what other prisoners might think. She was experiencing a strange, good feeling. She was in love with the joy of spiritual practice, the only joy she could reach now. She had gone to extremes and left reality. Nothing mattered to her anymore. She had, in her own way, worked out a way of unloading her own misery. Everyone wondered if she were mentally ill.

At this time, I was transferred to a crowded, chaotic cellblock where prisoners had to sleep crunched together on the floor. The traitors would smell friendliness and immediately report us to be transferred and separated. I had to live alone again, independent of others. I didn't know anyone in this cellblock except Farah, my hometown friend from Borujerd.

I was soon aware that the desire to be myself was rushing out away from my heart. As hungry as I felt to learn, I searched to find something to read. In the few outdated magazines available in the cellblock I found pieces of poems and excerpts from Persian classics.

This two-story cellblock was tucked into the folds of the hills. I was located in a cell with two small, filthy windows. The unwritten laws of prison forced inactivity, for activity was a sign of life. No one wanted to wash the windows, not wanting to signal neatness and organization.

I wanted to wash the dirt away from those hard-to-reach windows that had blocked the sky. It was not all about the worth of seeing a piece of the blue sky from the upstairs cellblock, but it was as if I looked for ways to purify myself.

One day I thought I heard Sister-in-law's voice when she was singing a song. She must be in the downstairs cellblock. Since she had gone crazy in Cellblock 8 a few months earlier, I hadn't heard anything about her.

It had been just two days after we'd been transferred from the Unit when Sister-in-law entered. Haji must have transferred her for a specific reason, perhaps to break her by making her despair.

Sister-in-law had high expectations of her heroes. In her mind, as it was in our own minds too, political prisoners would sacrifice themselves to achieve goals for humanity.

When Haji transferred her, she had anticipated a merry reunion with Hamideh and me after more than two years of separation. Her happiness shone through her honey-green eyes when she walked in and ran to hug me, then towards Hamideh.

Her smile dried up little by little as she saw our faces were pale and lifeless. Evidently we were cold and depressed, our dead eyes set back in our long faces.

"Is it true?" she cried, her voice shaking. "I want to hear it's all lies."

She looked at each of us again in disbelief. Up to five minutes before, we'd been her champions that she had wished to join.

She couldn't accept all the changes so suddenly. Once she realized the news about us might be right, she fell to the floor and screamed from deep in her heart. "No... it can't be true..."

Now that those she had greatly admired for two years were broken, she must grieve her loss.

Soon the warden took her away from the cellblock, for she didn't stop screaming for two days. I heard no more about her until now. Sister-in-law was here, in the downstairs cellblock of Evin.

After a few days of thinking, it was impossible not to do something. I wrote a twelve-page letter explaining how I could help my former cellmate restore her sanity. I asked the warden of Evin to transfer me to the downstairs cellblock to be with Sister-in-law.

After my first letter was ignored, I wrote a new letter, this time to Sister Mohamadi, the warden in charge of my cellblock, using a health issue, requesting sunlight in the prison yard, which was often available at the downstairs cellblock. This was approved by Evin's doctor and before I got to know the prisoners in this cellblock, I was transferred to where Sister-in-law was.

Before I left this cellblock, I wrote a calligraphed line of a poem on a small piece of paper for Farah, my hometown friend.

"I feel alive only if I keep going, if not, I will be destroyed, annihilated."

The first face I saw when I entered in the new cellblock was Nasim's.

The memory of the crowded bookstores, Kati, the men in black, and being arrested on Farvardin Street, all appeared in front of my eyes. Now Nasim, who was our look out, was here in the same cellblock I was in.

"Oh, Nasim." I exclaimed and ran to hug her. I had been longing to see a friend I could trust and here she was just a yard away from me.

Nasim frowned and pulled herself back and coldly walked away.

"I don't know you," she said with her hands rising at both sides.

I suddenly realized I shouldn't have run to her. I had no idea what her condition was or if she had given her real identity.

I found Sister-in-law in the last cell where I was assigned. The guards had chained her to the cold radiator attached to the wall.

Unbearable. Her honey-green velvet eyes were saddened under a layer of dull ash-gray. Nothing, no hope, or anything close to it reflected on her face. She was cursing the men in power as if she were an unknown creature lost on a foggy road in the middle of nowhere, groaning to release herself from fear.

Her sister, Monir had been standing right there, two feet away from her, for the past three days. Nothing was left of Monir's beauty, just a trace of soft skin on her cheekbone.

When they released Sister-in-law from her chains, I walked towards her in the yard. She recognized me. She talked loudly then remained quiet for a few days. I wanted to do anything I could to help her to get better. I felt responsible for what had happened to her.

My wish contrasted with her sister's, who spent most of her time with a group of neutral young girls. Yet, Sister-in-law and I walked together and I listened to her stories of how everything talked to her. She saw signs everywhere and believed the faces on TV told her to do certain things. That was why she acted according to their orders.

She sometimes communicated logically and told me about that shocking moment in Cellblock 8, and what had happened to her in a solitary cell in Gohar-Dasht. She had spent months in total isolation. Sister-in-law was a kind, loving, idealistic woman. She had a son and a husband waiting for her. Seeing her health gradually improve made me optimistic that she would become normal one day.

As it was the prison policy in Evin to transfer the prisoners to prevent any strong bonding among us, Sister-in-law and her sister were transferred with almost one forth of the prisoners to the upper cellblock. Sometime later, I heard Sister-in-law screaming as if her situation was getting worse.

Once, the guards held a religious class for prisoners in the downstairs' hallway and allowed prisoners from upstairs to participate. Among them was Sister-in-law, who refused to go back to her cell after the class was over. She was so strong that a few women guards couldn't make her move.

"Don't touch me," she screamed at the face of the woman who was going to pull her arm.

"Let me talk to her, please," I requested.

"Be quiet," a guard shouted.

Sister-in-law turned back and smiled at me, then stood confidently, held her head up and walked towards the stairs.

She told me later that she knew from my voice that I wanted her to go back to her cellblock and she did listen to me.

I had met Sister-in-law prior to the time we were arrested. She was an idealistic young woman, hungry to find meaning for her life. As they were intended to do, Iran's political prisons turned her lifeless, as they did with many more inhabitants.

Time passed. I hadn't talked to Nasim, who denied knowing me until a day in the yard when we met behind a dozen rows of hanging clothes under the sun.

At noon prisoners were having lunch. I found Nasim seated on the ground behind the wet hanging clothes, in order to be hidden when she was talking with me in private.

"I couldn't wait to talk to you, Nasim."

I cried and hugged her, a long hug. Nasim's eyes filled with tears, but she avoided letting her emotions out.

"Tell me Nasim," I said. "What happened to you the day I was arrested?"

"Nothing happened to me then, and Kati who escaped that day...," then she didn't finish her sentence and I preferred not to ask.

"Well, and here I am with you. I was arrested two years after you, but my husband... Do you remember Nader?"

"Of course. What about him?"

"He was arrested the same summer and two months later he was executed."

"Oh, my dear, I'm so sorry...Nasim."

"Well, you know... that's what we all have chosen to end up with, right? Mehri, now you tell me about yourself. Where were you before coming to Evin?"

"I will tell you, Nasim, but promise me not to spread it, otherwise, I will be in trouble. Would you prom...?"

"...Yes. Of course. What is it?"

"After seven months being in solitary, a group of us went under a long term interrogation and were severely tortured in a secret place called the Unit. They kept us there for fourteen months that included suffering in complete isolation, in a place called the Graves."

"Graves?"

"That's what Haji, the warden of Qezel, called them. We had to sit all day in one spot. We were not allowed to move or talk to anyone, like dead bodies in graves. Very hard to handle. Very hard to be in that hidden place. Nasim, if my interrogator finds out that I have talked about it, I will be in a real mess. Please don't mention it to anyone."

"OK... we better separate now. We'll talk more later. We shouldn't be seen together."

I felt a distance from Nasim. Her cold reaction to my report was how political prisoners would react to another's hardship when they had no real sense of the experience. They expected everyone to come out of all that horrible experience with their heads up.

At the last moment she turned back and teased me, pointing to my clothes, "Fashion still kills you, doesn't it?" She laughed in a soft voice and disappeared through the rows of dresses hanging out to dry. I watched her sandals trailing a half moon shape over the drips of water on the ground. I then looked at what I wore: a gray tailored cotton shirt over a black skirt patterned with small flowers, which my mother had sent me.

Deep in my heart I wished to survive the prison without loosing more of my sincerity. Maybe no one looking at me could guess what was in my mind. Certainly Nasim couldn't.

Two days later when rows of hand-made tablecloths were spread on the floor at lunchtime and my forty cellmates sat tightly around them, Nasim's close friend, a short intellectual woman, located herself opposite to me and said,

"I've heard about the Graves in Qezel. I'd like to know more," she said with a silly smile.

I stood up, for my food stuck in my throat. I casually excused myself to leave the room and strictly avoided talking about the Unit after that.

Being transferred from one cellblock to another was like circling around one's own tail. I entered into a new cellblock by fall to find Sara and Pooran from the Unit. I was so happy to see them.

Sara, a hair band over her head, looked like a fit, classy model. She slowly smoothed her long black hair to settle it behind her neck. It was not so long ago that I saw her sitting on a chair, an object for Sameen's play.

She looked up and saw me at the door staring at her.

"Mehri! Oh Sister Mehri!" She ran to hug me.

She looked fifteen years older than her age and the glow in her eyes had disappeared. Pooran joined to welcome me with her permanent kind smile. Her thick black eyebrows were the same as before, but nothing else. She looked old and caved in. Both of them were laughing, a look of exhaustion behind their skins, a deeper tiredness buried in their eyes.

To ease their life Sara and Pooran had isolated themselves from other the prisoners, since the mood in this cell was worse than the others. A twenty-year-old traitor intimidated her forty cellmates, so that when she entered the room they all shut up including a pregnant woman and a seventy-year-old lady who was called "mother" by the prisoners.

I filled my time by reading short poems I found in magazines; I drew and made calligraphy with a pencil. Occasionally prisoners came to see what I was doing and looked at my art.

From the plastic bags that came in with our daily bread, Sara sewed two raincoats for herself and me. When the cold breath of winter held the prisoners inside, Sara and I were in the yard. We walked together when the snow or the rain pelted down. At early hours when the guards opened the door to the yard we ran out as if to catch up with life somewhere outside the walls.

Behind the two-story cellblock, the surrounding tall brick walls cut the blue sky into a small square. A bit of bare land on the hill cut into that square.

While walking, I memorized a poem written by a poet, Khosh Amal. With her frozen hands, Sara held the small piece of paper, and, with chattering teeth, I recited the poem back to her.

even if I'm a small spring, I can find my way to the sea
if love rises up, I can fall for it
if there won't be eagerness of life, in the prison of existence
I can die for the hope of a perfect sweet love

When Sara was there, my life was pure and simple. Sara and I walked in the prison yard, looked at the sky and talked about a possible day we might live outside of the prison. The two of us promised if we would ever be released she would make a netting jacket for my beloved father and I would make a painting for her.

The main traitor in our room used to belong to a communist group, Paykar, and was now religious and spied for the wardens. There was an empty circle around her wherever she walked with her head tilted up. Other collaborators talked to her with respect, out of fear, yet she never acknowledged them. She kept glaring down at the prisoners who she believed were resistant.

One day, suddenly one of the guards came in and took away my notebook, which I had filled with sketches, calligraphy, and poetry lines.

A regretful feeling entered my heart at losing the notebook. I became tired of all this oppression and lay down on my stomach and began to sob, hiding my head under a pillow. I cried and screamed nonstop as I had never cried before. For two hours tears poured out and ran down my chin, like a new stream of water gushes out from beneath a hard rock. No one dared to comfort me in the presence of that traitor. Without knowing it, I had released some of the tremendous tension that had built up in me and I felt stronger afterwards.

"Oh damn you foolish spy," I said this to the traitor girl in my thoughts and it transferred to my eyes. She sensed my readiness to fight her and walked away and didn't bother me after that.

Soon Sara was called out with a group of the prisoners who were supposed to be freed. Her four-year sentence was over. Sara left us for good with tears and joy. I gave her my mother's number to call my family. Later, I heard from my mother that she and my father had visited Sara in her father's house in Tehran.

One evening when I was walking towards my cell, I saw Badri. She was among the newly transferred prisoners. I wanted to fall on my knees to ask her forgiveness. I couldn't justify the terrible thing I had done to her. I was ashamed that I had lashed her feet out of fear of Sameen, the interrogator. I knew I must talk to her.

Greeting her and remembering the past was a difficult moment. We walked in the yard together. As I tried to say something, words became meaningless and I failed to speak. I was full of shame.

Above all, I was afraid of how she would receive me.

"Please forgive me, Badri," I implored her. I was crying and didn't know if she could understand my position in the Unit. Tears flowed down Badri's face.

"Mehri, that day when Brother Sameen asked you to tie my hands I didn't expect you to do it. It hurt my feelings so much. I didn't expect anything like that from you. I didn't…"

"My God, she doesn't even know that I lashed her. Should I tell her?" A voice in my head was telling me, "Admit… admit that you have beaten her…" I screamed in my heart, "I must admit," but I realized I was not able to say it out loud. I wished that painful memory would be removed from our hearts.

"Badri, Badri jan," I sobbed, "please, forgive me."

My voice broke into strange sounds. I reached into my pocket for something to wipe my face. I looked down, not wanting others to see me in tears. I was embarrassed to confess that I had harmed her more than she knew. In one way it comforted me that she didn't know — or I fooled myself that it did.

Among the new group, I also found my friend Farah, from Borujerd. This was the second time I was in a cellblock with her. After a warm greeting she said, "One day I climbed on a chair to hang my clothes in the yard and secretly looked inside. I saw you were writing something in a notebook. I was so happy to see that you were using your time well, not sleeping all day, wasting your time like many."

After a swift glance at my face, she whispered, "I'll talk to you again, soon," and left the room. When in the early morning, we met in the yard, not many prisoners were out yet.

"Mehri, I must tell you I have heard about you as a…" she paused and then said, "a Broken."

A wave of sudden blood ran into my face,

"I have been watching you," she continued, "and I can say in confidence that I don't believe it. But what's your problem? Do you have any question about the organization? What is it? Can we talk about it?"

I couldn't tell Farah about the Unit. How could I know she'd keep it quiet and not betray our confidence? I couldn't tell her what caused my suffering. It was my own secret to keep.

But it was a fact that the Mujahedin's leader's strange marriage was a question for many of the followers. We could talk instead about that which kept many from embracing the Mujahedin leadership and how the topic was used by the regime for propaganda.

The wife of the leader's longtime second-in-command suddenly divorced her husband and married the leader. They claimed it as an ideological revolution to justify what appeared to be inappropriate behavior. This strange incident left the followers puzzled. The leader and his new wife even went so far as to order all Mujahedin couples to divorce each other and "marry" the leader, a shocking suggestion given Iranian cultural norms.

In reality, it was difficult for me to think about the politics outside of the prison. It was the hardship of interrogation in the prison that made me pretend that I was broken. Farah changed her tone, "Yes, yes, the leader's strange marriage. I understand. But look, Mehri, we don't know everything. We don't know what's going on outside. Our source of news is the regime's propaganda, their media, newspapers and TV. The regime's news is not reliable. Do you know what my source of the true news is? Well, yes, the regime's newspapers. But only what they quote from the opposition, and that's how I read newspapers. Our leader's marriage was ideological. An influential writer has said so. Mehri, come on now. Stop thinking nonsense."

I wanted to stop the conversation right there as well. All that wasn't helping the movement for democracy we had started in the first place. We needed basic morality to survive as a community. If it hadn't been for the higher-ranked Mujahedin, their betrayal and lies, my friends and I might have been in a normal state of mind like Farah herself. The leader's strategies left the followers like injured solders in wartime. We were on our own to be ruptured by the enemy.

"I came to ask you a favor, Mehri," she said. "When you have a family visit, would you ask your Mom to go to my parents' house and ask them to send me some money?"

"Sure, I will tell my mother."

"My parents don't even bother to come to visit me,"

"Why don't they?"

"They don't care about me. That's why."

She pulled her hand with her short disfigured fingers out of her pocket to give me a telephone number. She didn't feel ashamed of being disfigured anymore. But could that be a reason for a family to reject their daughter?

"If your mom could go to our door, it would be even better. I want them to know I will return the money when I get out of here."

"I will ask my mother. I am sure she would go to your house, Farah, but maybe they can't make it here for some reason or don't have money to send."

Farah shrugged. "They have always been that way. They spend so much on my sisters."

"I'm sorry," I said.

"I was a black duck in my chicken family."

"Well, then don't be annoyed, Farah jan, now that you know. It's not you who should be blamed."

"No, but I need some money to buy necessary things. That's all I need from them now."

"I have a little money to give you," I said shyly.

"Thank you, and I have another request, Mehri"

"What is it?"

"I don't know if you can do it, but if you would, your prison sentence is almost over and you will be freed soon. I want you to take some of my notes out. I have done some research on the Quran and have come to some interesting conclusions. I would like to send them out. Would you take them with you?"

"I don't know if that's possible. You know the guards search the prisoners head to toe before releasing them."

Farah started to walk away to go back in the cellblock. "I really want to send them out," she said seriously.

Farah was right. My five year sentence was almost over. I had only three months left; yet I couldn't imagine myself being released. Was it really possible for me to get out?

A few months earlier, it was announced that Khomeini would pardon some prisoners chosen by the wardens and the interrogators from case reviews. That meant the prisoners who deserved to be forgiven would be rewarded and released before their sentence was over. I was called and sent to be questioned by a special committee. I guessed that must have been Abraham's idea. But I was certain Ashtari wouldn't let me out. Blindfolded, I answered the man who wanted me to convince him I deserved my freedom.

"I was in charge of the Unit for six months," I replied.

"That was two years ago. What else have you done?" he said.

"Nothing," I replied, feeling released.

He then called upon someone to come into the room. It was Pooran, from the Unit who was with me in Evin for a while. The man asked Pooran about me and she said kind words. Her presence softened the painful memory of the time we were in the Unit. The man left the room and allowed us to remove our blindfolds. There was a kind emotion in Pooran eyes. She was so grateful and passed me a fine hairpin to keep as a memory. I was about to cry; seeing her free soul revived my hope. A warm feeling entered my heart, for life offered a similar journey to both of us.

I was not only denied release but Abraham was also asked to send the resistant prisoners in the Unit for a re-trial. I was one of those he tried successfully to save from a new trial. He convinced the judge to accept my five-year sentence as my re-trail, for Haji had changed my sentence from one year to five in my trial in absentia.

After that I lived the days counting from six months to five then four and now three.

It was an absolute condition for all prisoners to confess their political errors and condemn the activities of their political groups in front of a video camera before they were released. During that time, it became acceptable for prisoners to do so as the price of their freedom.

Finding a way to avoid this "confession" occupied my thoughts for months. I had to either fake the confession and get released or refuse it and stay in prison. Neither was a good choice for me and I had no power to change things.

The crowd in the cellblock was excited, for it was announced they should get ready to go to Husseiniyeh, Evin's gathering place for religious ceremonies and lectures. Covered up in chadors and blindfolds, we headed up to the hills.

We passed through a few hallways and stepped outside. The fresh air flowed over our faces. When we were told to take off our blindfolds, we all turned towards the city of Tehran. Farther down the hills to the right, lights were blinking in Lona Park, an amusement park not too far away. The traffic light changed to green, yellow, red and then green again. Life was going on out there.

I looked up at the sky where millions of stars were blinking. As we walked up the hill, our shadows darkened the moonlit road. The young girls were chatting with their friends in groups of two or more. The cool night air brushed against our flapping black chadors until we arrived.

There were many other prisoners sitting on the floor inside the large high-ceilinged, gym-sized room, facing the stage. Prisoners in masses of hundreds were about to listen to some boring speeches of a new Repentant, a newly arrested prisoner or the warden of Evin. Male prisoners sat in the front rows and women were located behind them in the back.

I understood why prisoners liked to come to these mandatory gatherings. They enjoyed a touch of life and the fresh air during the walk. They also put up with the speeches for the opportunity to secretly glance around, searching for someone they might know. Most prisoners had a family member or a friend, perhaps a former cellmate they were looking for.

Among the crowd, I saw Hamideh as she helped the guards pass out a plate of dates among the prisoners, a happy expression on her face. With her smile, she asked for nothing but the guards' approval.

Soon Hamideh was transferred to our cellblock. She yelled at the upstairs prisoners accusing them of looking out from their windows to the downstairs prisoners in the yard. She cursed them loudly to proclaim her status as a super traitor. It seemed as if she had decided that nothing but her total cooperation with the wardens would protect her from misery.

Turncoats of this kind, who used to be in the higher ranks of the Mujahedin in Qezel, had made cellblock 2 an uninhabitable hell for the prisoners. Cellblock 2 was known as the worst cellblock in Evin. The competition among the traitors to harass prisoners was a proof of their redemption. Roya, in response to one of their verbal attacks, had revealed publicly that these super traitors used to be her leaders in the Mujahedin organization in cellblock 4, so that they would leave her alone.

I found Hamideh in cell number 1, sitting at the end of the cell under the light of the window by herself, her eyes fixed on the wall.

"Hamideh…" I called her name and awkwardly sat beside her. She was not a trustworthy person, for she had deeply wounded others and in her position she couldn't trust anybody. The tone of my voice made her turn and see the empathy in my eyes. The silence between us continued. We looked at each other and cried. It was as if we cried for the death of goodness, sisterhood, and humanity.

I had no doubt that she was suffering.

Very soon, I heard her screams from the storage room where she had locked herself in. It was as if her feelings had resurrected the goodness in her or her conscience had awakened.

PART 15

Last Days

(1986)

At the beginning of the spring 1986 and the Persian New Year, excitement rose in Evin again. Prisoners were going to have visitors outside the regular visiting salon. Our families sat in groups on blankets with some distance in-between them. The hills of Evin filled with women covered in black chadors, embracing their daughters.

My sister, Shirin, who could never imagine the regime's brutality and my younger brother, Shareef, had come with my parents. This was a sign of some changes in Evin. During the last year, they also had been releasing prisoners whose sentences were over.

I was called to the Releasing Room, with a group of prisoners. From below my blindfold, I read the paper that had been placed in front of me. "I proclaim that I will not do any political activity against the Islamic Republic of Iran, otherwise my brother Ahmad, who was my guarantor, will lose his house he has put up as security for my release."

I also would not have permission to leave the country for two years. During these two years, I must report to the closest jail center run by the Revolutionary Committee every month.

In addition, I had to answer one single important question: "Do you agree to do an interview and confess?"

The pen in my hand drowned in my sweat from spinning around my doubts. If I wanted to get out of prison, I had to say, "Yes." Saying, "No," meant no release whatsoever.

While wishing that a miracle would prevent me from doing an interview, I finally chose to answer, "Yes."

In an old Persian story, a man was going to be executed. The warden told him if he had a last wish, the warden would make it to come true. The man asked, "Would you untie me from this pole and tie me up to the next pole?" The warden wondered and said, "You could have wished for better things. What difference would it make to be tied on the other pole? You are going to die anyway!" The man said nothing.

The warden untied the man to tie him to the next pole when suddenly a messenger arrived hurriedly on a horse. "Hold on! Hold on!" the messenger shouted. "The King has granted this man's life. He is free to go." The man smiled at the warden and said, "You see, from this pole to the next there might be salvation!"

I had two months left from the time of signing the paper to the end of my sentence. I was thinking of how to resist doing the interview when I recognized a voice arguing in a polite manner with the man in the room.

"I haven't done anything wrong," she said calmly with confidence, "then why should I do an interview? No, I don't accept doing an interview."

This was Sohayla, my blue-eyed friend from Cellblock 8, who had asked me once to take a turn participating in the prison's religious ceremony. She now had refused the regime's obligatory interview as the price of her freedom. Ironically, I was the one who had resisted participating in the regime's mandatory religious ceremonies and now had ended up compromising.

I didn't expect any prisoner to refuse signing this paper. Everybody who was released in my cellblock had signed the paper and done a video interview before getting out.

We were ordered to stay in line in a row and hold on to the chador of the person ahead of us, in order to go back to our cellblocks in a group. Someone held onto my chador and stood behind me.

As soon as we walked out, she whispered, "Mehri, this is me, Sohayla."

I wondered if she could see through her blindfold. At least one guard must have been watching us.

We were blindfolded and I couldn't see anything. I didn't know how Sohayla had recognized me and could talk to me without fear. I didn't respond, but from under my chador, I looked for her hand to squeeze it.

"Azadeh is with me in my cellblock," she continued. "Not a day passes without her mentioning you. She says, 'I wish to see Mehri at least one more time.'"

I felt frustrated not being able to talk to her and send my regards to my former cellmate, Azadeh. The time of our sisterhood seemed a long time ago, as if it were another lifetime. Sohayla heard me crying and squeezed my shoulders. I heard a few footsteps. "Good-by Mehri..." She whispered as she walked away.

The rest of us continued dragging our slippers on the hallway floor breaking the tedious silence, our black chadors sweeping the dust of the hallways.

Sohayla and I had both changed. Sohayla, who was suspected by some as a Broken, had grown brave and confident. Her fate had turned around. She was now simply a free human. For her, there was a choice. But the pain of my wrong doings could never be forgotten. No matter how much I had yearned in the prison to remain a kind human, crumpled with pain, I would have to carry a load on my shoulders.

Who could have foreseen this and know our future?

Would it be possible for me to be free again? How?

My last months in prison were slowly passing. Months before my release date I surrendered all my thoughts and lifted my hands up for the first time, "Please, my Lord, send me out of prison without doing the interview." I never stopped asking God for this one favor every single day.

On a normal day in May 1986, the bright morning sun found its way through the slightly opened windows inside the dim cellblock. The end of my five years in prison arrived without my having been called for an interview. This was absolutely a miracle.

The intense world of the prison had buried my emotions, thoughts, and freedom for years, yet this last day was unbelievably grueling. Prisoners were doing their daily routines. Minutes passed by slowly, and seconds felt longer, until my name was finally called.

I still couldn't believe they were letting me leave without videotaping me condemning all the political activists.

The more popular the prisoner was, the more prisoners would follow her to the door. A few prisoners gathered to say good-bye to me. Some stood in the L-shaped hallway waiting for me to pass through, and a handful followed me to the end. At every minute I was expecting something to happen and interrupt my departure from the prison.

When I put my feet on the first step to go up, my eyes filled with tears, but I kept myself from crying. I looked at the girls I didn't know well who stood on the side of the stairs in order to register every face in my memory. It was hard to believe I was leaving the prison with so much pain.

I went up about fifteen steps and looked back again as if I haven't seen it all before. Then I disappeared behind a door and walked into a small room at the top of the stairs and cried. A woman guard who stood there let me go without searching my belongings. I regretted not taking out Farah's notes, the result of her research on the Quran.

I put my blindfold and chador on. Hearing the sound of footsteps coming from the other side of the door was like the tick-tock of a timer getting close to the moment of my heart's explosion.

Despite my longing to be released from prison, my feet wouldn't move ahead. I was full of regrets. The war between my head and heart was tormenting me more than ever.

I don't know how I walked out of the prison. My feet stuck to the ground outside the door. I dragged them to reach the white car waiting for me. I opened the door, dipped into the car and into my mother's open arms and cried, my tears like a calm rain.

The world I walked into didn't belong to me anymore. The warm sun, the road, my family, and the freedom felt strange. The prison was pulling me back to my memories of the injustice, my friends, my secrets, and my lost self.

My mother didn't let go of me. It seemed as if she were afraid of losing me again. She held me for the entire hour that it took to get to my sister's house in central Tehran. The first one to run to embrace me was my sister, Shirin. She ran down the five steps and collapsed in my arms. We held each other tightly and cried.

Shirin was one year older than I. We had grown up together. Some regarded us as twins because we wore identical clothes and sat in the same classroom for many years. When I became religious at nineteen, our ways separated us a bit. A year after the revolution, my sister gradually became religious too, under the influence of her husband's family, and she wore a black chador and became pro-Khomeini.

Then I went the opposite direction and opposed the Islamic regime. But our different political views didn't keep us apart much. Our relationship was based on trusting each other's good intentions. She was my dear sister and I loved her.

Her long black eyelashes were wet with tears, and her bright hazel eyes filled with love and passion as she comforted me. The only time that the authorities allowed it, she came to Evin at the last New Year to be with me. Her naïve question about whether there was torture in prison made me laugh.

Her adorable baby daughter, who was six now, sat against the wall. She was giggling and looked at me with interest. I just couldn't believe this was my sister's child who had grown up. My sister now had two more daughters, more evidence of time passing.

For two days in my sister's house, I felt empty inside. I was unable to move or walk and I fainted a few times.

The first night after my release date, I dreamed I was inside somewhere behind some closed walls, working unwillingly. Beside the building there was a body of water as vast as a sea. On the surface of the water, there were many small wooden rooms far from each other. Inside each room there was a girl. I was on a boat passing through. Each girl extended a hand towards me, asking for water to drink. I yearned to give them water but I couldn't. After a while, cars and buses came and the families of those people told me, "Your parents are waiting for you in a bus behind the door. Just go."

I couldn't go. My eyes wandered around aimlessly and I felt sad. There was a lump in my throat. I was allowed to leave. Everybody else left, except me. I remained there alone. My parents came, and each taking one of my arms, they asked me to go with them. I dropped to the ground crying. I woke up tired, with a terrible headache.

Since I woke up with nightmares and wasn't able to sleep, my mother took me to see a psychiatrist. His diagnosis was depression so he gave me Diazepam pills. The pills didn't help me feel normal. After a while, looking in the mirror, I noticed my eyes were dull, my skin yellow as if I were a drug addict. I stopped taking those pills.

My days and nights passed in confusion and nightmares. I was astounded at the changes that had taken place in Iran while I was in prison. There was a pall of fear over the entire country. Anyone whose ideas differed from the regime had to flee or risk arrest and possible death. Repression of ideas and censorship were the order of the day. An immense political silence dominated the country as if nothing had happened, as if there had been no mass murders, no torture, no violence, and no oppression. It was as if the country had been under Khomeini's control forever.

The Iran-Iraq war was still going on and the state-run media covered the war by trumpeting Iran's victories. The names of streets and avenues were changed to the names of men killed either in the war or by assassins from opposition groups.

My sister's husband, H.K. who had visited me in prison, welcomed me warmly. I asked about his family, especially his mother, one of the rare, wise and understanding humans I knew. Then he told me the shocking news about his younger brother Mehdi.

"He made up his mind to join the Basij militia to defend our country," he said. "He left school to join the army and was killed in the Iran-Iraq war."

Whatever political disputes we had, I always admired Mehdi. He was the second youngest in their family, a humorous young man and a playwright. He was, after all was said, one the most passionate men I had ever known. Not often had I met anyone with such qualities. I told H. K. how sorry I was and cried for his brother

With my parents, I left my sister and her family and went to my father's house in Borujerd to see the rest of my family and relatives. I was surprised that my sister Ziba, who was nine years younger than I, was happily married, and my mother hadn't told me.

This sister had her long black hair in a braid down her back. She stood tall and fit, looking at me with her large sparkling brown eyes. I hugged her again and again and remembered our trip to Esfahan and harbor cities on the coast of Persian Gulf in the south before I got arrested. My then thirteen-year-old little sister was now a highly attractive young woman.

My cousin Farzaneh, whose picture was shown to me by interrogators in the Unit, came to visit me. She revealed that she had been in prison for four years and was released a year before. Her brother had already escaped to Italy and then immigrated to America. Farzaneh's best friend had betrayed her by informing on her and had caused Farzaneh's imprisonment. That's how the interrogators knew Farzaneh was my cousin.

With all this information no one gave me any answers to my questions about Hussein, my fiancé. No one talked about where he was or how he was doing. As it was not wise to mention his name in prison, I had asked about him only once during visiting time with my parents. Using sign language my mother had told me that Hussein had escaped the country. And recently after I came home my aunt, his mother, didn't talk at all when she came to visit me. She sat and listened to me, just shaking her head in regret.

"My dear auntie, I never mentioned Hussein's name to my interrogators or any authority in prison. Never," I said.

I was so proud that I had kept his name a secret, not giving up any information about him. My aunt sighed deeply and remained silent.

I saw Hussein in my dreams over and over and started to write them down in a notebook. There, he always had very large eyes. They were filled with a sense of tranquility and he was always going somewhere unknown. In one of those dreams, he invited me to go with him.

I wanted to go so badly, but something pulled me back, and I saw he got frustrated with me. I finally agreed to go with him, but on the way, I asked if our families knew where we were going. He said they didn't, and I turned around to go back home. When I got there, the television was on at high volume and no matter how much I tried to turn it off I couldn't.

My mother invited all the relatives and neighbors to our house for a party. As always, she showed great energy now that she had a good reason for celebration. Under the cover of assisting my family, I avoided the crowd and spent much of the time in the kitchen helping with food preparation.

All this didn't help me stop thinking even for a minute.

The shadow of the authorities was everywhere. Yet I had to make a decision about the direction of my life. How would I be able to live with the limitations the authorities put on people? I wanted a better and meaningful life, but how could that be possible without freedom?

My answers got lost in the darkness of my doubts. If I wanted to choose a rewarding life, I needed courage and strong faith and I knew I didn't have enough strength.

I saw how the material world seduced everyone and kept them busy all the time.

The unanswered questions from my teen-age years still were with me, "Why are we here?" "What is the purpose of life? Is this all? To have a home, job, education, get married, and have children, some fun, then die? Is that all?" I couldn't buy that. The complexity of the world told me there must be a purpose beyond all of these things, and I wanted to know it. But where could I find the answer? And how?

In the morning, I opened the windows to feel the cool morning breeze that touched the jasmine in the yard and brought the aroma inside. In the evenings, sitting alone in my room, I looked at the tall, blue mountains full of pleasant memories from the days before the revolution when we marched towards the mountains in a group of twenty with bright faces and happy hearts.

At dusk, the sun kissed the peaks of the mountains and when the dark spread everywhere, the bright stars and the moon broke the black of the night.

From early morning until night, I thought of my friends in prison and talked to them in my notebook. I filled my notebooks by expressing my feelings to Roya, Azadeh, Lily and Sohayla when the moon and stars were revealing their beauty in the dark nights. "Azadeh, you called yourself Liberty. Did you know that you weren't fiction, a made up story, or an illusion from far away dreams and long ago days? Did you know the image of your kind, brilliant eyes has never turned pale in my memory? If you only knew your name is a constant echo in my head. If you only knew every morning when I open my eyes to those dark-blue mountains, a lump closes my throat. Now, where are you, Liberty? Where are you, Liberty?

"When I stand in wonder, looking at the tireless flight of a group of white birds above the roofs, how is it possible to live in peace when you are on the other side of the mountains, locked in? How is it possible?"

I was thirsty for the books that I had been deprived of in prison. I started to look for Dr. Shariati's books about Islam to find some answers for our cruelty, wars, genocides and misery. I wanted to know how life could become so senseless. But strangely this time there was no answer in his books. Above all I wanted to know how under the hard and isolated conditions in prison I could have remained a virtuous person? I assumed something must have been wrong, that I had lost myself.

When I was not reading or learning, I felt I was wasting my time. My mother often looked at me with pity. Everything about me increased her concern.

When one of the old neighbors came to visit me, she scrunched her eyebrows, as soon as she saw me, "No," she dragged the "o". "This is not Mehri. No, I can't believe this is her."

"See, darling," my mother said, turning to me. "You should eat more. You look too skinny, as Mrs. Hatami says."

I thanked Mrs. Hatami for coming to visit me and excused myself to let them chat. I heard my mother telling her how I liked to clean the house and organize things and even how I brushed my teeth for one hour after each meal and even more strangely I rested on the floor while brushing my teeth and my favorite food was fresh tomatoes.

I had many friends, but the first one I wanted to visit was Nasrin. Her father opened the door and almost screamed.

"Oh, My God! Mehri. How old you have become."

Nasrin's mom ran out of the house and before saying hello to me, she scolded her husband. "Be quiet. No, she isn't. What are you talking about?"

She then looked at me in tears. She, Nasrin, and her sister were all crying. They held me one at a time and wouldn't let go.

"Come in dear," the mother finally said. "We've been waiting for this moment for five years. Come in sweetheart."

I had been home a little over three months when one day my mother needed to tell me something important about Hussein. The way she started, looking too serious, I knew it was bad news. I felt as if I was going to pass out and I sat down before she began.

"A few months after you were arrested, Hussein called me one day and asked me to tell his mother to come to our house the next day at 2:00 p.m. so he could talk to her on the phone. It was dangerous for him to call his mother at their home." My mother drew a deep breath and went on, "The next day your aunt came and waited here until night, but Hussein never called. That was it. We never heard from him again."

I was confused and didn't know how to make sense of the news, but my mother went on.

"They wanted to arrest him, or else he was threatened with assassination. In a court a judge sentenced him to death in absentia. If they saw him anywhere, they would shoot him. This was what his friend told your aunt, later."

My Mom was trying to make things easier for me. I felt dizzy and tired, but I didn't want to cry or believe in what I had just heard. Why I was so certain Hussein was living out of the country, safe and secure? There were many possibilities. Hussein might have been arrested with a fake name or hidden somewhere, here or in another country.

"One of his friends came to your aunt's house a month later," my mother continued. "He didn't know the details but he was certain that Hussein had been assassinated in Shiraz."

"No, it's not possible," I cried, releasing the pain in my chest. "It's not possible, Maman. What about my aunt, Maman? Did she believe this?"

My mother shook her head and said nothing.

"Oh, my poor aunt. How could she handle this? This is cruelty. This is so unfair."

"But listen, Mehri," my mother said. "Your aunt doesn't want to talk about this. Do you understand? You shouldn't tell her anything. All these years she has been quiet. No one dares mention Hussein's name in front of her. Your grandma doesn't know either."

"Oh. What a tragedy, Maman."

"Now listen, my daughter. It has happened. We cannot do anything about it."

"I just can't believe it."

I stopped listening to my mother who had hidden this secret from me all these years. I wanted to run away from home. I didn't respond to my mother begging me with her eyes to stay. Blinded with tears I walked out of the house into the street, thinking of the afternoons when I walked there with Hussein. I wanted to see signs of his existence. I walked around the same street over and over.

I stood by a shop window to avoid attention and looked out at the gray reflection of the pedestrians in the glass. The world had sunk into darkness. I wished it were possible to give up my life to bring Hussein back. He was an articulate, well-read young man with so much kindness. He didn't deserve to die. There was nothing I could do except sob. My tears splashed on my black chador then on the black pavers of the sidewalk.

I didn't return until sunset. My mom worried and stood at the door waiting for my return. I entered and went to the room, where for the last time I had seen Hussein's happy smile.

How could I face my aunt now? When she came to visit me, I didn't know the men in power had already spilled her son's blood on the streets, far away from home in a strange place. I didn't know, and I talked to her about her son. I was so proud that I hadn't given his name to the interrogators. My dear aunt sat quietly, pale and patient and didn't cry in my presence.

My dear aunt knew about Hussein's love for me since we were both eighteen, but she didn't know I wanted to be her son's wife. I wondered if this would make her happier now that she knew he was gone. Her dearest child was gone.

The memory of my prison time, my breakdown, the outside world, the loss of my dear Hussein, all seemed like a delirious nightmare. I got up, went to the window and looked at a crow sitting in the yard. It was long before arrival of the fall, but I was shivering from the coldness of these tragedies. I didn't know any other way to cope with all this except to think about some advice I had given to a cellmate while in Evin prison.

Tara had lost her mind and was seriously ill for a while. After a few months she got well and came directly to me expressing her regret for losing her peace of mind.

"I am inspired by you, by the way you have attained your peace," she told me.

I looked at her, surprised at hearing what she just said. When I arrived in Evin, Tara was overwhelmed and out of control. She sometimes walked around, loudly cursing the regime and the authorities.

I was new to that cellblock and soon she picked on me, accusing me of being a spy. The second time she cursed me, I told her, "Leave me alone, Tara, or I will respond to you the way you deserve." After that she let me be, as we were in the same cell. Gradually she regained her sanity and then showed her kind nature.

Tara asked me, "What is keeping you calm? How can I reach peace within me and be happy? I want to know how did you do it, Mehri?"

"You are right, Tara. Something has changed in me since the first time we met. I need to admit that I always wanted to live for nothing but goodness and truth and I still long for recovery."

Tara was listening carefully.

"I don't think there is anyone who hasn't gone through shame and humiliation in different ways," I said, "but all of that can pass and even be cured. But, yes, there is something greater than our mistakes."

"How? How do I do it?"

"This is one of those things one can never reach through words, but the process of my recovery happened through attaining my faith in God and being more truthful to myself. That was how I tried to correct my mistakes."

"Then it will all be peace..." she mumbled.

With the bright sunlight and a cool spring breeze, the sadness in Tara's eyes came to an end, at least in that lovely morning.

I understood how the frustration of prison caused her to lose her mind. It was the same with my friend, Sister-in-law. Tara longed to live the truth. I had sensed this from her compassion and liveliness. The uncertainty and severity of prison, where friends hid their real selves from each other, could damage a sincere person like her.

Those days in prison, I had no other way to move on except to strengthen my faith. Now that I was out of the prison, I had to handle the news of Hussein's death by doing something. I thought about immersing myself in teaching while practicing my religious duties.

I went to the Department of Education in Tehran with my father to get my teaching career back, but I was informed I had been banned for life from teaching and any other public and governmental jobs.

When we were about to leave the building, we saw a young religious man I knew at my former school. I was in my black chador and he was in his new gray suit. He used to wear cheap tailored shirts and pants and look at the ground with a frown while speaking to women. Gazing into my eyes, he offered to help me. I refused his help and asked my father if we could leave.

Before I got arrested, the young man had reported me for taking my fifth grade students on a field trip to see a play written by Samad Behrangi, an author with socialist leanings whose work was banned by the Shah. Even though his play was just an innocent children's story, "Oldooz and Crows," it encouraged independent thought and concern for others.

Despite my having secured the permission of the children's parents for them to attend the play, school officials aligned with the government's policy were not pleased that I had done this. A few days later, I learned I was demoted from my teaching post to that of an office secretary and transferred to another school. The same young Muslim man caused me to lose my teaching position because I disagreed with the government's censorship policy. This had happened a month before I was arrested on the street.

Through it all, the Iran-Iraq war continued. Early in 1987, Iran attempted to capture the city of Basra in Iraq. Iraq countered by attacking Iran's cities, bombing civilian neighborhoods.

One morning, a whistling sound followed by a fiery explosion made the war real for people in my city. Screams came from every direction. The streets were still filled with smoke when my parents, my sister, and I rushed out of our house to escape in a taxi. Many other people without a car managed to hire taxis to leave the city and camp outside or rent rooms in nearby villages.

My younger brother, Shareef, who had a house outside of the city welcomed the entire family. Twenty of us stayed in my brother's house for a few weeks during the Iraq missile attacks. Even though the city seemed evacuated and was almost empty, fragments of the missile had killed some people who were close to the explosion.

Among them were two young women who were our distant relatives and had stayed in the city.

The bad news spread quickly. Some houses were destroyed and some were partially damaged. My brother who had gone to the city to check out our houses told us that pieces of broken glass were scattered everywhere in my parents' house.

Every evening we built a fire outside my brother's house and discussed the war with neighbors. The older ones carried the pain of insecurity, the loss of their houses, the fear of losing their families and their own lives. Free from school, teen-agers and children treated their time like a holiday and enjoyed themselves.

One night when young members of families gathered around the fire, a girl in her late twenties who knew Hussein and me during the revolution time, stood there beside the fire. She looked at me with strange expressions in her eyes, which I couldn't comprehend. She at last opened up and criticized me for not getting executed and being released from prison.

"You yourself came out of prison and made poor Hussein get killed. He was killed because of you."

Hussein's sister looked at me and was disturbed by the girl's tones and words. She repressed a sob. I felt pain in my heart and wanted to cry, but my cousin and I both controlled our emotions and remained quiet. I felt grateful that I had never given any information to the interrogators about Hussein.

My aunt's family didn't like anybody mentioning Hussein's death. They wanted to believe that Hussein was still alive and one day would come back. His mother suffered day after day, not accepting the reality of our loss, the dearest in the world, Hussein.

My older brother heard the news of the missile attack on Borujerd and came in his car to take those who wanted to stay in his large house in one of Tehran's suburbs. At the time of leaving, I cried at being separated from my family and relatives, especially my aunt, Hussein's mother. My second brother, his family, and I left our hometown for Tehran.

In Tehran, I became more independent by tutoring for private companies while I lived with my older brother and his family. During this time, I ran into Marjan who was a secretary in a vocational training center. After I'd been transferred to Evin, I never saw her in prison again. Three years had passed since then.

She told me that most of my friends were released from prison about the same time as I was. Through Marjan, I found Roya and Lily. We always met in fear of arrest, since we had to show up and sign in each month at the local jail. We decided to keep our reunion and friendship a secret and not to mention each other's names to the interrogators, who questioned us every month as part of our probation.

After a few months, I didn't wear a chador and dressed in a simple manto and scarf. But after the Revolutionary Guards followed me with their car, I changed my clothing again to blend with more sophisticated women in a new, stylish hijab and gradually showed some of my hair and applied a little make-up like most women.

Marjan who had an apartment in a wealthy part of Tehran asked me to live with her. After six months, Roya also came to live with us. Once in a while, we briefly talked about the past.

Roya often shook with laughter when she talked about such people as the Mullah from the village who couldn't pronounce some words correctly in Farsi. This Mullah was our religious teacher in Public 4. For a long time afterward when speaking about prison, we would go off into hearty laughter, remembering the ridiculous side of that harsh reality. Yet whenever we remembered how days passed in the Unit, sadness was all we were left with.

Roya had a realistic stance on the torture. "The main reason why torturing your friend was so hard on you was the fact that you knew that you might be next. At the end of the day, accepting the torture of a friend became easy, as it was not your own," she said. None of us wanted to remember how we were manipulated.

Fifty miles away from Tehran, in my brother's house, we had gathered for Friday lunch with my older sister Shirin and her three daughters. Kids were at play outside while the television showed the victory of Iranian forces at the Iran-Iraq border.

Shirin sat on the floor, watching the news quietly. Talking about the war was still taboo among the followers of the regime, one of whom was my sister. Yet, I couldn't resist saying something against the war.

"These poor soldiers shouldn't be sent to fight and kill the Iraqi people, or better I should say the war shouldn't ever have started," I said to my sister.

"Basijies and soldiers don't feel that way. They are following the Imam's command and that's why they go to war," Shirin said.

"You talk about the war, but do you ever think about it? What is it about the war that you are defending? Don't you see the signs of destruction everywhere? People had to emigrate from border cities after they lost everything. Perhaps as many as a million people have died, many more are wounded, and millions of refugees in Iran and Iraq are suffering."

"Do you think I enjoy it? No, but Imam Khomeini says we must fight. He says we must win it. There is no other way."

"Shirin, why do you blindly defend something you don't know enough about? Are you defending a man who doesn't care about people's lives? Crippled men, widow women and orphan children?

Can you sit down and think of these and be proud of this war?"

Shirin stood up, "I'm going to watch out for the kids," she said and walked out of the room.

Through the window I saw her walking towards the end of the yard in the safe suburban town, our wartime shelter outside of Tehran.

The war news was still on the TV screen. There was hard fighting there. With background marching music in high volume, young soldiers were running over dead bodies under gunshots screaming, "God is great."

I wanted to put my hands over my ears and scream as loud as them. Unexpectedly my brother's wife came in.

"Shirin is crying, Mehri."

"Is that right?"

"She says she couldn't defend her beliefs the way you can."

"Oh, dear God."

I never wanted to hurt my sister's feelings or humiliate her. Ever since the last time we fought as children, I had never raised my voice to my sister. I hadn't said that about the war to make her cry. I wanted her to think.

That day I decided never to discuss politics with her unless I did it in a kind manner, and then only if she initiated the discussion.

In a month, on August 20, 1988, the eight year war between Iran and Iraq ended. Many, including my sister, regretted the futility of this long war.

Censorship precluded my knowing about the most horrifying mass killing in the political prisons of Iran in that same summer of 1988. According to Amnesty International 2,500 political detainees were executed in the matter of two months. Some believed the real total was much higher.

Details of the mass killing emerged only some time after the event. Walking with Roya on a major street of Tehran, we ran into one of the former prisoners of Evin. She and Roya chatted. Roya learned of the execution of her dear friend in Evin.

Mujahedin had stablished an Iraq-based garrison, in Iraq close to Iran's borders. The mass executions happened after the armed incursion into western Iran by the People's Mujahedin of Iran. The

Mujahedin attacked the borders in the west of Iran a few days after Iran's acceptance of UN Security Council Resolution 598 calling for a ceasefire between Iran and Iraq.

After the Mujahedin force was repulsed by the Iranian army, the regime took revenge by executing prisoners who still were sympathetic to the Mujahedin. Even though, those executed had already been in prison for some years and had no knowledge of the attack.

Before the executions took place, prisoners were interrogated for a few minutes by a commission made up of clerics. The prisoners were questioned regarding their past activities, beliefs, their attitudes regarding the Islamic Republic of Iran and whether or not they performed the daily prayers.

While many prisoners were under the impression at the time that the questions were asked with a view to granting amnesty, the commission ultimately became known as the "Death Commission."

Khomeini made a fatwa, a religious edict, to execute any prisoner who failed to fulfill their religious obligations. Most of the executed were supporters of the Mujahedin, but hundreds were members or sympathizers of other political opposition groups, mostly communists.

The authorities stopped all family visits without warning or giving any reason. They also stopped providing newspapers to prisoners and removed television sets from prisons. For weeks no one knew what was happening, and it was only later that their families were informed about their children's executions. Khomeini died a year after, in June of 1989.

Roya encouraged me to take art classes and use my art to make a living. While I took many private art classes with professional artists, I earned a high salary working as a designer in an export company.

After a while Marjan, who had some money, paid for an illegal passport and escaped to Turkey. For security reasons, she didn't notify anybody, including Roya and me. We had to leave her apartment that same day. I found a small suite and Roya rented an apartment.

Roya built up her own circle of friends, socialized with musicians, took singing lessons, and became a member of a literary club devoted to Hafez's poetry. I worked, took art and English classes and experienced life like any other common woman. During this time I ran into Sister-in-law. She was on medicine and had regular relapses.

I spent four years waiting to register for the university entrance examination, a bureaucratic nightmare since my high school diploma had been lost in my apartment in Tehran after I was arrested.

Among many thousands of applicants taking the Concour, a comprehensive exam, I received the 75th highest score in the first exam round. I then took a required second round of testing for art majors.

When my name did not appear among the accepted applicants published in the newspaper, I suspected the government had interceded with their "ideological filter," denying me entrance. Following up, I found that this indeed had been the case. I then wrote a two-page letter to the Ministry of Education and Training in which I argued that if they denied a person with a political record, such as myself, the right to enter a university, they would be giving me little choice but to leave Iran.

The school year had already started when I received a congratulatory acceptance letter in the mail, but I had to wait until the following year to become a student at the Art University in Tehran.

I lived fully submersed in my studies and became an honor student at the Art University. But all this didn't satisfy my thirst to live the life I wanted.

Men approached me inside taxis, at work and walking on streets. It was four years after my release, when I was in my early thirties that I started to date with the constant fear of being arrested. After a Revolutionary Guards stopped me twice, I realized how dangerous it was for men and women to socialize. Once on the street a guard separated me to find out how I was related to the man I was walking with in the street. I had just met his family, but he had to tell the guard I was his fiancé. The guard found out that he was a young doctor and said he would let us go for a bribe. It took us an hour to talk our way out of the mess.

Later, I made an escape when the guards stopped my car in the Mohseni Square to arrest me for applying some lipstick. An opportunity to escape arose when they were distracted, and I stepped on the gas. I made it through a traffic light and was lost among the heavy traffic. It was dark and I couldn't see the cars behind me. I imagined them catching up with me to shoot at my car. After driving in fear for half an hour, I arrived, my knees trembling, at the house of Sister-in-law, who had invited her family and me for dinner.

I had thought that if the guards would arrest me on the street, no one in my family would know what had happened to me. On the other hand, Sister-in-law was waiting for me and she would be distraught if I didn't appear. On top of it all, I feared the consequences after my arrest when the guards would learn about my prison record. I would rather die than be arrested again.

The Islamic regime tried to uphold their own commandments written by Mullahs, called Sharia laws. Iran's society now reflected their religious teachings. People lived a lie daily in the street, at work and even in their own home by concealing their emotions and thoughts behind a mask. As a result, using drugs and alcohol and engaging in immoralities of all kinds was wide spread underground.

Artists and intellectuals taught art, literature, dance and music in underground classes and gatherings at their homes. If the guards showed up at parties to arrest the hosts and the guests, people tried to pay them off, but in some cases they ended up in jail for a few days.

The regime's attempts to separate men and women caused a negative reaction to these limitations. Immoral relationships became the norm everywhere. This flood of moral chaos enveloped me, as it did many others, in dead-end relationships until I turned my back to all of it and left the country at the age of thirty-five.

PART 16

Leaving Iran

(1994)

Ali used to live in the neighborhood where I grew up. He had twice proposed to me through my mother. After he had lived in America for eighteen years he came back for a short family visit and learned about my release. He called my mother asking to meet me to propose again. I wasn't interested in getting marring to someone I didn't know.

After I met him in Tehran and sensed how he and I looked at life differently, I was sure he would not be the right choice for me. Besides my first impression, it wasn't possible to get to know him in such a short time as the month he was going to stay in Iran. Yet when faced with his constant perseverance, I put aside my intuition and agreed to visit him a few more times, for his family's persistence was wearing me down.

When we arrived in Borujerd his family treated me as his fiancé and suddenly I was pushed to the extent that I found it impossible to refuse his proposal and I decided to go along with their wishes. That was how I became engaged to a man I didn't really know. This news surprised my close friends but my decision stemmed from a deep desire to get away from Iran.

Ali and I went back to Tehran to get my passport. The immigration office informed me I couldn't leave unless the prison authorities at Evin that dealt with political prisoners allowed them to issue me a passport. Ali's mother insisted we should get legally married before going to Evin.

The building for obtaining the permission was in a district far from the actual prison. Two women in black chadors searched me in a room behind a curtain before we entered into the building. Inside they gave Ali a small jacket to cover his arms since he wore a short sleeve shirt. It was hot inside the building and the old jacket stuck to his tall figure.

Ali didn't look well after a man registered our names and left his greeting unanswered. His face paled, his eyes darting around the room looking at the bearded staff's bitter faces.

We both sat on two chairs waiting as the man had ordered. Coming back from my thoughts about what might happen, I saw a man standing in front of me. I looked up to see Abraham in a long sleeve white shirt buttoned up to his neck, a few pounds heavier since I'd seen him in Evin eight years ago.

"What are you doing in here, Mehri?" he asked me, looking at Ali.

While I stuttered looking for words, Ali answered.

"We are married; we are here to get my wife a passport."

"Follow me," Abraham said firmly and walked towards the end of the hallway and entered into a room.

"Wait here until I call you." He went in and closed the door.

"He was my interrogator in prison, very religious," I said hurriedly before the door opened and Abraham called on Ali who was now shaking.

I waited outside gathering my thoughts about what to say if he would ask me about my friends. In those moments, I wished I wouldn't have visited my prison mates. Now I had to lie and deny seeing them.

When the door opened Ali hurried out.

"Come in, Mehri." Abraham said.

I went in and sat on a chair. Abraham politely asked me about my plans. I got the courage to ask for my passport, "My husband lives in America, and I need a legal passport to go and live with him."

After giving me some advice Abraham sent me out. He had requested Ali to take the best care of me and play the roles of a father and a mother in addition of being a good husband for me. Abraham left his room to return with a letter that allowed me to receive my passport.

In the month Ali and I spent time together in Tehran, I gradually felt more affection for him. When we returned to Borujerd, the beloved city looked poor and undeveloped after the war. I wanted to visit my relatives. My uncle and my aunt still lived in the same houses in my childhood neighborhood, where the streets seemed smaller and shorter.

As I entered my old street, Mrs. Khandani, my elementary school principal covered in a black chador, walked out of her large house and closed the gate behind her. I said hello to her, and she greeted me warmly. Her tall figure in a fashionable blue suit from twenty-five years earlier appeared clearly in my mind. She must be retired now. I wondered if the "*Three Bears*," my membership gift to Mrs. Khandani's school library, was still on the shelf in her old office.

I looked back and saw Mrs. Khandani's shrunken figure get into a taxi. The black chador didn't fit her strong character, yet she had no choice except to wear it.

I reached for the doorbell of my aunt's house. One of my cousins opened the door and I walked through the hallway to the yard. This was the same yard Hussein and I, along with our cousins, had played together when our families gathered some Fridays to have a big pot of home-made Reshteh Soup or plenty of Kabob.

I saw my aunt walk out of the kitchen at the other side of the yard. I ran towards her crying.

"My dear aunt," I said.

She had received an invitation and she knew I was going to get married. She stood frozen in silence. Filled with my own deep sadness for losing Hussein I cried in front of his mother.

"My dear aunt, please forgive, me. Please, forgive me, please." I cried harder and didn't let her go as I hid my face in her embrace.

I felt guilty for getting married. I was sure it was more painful for my aunt to see me in a white dress beside another man and not her son, Hussein. Yet she came to my wedding ceremony. Sitting in my puffy wedding dress, I was grieving in my heart. The local musicians played happy songs and our families danced, while I couldn't turn my eyes away from my aunt's sad face.

Three months later, I was in America in the house of my husband. The next morning after my arrival, Ali woke up to go to work. He dressed and stood at the bedroom door. He wanted to say something but had no clear idea what it was. His frightened eyes, dark irises in circles of white, jerked around.

"Don't open the blinds or curtains and don't answer the doorbell. Don't even walk out of the door to put the trashcan outside. There might be a big black guy with a gun outside the door waiting. As soon as you get out, he will grab you." He then went on and described all the possible criminal scenes that could take place in America.

He paused after a few minutes, lowered his voice and put his head down then talked to himself, "I am getting scared myself."

He turned toward me, bitter-faced but he didn't see me crying. His cold eyes looked beyond me as if he was blinded with his own fear.

My English from high school and a year of studying in a private institute in Iran didn't make much difference. I couldn't understand what friendly Texans were saying. My priorities were to practice English, learn computers and the names of the streets. Only driving was easier than driving in Tehran's streets overloaded with cars.

America was different from Iran in the relaxed faces of the people and their easy smiles. The food stores were huge and overwhelming, with too many choices. People didn't stay in long lines to receive limited sugar, milk and detergent or to put gas in cars using coupons. Essential medicines were not hard to find. Everything was so available and most people didn't live under daily economic pressures.

For Ali my driving distance across the city was too far, learning English was not necessary, and taking college classes was not meant for a married woman. He demanded I quit thinking about art and that I must stop my education, "You are my wife, and I will tell you what to do. Will you stop thinking as a student and listen?" he said this twice, yelling each time.

In Turkey, where I had to get a visa from the American embassy he yelled at me for getting cold and he didn't allow me to buy a pair of walking shoes with my own money when my boots hurt my heels. He instead asked to keep the money for me since I would lose it. Ironically, I did lose it in his pocket, for he never gave it back to me.

At the climax of the political unrest in Iran, in 1981 the leaders and members of the Mujahedin organization, if not executed in prisons or killed in the streets, had to flee to France and then became refugees in Iraq. Members in the United States solicited money for the cause. They demanded people donate money in support of the Mujahedin military settlements, its residents, and their war expenses in Iraq. Ali and his friends had to pay some of their monthly salary. Ali questioned their manner of collecting money yet he and his friends felt obligated to hold their tongues in their presence, for the "Mujahedin were sacrificers of their lives and were the serious opposition forces against the Islamic regime," they were told.

There was a woman who looked down on anyone who was not a member of the Mujahedin organization. In her mind everyone, especially the former political prisoners, should shoot at the members of the regime until the last one of them fell on the ground, slaughtered.

She said, "You were useless. If not, you would have been executed. Instead they set you, and those like you, free. Why?"

She made me feel guilty about living, and her snapping eyes and sharp tongue didn't leave me any ease. She pressured me so much that I decided to join the fighters in Iraq and put myself in the front lines.

By all means, it didn't pain me to do so, for at least I could do something with my life, rather than waste it in a failed marriage. I told Ali, "I'll go only if you, yourself, will take my suitcase to the airport."

He hated to see me leave him, a fine prosperous husband who had brought me out of Iran. Yet, he too, couldn't bear the tension of my emotions, for I cried days and nights as I regained my focus on the people's rights against the cruel Islamic regime and its men. And when the time came for him to make a decision, both he and I cried and said good-bye at the airport.

Ali released me but later regretted his decision. He called the center of the Mujahedin in Washington, D.C. many times a day and asked me to come back home. Almost every time he called to speak to me, the woman who took me there, herself a former political prisoner, rejected him.

"He makes me sick!" she told me. "If he thinks he would die without you, then let him die! My husband and I divorced each other, for it was the command of our leader. We have sacrificed everything we had; our children, our home, our family and any kind of attachment that kept us from fighting."

"I know, but I cannot do this to him."

One-day Ali's friend called and informed me that he seriously feared for Ali's life. He was certain Ali's pale face and blue lips were signs of a coming heart attack. I felt obliged not to cause the man I had married a serious problem; I didn't want to do that to anyone.

Both sides of the equation, my husband and the Mujahedin, pulled at me with no recognition of my individuality, mind, and feelings. The Mujahedin didn't care about anyone. It was clear that what they had done during all these eighteen years was attacking, killing, ruining and destroying. Putting themselves above others, they hoped to be admired and attract more members to get power over Iran. Their way to political power was based on force and propaganda. I came back home feeling empty inside, to find Ali impatiently waiting for me at the Houston International airport.

For two years my attempt to have a peaceful and meaningful married life failed. I didn't belong to his world and he didn't to mine. American law allowed me to get a divorce, even if it took me a year because he resisted.

It didn't shame me to break the news to my mother whose first suggestion for a wrong husband was always: "Get a divorce." I left three years of my mid-thirties life behind in Texas and moved to start an independent life in the sunshine of the golden state of California, where my cousin and his wife kindly hosted me for a few months.

I struggled in California, enduring years of exhausting academic studies. I lived on student loans and exhibited my art inspired by my prison experience but didn't openly discuss my time in Khomeini's jails.

Finally in the winter of 2001, after seven years living in America, I bought a ticket and packed my two suitcases with souvenirs to go back to Iran to visit my family, whom I missed greatly. Two weeks before my departure, a serious student movement shook the country for the first time after years of silence. The regime's Revolutionary Guards attacked the protestors in their dormitories and arrested hundreds of young university students in Tehran. Four of them were sentenced to death.

Iranians around the world reacted to the regime's violence against protesting students. There was an immense rally in Los Angeles in front of the Federal building to protest the execution of the four university students. I participated.

Westwood and Wilshire Boulevards were loaded with chanting people marching from the Federal building to the streets around UCLA. The sun was setting behind the tall buildings when people lit candles and walked back in silence—a dramatic scene, shadows of people in the light of candles.

A group of human rights activists collected signatures against the Iranian regime. I signed the petition and stood next to their tent observing the event. At the moment of dusk, I felt the weight of the presence of someone who was staring at me. When the staring took longer than normal, I became curious. As I turned to my left, my face went numb and I froze in my place. It was the infamous interrogator, Ashtari from the Unit, standing twenty feet away.

I didn't trust my eyes. It was impossible. I denied what I saw and turned my face, wanting to believe I had seen nothing.

"Was it really him?"

He was a short man with a thick beard, and straight full hair over his forehead. He wore a black shirt and black pants, just like Ashtari without his coat. That's all. But why did he stare at me for so long with his dark sharp eyes?

"It must be him," I thought. "He was staring at me because he never saw me without a chador."

I turned to check on him again. He was still looking at me. Our eyes met for a second and I saw him walk away from me and into the crowd. "It was him."

He disappeared the same way he walked with stealth in the Unit, where no one could ever tell how he appeared in the room. He was just there when he suddenly caught us.

I looked around but he was gone.

The crowd collecting in the middle of Wilshire Boulevard chanted and shouted against the murderous regime. They didn't know one of the murderers was right there just a moment ago and walked away that easily, and I didn't tell them.

I was going to leave for Iran in a few days. I thought about the possibility of getting arrested in Iran and going back to Evin. I tried to call friends and family in Iran and the Iranian embassy in Washington, D.C., to find out if my name was on a black list, among those who were prohibited from leaving Iran. No one could guarantee I would get out if I would go back.

Two days before my trip I called my mother and told her I couldn't go to visit them in Iran. My mother cried out and grieved, "My dear, everybody is celebrating. Please don't disappoint us. All your brothers and sisters and their families are going to come to the airport."

"I'm so sorry Maman, not now. I can't come now. I do apologize for ruining your plans, but Maman joon, I'm afraid I cannot make it now. I have to wait a little while."

I made the excuse that my ex-husband could stop me at the airport and I could be detained in Iran without my passport for numbers of months or years.

This was a true possibility. My friend, who was a lawyer in Iran, told me my ex-husband could claim he was still my husband and according to the regime's laws husbands could prohibit their wives' trips. My legal divorce in America didn't mean anything to Iran's judiciary system. I had to get another divorce in Iran.

Four months later I told the head of the human right activists for Iran about seeing Ashtari in LA.

"Oh you should have told me, Ms. Dadgar. We are looking for them. We are collecting evidence to prove to the FBI that these criminals are coming into the U.S. freely. We could have gotten him arrested."

"I'm sorry." I said. "My mind didn't work then."

I couldn't explain to him that I owned the Unit's secrets and Ashtari was one of them. Ashtari was my own misery and terror, braided into my past and present. But how could I keep carrying this burden unless I was still living in the darkness of fear? And that fear was the means of Satan's ruling me?

Lonely and broke I felt there was no way out of my difficulties, but I continued my study towards a master's degree in art. Even if I had forsaken all my religious practices for years, I asked God to help me go on. I pledged I would fast for forty days. In return I wanted all my misery to go away.

During this time I found a new place to live through an organization in Hollywood who matched landlords with students who needed rooms. Landlords met with students in a conference room to choose their tenants. The room was mostly filled with young Caucasian women in jeans and T-shirts, marked with wrinkles and folds. The smiling, chatty girls were picked quickly. I was left out, dressed in an elegant suit, too distant to please a stranger.

The organization called later to connect me with an old, rich Jewish man in Hollywood. Soon, I was in Hollywood to meet the man.

The heavy, carefully designed wooden door opened with a squeak. A thin old man, little more than five feet tall and a black dog behind him appeared inside the dark hallway. As if it were in the house of Miss Havisham in Charles Dickens' *Great Expectations*, there was something unknown here to be discovered later.

I followed the old man who said, "Come in. Let's sit somewhere." He passed through a large formal dining room with his short steps to reach old, casual chairs in a smaller, dark dining room lighted by a small window. He opened his newspaper and started to read and completely ignored me. I sat there waiting for him to finish reading his newspaper. His reading took a long time so I made myself ask, "Did you go to that organization's meeting too? I didn't see you there."

"No," the man said and kept reading.

"How do they know you, may I ask?"

"This is not the first time they sent me someone to live here. You are the third girl."

"I am an art student in the master's program, busy with study, no guests coming over. Do you think you want me to move in?"

"There is another girl I am going to meet tomorrow."

"Oh."

The man continued his reading, showing no interest in talking to me.

At last he put the newspaper aside, rubbed the dog's head and pushed his chair back to stand up.

He was small but fit. In his green eyes there was no sign of kindness, but indifference or rather bitterness. The man had short, white hair, but not many wrinkles on his face for a 98 year-old-man.

"Let me show you your room," the man said.

He walked towards the wide stairs to the second floor of his huge house. I followed the man and his dog through a long hallway until they stood in front of a door. The man opened the door and entered into a small, nicely furnished room with a shower and bathroom connected to its right corner.

It was a perfect place for me to continue my studies without being worried about my rent. The man was so wealthy he would ask for no rent. He once told me that providing room and board was his contribution to education and art, besides his donations to fine arts museums.

The man gave me a tour around his impressive library, the living room and showed me his art pieces on the walls. An original bust by Rodin caught my eye before we walked towards the pool in the yard.

"I will call you." The man said with a cold voice and shut the door.

I left with the feeling of butterflies in my hungry stomach. I broke my fast at Brentwood where I had rented a room in a two-bedroom apartment belonging to a middle-aged woman. I no longer could afford to pay rent. I couldn't find another job after I had quit my designing job in a sign company, and my financial situation grew worse and worse.

"Would he choose me over the other girl?" I wondered.

I prayed, "Please God, make it happen." I was desperate.

The man called the next day and asked me to move in.

I left my few pieces of furniture behind and moved with boxes of my personal items, books, paintings, family pictures and two large suitcases of my clothes.

In the large house, I thought I smelled a dead mouse when I walked in. The man's housekeeper, a sweet, young Spanish woman came in that day and worked hard to put a shine on every floor and every object. The bad odor was gone for two days.

For the first week, I spent most of the time in my room unpacking or at the university studying. The old man made our dinner of broiled fresh salmon or lamb chops served with a big mixed salad of kale, beets, beans, nuts and balsamic vinegar.

After dinner I wanted to wash the dishes, but he wouldn't let me. He left the dishes and the remaining vegetables on the kitchen counter for the housekeeper who cleaned the house once a week. This brought back the smell of a dead mouse in the house.

The second week when he noticed I wasn't eating during the day I had to explain I was fasting.

"Not eating and drinking during the day, but eating at evening! This is ridiculous. I never will believe in such a thing. It is unhealthy," he said.

After that he criticized me constantly, for eating before dawn, for not eating during the day, for washing the dishes, for not washing the dishes, for helping him, for not helping him.

The old man's wife and his two daughters had left him many years ago. They suffered and became alcoholics, never wanting to see him again.

For a while, I avoided coming home until dark, so the man's cold eyes could not stare at me for some wrong he said I had done. I couldn't bear the insults, either in his eyes or words.

Once when I came home from a tiring night after studying at a local bookstore, suddenly the light in the hallway went on, "Why do you come home late and sneak in the dark?" he yelled. I had expected him to be in his bed after nine.

I had twelve more days to fulfill the forty days of my pledge with God, but I stopped fasting to remove his reasons for criticizing my eating schedule and reduce the pressure.

At the start of World War II in 1939, before the camps became places where Jews were either killed or made slave laborers, the old man had escaped from Europe to America at the age of thirty-five. He started a business that turned into a large food distributing company. He married an American woman who gave him two blue-eyed, blond daughters. If I hadn't met him, or didn't live in his house or didn't know about his family, I would have believed a man who had escaped from the Nazis and lived this long would find his way to kindness.

But who is to be blamed for a heart that grew harder over the years? In his house I answered my questions by writing poems.

who may ever believe a swallow would fly to the horizon
if the sky wasn't boundless
or Lilacs could bloom
if the morning breeze wouldn't blow smoothly
who may ever believe a stream could chant
if the earth was not a cradle

When I talked with a friend on the phone, she detected that I was falling on my knees from desperation and urged, "Oh, Mehri please, move out. Don't stay there even one more day."

The day I moved out, with the kind help and invitation of my cousin's wife, the old man stood at the door with his cameraman friend, whom I didn't like. The cameraman had come over for dinner once with his well-mannered wife and had stared at me the entire time. He worked in the movie industry in Hollywood. "I look at you from the camera angle," he said lustfully when his wife was not around.

I heard the old man saying in regret, "If I was young I would propose to you."

The cameraman released a short laugh with a malicious smile. I would have expected to hear anything else but this, for I thought the old man hated me. I looked at the black dog. No doubt, I was going to miss him.

Two years later, I invited the old man to my art exhibition, as he had requested to come to my thesis show. He apologized for his unkind behavior.

"I am not sure, but I may have hurt your feelings because you were a Muslim and I hate what Muslims are doing. Read the newspaper; see what's going on in the Middle East. Violence and killing is everywhere," he said minding his words.

His pale green eyes shone with a ray of kindness and I pictured him as a sweet young boy under his bitter mask.

What could I say to the old man? I had no experience with religious hatred back in old Iran. My mother always shopped at the Jewish merchants in Borujerd's Bazaar and my father never spoke ill of any race, ethnic group or religion. He was good with people regardless of their belief.

At the beginning of the spring of 2003, I rented a two-bedroom house from a kind American couple and taught art privately, besides teaching the Farsi language in a language institute in Beverly Hills.

During the search for the house, I had met a tall man, who took tango lessons for fun. He was a film lover who lived with the dream of becoming a movie director for which he had studied at Stanford and the University of Southern California.

He invited me to take tango lessons with him. I had cheerfully danced and laughed with him in a wide, shiny-floored studio where the tango teacher called him, "The tallest man in the world." Half American and half Swiss, he had a delicate face, a good heart and lived with his brother. Their way of life drew a picture of two lost birds from a flying formation of birds in my mind. Except they belonged to the American generations with great dreams. From the time their parents died in their mid lives, the brothers lived in a three-bedroom house in the wealthy part of the city.

The second time we met, he talked about a woman. "I loved her for five years, but she didn't love me."

After a few times of going to dance class together, I didn't want to continue to see him since he talked nonstop. But my friends criticized me for not appreciating a man who can talk with women.

He was caring, sweet and intellectual when it came to art and film. He gradually won me over with his kindness and I fell in love with him. After a few months when I thought we were going to get married, I asked him about the woman he had once told me about. I was sure nothing was there and his love for me was pure. But I wanted to hear him say out loud, "Of course there is no one but you. Are you crazy?"

"James?" I said.

"Yes, dear."

"Remember that night after our second dance class, you talked about a woman you knew in the past?"

"Yes, I remember."

"What happened to that woman?"

"We still talk daily."

"Daily?"

"Yes, she calls. Sometimes she calls eight times a day."

"Oh, but I never saw you talking to her." And I suddenly remembered he always turned his cell phone off when he was with me.

"You didn't want me to know? Why?"

"Well, I only didn't want her to take away from our time together."

"But you called to your other friends. Do you see her at all?"

"Yes, I take her to good restaurants since she doesn't have money to go by herself and most of the time we eat lunch together."

"And you never told me anything." I murmured.

I cooked dinner for him, but we never lunched together. In a few incidents when I called to invite him for lunch he told me, "I have already eaten something," or "I'm sorry I can't. I'm busy."

"Why didn't you tell me?"

"I promised her."

"Promised what?"

"That no other woman would keep us apart."

"No other woman?"

My heart shriveled. I could not believe what I had just heard. How could he possibly say that? How could he hide this from me all along when we saw each other every day? What a fool I was.

I walked out of the room.

I loved him. Oh, I loved him so much that I couldn't be angry or harsh with him. I was convincing myself, "That it is what it is, but what should I do now? I must talk to him. Maybe he doesn't know how hurtful it is. I should tell him it will hurt our relationship if he continues to see that woman. I know he loves me. He said it many times. If he finds out how I feel he will want to do something about it. I am sure he does. I will talk to him. What I want is natural and he will understand." I came back into the room.

It was eleven at night, the thick curtains were down, and the room was softly lit. He was lying on the couch. We talked all night. I tried to convince him. I gave examples, described my feelings and asked why he needed to see another woman if he were in love with me. And he kept saying, "She needs me. Do you think I simply can tell her to take a hike? It's impossible. She was in my life before I met you. You must understand the situation."

"But you should have told me. It was my right to know."

"I was afraid you would get upset."

Many hours passed until I dared to ask the last and most important question. I drew a deep breath, and asked slowly, "Do you still love her?"

Struggling, he searched for the right words, but he seemed tired of the discussion and preferred to say it all at once, as if he had his last, strong weapon to shoot me down and win the war.

"Yes, I think I do love her." He emphasized each word.

"Oh, my dear, how could a man love two women at the same time?" My voice came out weak.

"It is possible, like the life of Doctor Zhivago," he replied. "Remember, Zhivago loved two women. One was his wife and the other was his love, Lara."

"Oh, James, are you saying you are seriously in love with her?"

"Yes, but my love for her differs from the love I have for you. You are my wife and she is Lara."

I was about to cry.

"No, no," he said, "I think you are Lara. You are my love and she is like my wife. She will stay in my life forever, but you are the one who gave me incredible happiness and you are different from any other woman I've known."

The room seemed to be out of air for me to breathe. There was a pain in my chest and my mouth was dry. I didn't want to get angry. I just sat at the edge of a chair and cried. It was seven in the morning. The sounds of cars and traffic had already started. The light came in through the sides of the curtains from the large glass windows and the birds sang in the early summer morning. I felt the pain of Lara and Zhivago's wife both at once. The sounds and light of the morning no longer gave me joy or warmth.

I had pleaded to make him see where he was taking us, and he put me off. He had the last word before leaving. "She will be in my life forever. I promised her."

A few weeks later my mother called and insisted on visiting me in Dubai.

"Haven't you always asked us to come to Dubai to see you? Now we are ready, my dear. Let's visit each other in Dubai soon."

She was right. I had asked them to visit me in another country, but she always refused, "No, no darling. We are too many. But if you come to Iran all the family can see you."

Not wanting to make my parents worried, I hadn't told them that I would never feel safe to go back to Iran as long as the Islamic Republic regime was in power.

The airport in Dubai was not too crowded in November. I followed the signs for my luggage while my heart pounded with the pleasure of thinking of my reunion with my mother, my younger sister, and my dear father after nine years. When I passed the crowd of passengers into an empty space in Dubai's contemporary airport, from a distance I saw my sister waiting for me with her nine-month-old daughter resting in her embrace.

The happy moment had come. I left the cart with my suitcases aside and ran to hold my sister and her daughter tightly in my arms. She and I had grown older, but it didn't feel that we had been separated that long.

"Don't cry, my darling, not now in front of your child."

"Oh my dear you don't know how much I have missed you." My sister couldn't stop crying. I held her arm in my hands, "Let's go, my darling. Let's go. Where is Maman? Where is my father?"

"Maman couldn't make it to the airport, but father is outside with Mr. Abdullah, waiting by his car."

I couldn't wait to embrace my father and kiss his hands a thousand times. Oh, I was dying to see him. My love for him was as pure as his kind heart. He was my star of honesty, goodness and loyalty. He was my dear father. I felt so lucky and so proud to be his daughter.

Abdullah, my father's relative, had kindly provided a detached suite for us. We stayed there for ten days. He, his wife and two servants welcomed us warmly. The trip to Dubai was perfectly timed to help me forget about my bitter time with James.

I noticed my mother looked much older and thinner, but she hadn't changed in her manner. For three days, we laughed, took pictures and I shot film. My father, my sister and I took a tour around Dubai in the Persian Gulf on a boat, visited the Bazaar and purchased souvenirs. My mother couldn't go out with us since she had pain in her legs.

I was holding my niece and making her laugh when I noticed my mother and my sister whispering together.

"No. Don't Maman," My sister muttered, "not now, not today."

"What are you arguing about?" I asked Ziba.

She looked at me with sad eyes and my mother spoke, "We have something to tell you. But we don't know how to say it."

"What is it Maman, say it please."

"Don't you get worried my dear. It is about your brother Ahmad."

Ahmad was my older brother who put his house up as bail for my release from prison. I had stayed with him and his family for several months when Iraqi missiles started falling on Borujerd, my hometown.

"What about him Maman?"

"You know my dear, your brother Ahmad…"

"Ahmad, what Maman?"

"He…he got into an accident five months ago…"

"What Maman? Why didn't you tell me earlier? How is he?"

She waited then suddenly said, "He is dead."

My mother finished the news as quickly as she could.

"My dear. Your brother died five months ago. We wanted to be with you when you heard this horrible news."

"Oh, Maman."

"Yes, my dear."

I cried.

I hadn't seen my brother for nine years.

"Don't tell me that I can't see him anymore. No, Maman, don't tell me this. I want my brother. I want to see Ahmad."

My father, my mother and my sister were crying with me.

"No, no, he couldn't have died. I haven't said goodbye to him."

Feeling a deep grief in my chest, I collapsed on the bed.

"What can I say my dear?" My mother cried out. "I am a mother. I have been mourning for him a few months, but nothing can bring him back. He is gone. My dear son is gone."

My mother was right. I knew very well that death was the end and my brother Ahmad would never come back. My world faded into the dark cloud of my memory of him. My heart filled with sadness and I cried for hours. Grief surrounded me for the rest of our time in Dubai until we said goodbye in tears.

James called me the day of my arrival and I told him the news about my brother. He immediately came over to my house to show me his sympathy and love. Then he left.

My sorrow for my brother merged with the misery of losing James. Every moment passed in deep sadness. After a while I couldn't bear my life. I was desperate, and lost. I felt betrayed. I struggled trying to persuade myself not to see him anymore. I knew our relationship was over, even if James didn't want to accept it and insisted on seeing me.

I cried for days. With James's love, I had thought that misery would never confine me again.

The pain in my heart would subside if I could only think and gain perspective. I knew that I had strayed from my intended direction, from the time I first stood on my feet as a young, happy woman. I was no longer practicing my faith, nor was I contributing to the peace and freedom of society. I was just dragged down by my own misery. All that was left was my academic education.

One day at school while I carried a heavy pile of book and art supplies I cried all the way from a parking lot far from my class, until the campus police came to help and dropped me off at the health center where I met a psychologist. I knew there was something deep down inside my chest that needed to be cured.

In a dark mood over my lost love, I was comforted by the thought that I wasn't the betrayer. I became more hopeful thinking about higher goals. I knew it well: there was no way out of misery and loss, but to embrace life.

I didn't want to belong to the place of misery, and life was worth nothing without happiness. I had experienced living in a place of pure happiness when I was an innocent girl at nineteen, but did I deserve it now?

PART 17

Faith

(2003)

I was longing to leave my misery, but I wasn't aware of a way out. I implored God to guide me in the right path, "But You O, Lord do not be far from me: O, my Strength, hasten to help me." Bible - Psalm 22: 19

A week later, one of my Jewish friends who had married a Muslim man insisted on taking me to a mosque she knew, to comfort me with my own faith. Long dark fabric hung on walls of the large space. A handful of bitter men and covered women sat separated. A teacher preached and interpreted the Quran for them, as they listened quietly.

Two days later at a dinner gathering in my friend's house there was a middle-aged Iranian couple. I told them about the empty, gloomy mosque that horrified me. The man fixed his eyes on me, wondering if he should say something.

Finally he said, "Well, you know there is another place close to your house. People read the actual verses of the Quran without a teacher or interpretations. They say, 'We want to read and learn the scripture by ourselves.'"

His words filled me with hope. Since the time of the revolution, like most Muslims who used the Quran only as a decoration for their libraries, I had abandoned the Quran. Now it was my wish to read it again.

It was almost as if by divine intervention that I was guided to the way I had lost many years ago in my early twenties. I was ready to embrace my lost path after years of separation.

I participated in an informal group study every week and spent many hours reading the Quran in English. A small group of people gathered in a room, on the second floor of a residence, calling it the mosque of God. But the shock that followed was the tremendous new information that I learned from the Quran. It didn't take me much time to recognize the core of the corruption in Islam, and all other religions. Years of studying the Quran would come to form my views, which are harmonious with human rights and maximum freedom for all people.

I wanted to return to the time in my youth when I practiced goodness. For countless hours I woke up at dawn and read every day until the shift of dark into light.

It became clear to me that I'd been out of God's protection for many years and all the misery I had been through was the consequence of the wrong choices I had made.

I now had no doubt that Khomeini was a murderer, like the churchmen in the dark ages who imposed misery on Europeans through their oppressive rule. They were like the criminals who crucified Jesus for speaking the truth that didn't match their fabricated rules and religious theory.

I learned that all the divisions among religions are baseless and they all, with no exceptions, have been corrupted by innovations and traditional interpretations. Idolatrous doctrines have replaced the monotheist religions, including Islam.

I began to understand that the reason behind my suffering was giving power to other than God. The world of torture and famine created by corrupt religious men in power was in fact Satan's Kingdom. The soldiers of Satan advocate fear and terror. They fool the masses into not thinking for themselves. The first thing the corrupted Islamic regimes, false organizations, cults and many organized religions do is to blind their followers and make their decisions for them.

In my own life, losing my individuality and disobeying God's rule had left me with no protection. And when I was in the darkest time of my life in prison, I had only counted on my own limited power to face evil in the land of Satan.

My art now reflected a shift in how I viewed the world. It was just before I graduated from California State University Northridge in the Master of Arts program. Earlier that year, without realizing it at the time, an event occurred that would influence my art. I met an art connoisseur, who took an interest in my work. Reviewing my prison drawings, she encouraged me to explore them more.

I also felt I needed to somehow reconcile my past with my present. Maybe by bringing these experiences back into my life as art I could better deal with my memories. At least I was free now to do what I was not allowed to do in Iran. I was getting ready to give a testimony about the barbaric situation in Iran's political prisons.

My discovery of art began when I was six years old. My brother, Ahmad, introduced me to painting when, unbeknownst to him, I watched him working on one of his school projects. An image appeared through color on a white page in front of my eyes. Just by seeing him confidently applying the reds and greens to the blank surface, I was totally captivated by the creative process. In a sudden flash of certainty, I became involved in the magical world of art.

After my brother was killed in the car accident in 2003, in order to explore the mystery of human life and death, I created an art show entitled "In Search of Unification."

While in prison, the absurd difference between the external reality and my inner world threatened to destroy who I wanted to be. I now was searching to unify my life. After seventeen years, I felt I must document my prison experiences. For the first time since my incarceration, I depicted my prison experience openly in my art and acknowledged it as a difficult part of my life.

In some prison pictures, despite the layers of black chadors that covered us head-to-toe and the blindfolds, you can see that the free soul of these girls still persist. During the painting of "the prison pictures," the art connoisseur discovered some quick sketches of fancy, free-spirited women among my works. She encouraged me to pursue these in much more elaborate works that I would come to call

"The Ladies."

When I was a teen-ager my interest in art extended to fashion. When my mother might bring home a dress each for my sister and me, Shirin happily accepted it "as is." But I would always want to change it: make it shorter, tighter or in some way more stylish.

The girlish women in fanciful abstract poses satisfied my desire to depart from the mostly dark imagery of my prison pictures.

The Ladies depicted were not in prison. As prisoners, they would not have appeared to be individuals; they would be devoid of emotions or personality by virtue of their situation, an impression compounded by the fact that they would all be dressed the same in a black chador.

But now, they were able to express their emotions and themselves and wear fashionable clothes. This notwithstanding, their moods seem to range from joy to sadness, from anxiety to pride or kindness.

In the summer of 2006, my show made its European solo debut on the campus of New Hall, Cambridge University, England. I stayed in Cambridge for a month before I went to London to stay with a friend, attend a reunion of our high school friends, and release our sweetest laughter.

A young Iranian student spent hours giving me a tour of the historical Cambridge campuses. I was thrilled to see a happy young crowd in the town.

As I said good-bye to Cambridge, the polite taxi driver put my luggage into the back of his car. He was an English man, about thirty-five with dark hair and brown eyes. We had just left the old streets. The sky was soft grey and the air was windy after a quick rain. It would take more than one hour to get to central London.

At one side of the road people were waiting in train stations. The young man broke the silence by speaking softly,

"You must be a tourist, I suppose."

He turned back to the road just in time, since a young driver cut in front of him,

"Allahu Akbar!" The man mumbled.

I was surprised that the English man had used Arabic words.

He explained that he and his mother became Muslims some years before.

"Do you mean your mother covers her hair like Muslim women?" I asked.

"Yes, she only shows her eyes. She totally has changed her way of life."

I had always thought that the women in long black coverings in London were from Middle Eastern countries. I now remembered the way I had embraced Islam before the revolution in Iran in 1979. She too, I assumed, had questions about the purpose of life as I did. She must have been attracted to traditional Islam, not aware of its complex blend of right and wrong. I wondered how a European woman could accept such a way of life unless she was thirsty to find a meaning for her life.

"Have you read the Quran?" I asked.

He bent over, opened the glove compartment and pulled out a pocket size Quran.

"I carry it with me all the time."

"Oh, you carry it, not read it." I teased him. "I'm a Muslim too," I said in a low voice. "I don't cover my hair because the Quran doesn't command women to cover their hair."

He argued that the order was from Sunna, the sacred stories about the prophet Mohammad handed down through oral tradition; and I called Sunna false doctrine.

I opened my backpack and pulled out the best English translation of the Quran, by Dr. Rashad Khalifa, and read some verses aloud.

The young man kept his eyes on the road and stayed quiet. Thank God he was raised in a free country and allowed me to speak my mind. I had to tell him that there were so many fabrications and laws in the Muslim world that contradict the Quran.

"Terrorism cannot be justified by any religion of God. One of the major commandments in the Quran is to not kill since life is sacred, but look at how suicide-bombers break God's laws and how many Muslims defend them as motivated by despair and the belief they are fighting for the cause of God," I said.

I quoted the Quran, "The worshipers of the Most Gracious are those who tread the earth gently, and when the ignorant speak to them, they only utter peace." Quran, 25:63

He raised his hand and said, "But killing in the cause of God is a holy war."

"There is no such a term as 'holy war' in the Quran. Some religious leaders have not only added man-made laws to the religion, but also terms and false ideas. They use the verses out of context to justify their ways. Khomeini paraded as a holy man, but promulgated a fatwa, an unjust religious command, to kill thousands of the young, educated political prisoners in Iran in 1988. This can be only a work of evil."

The man didn't interrupt and kept looking down the road. I became quiet too. We had entered into busy streets. The ancient buildings towered over the narrow streets. The rain started and many umbrellas went up. People hurried up the sidewalks. The beauty of the London streets doubled with the reflections on the shiny wet streets.

The driver said, "I don't have the answer, but I am sure scholars have."

"Scholars…this is what happens when we give up our own minds and our own ability to understand God's words," I said with regret and shame in a low voice.

His face remained doubtful until we arrived at our destination. He turned to the main street, then to a narrow avenue where my friend lived. At the last moment, I decided to give him my copy of the Quran with the newest English translation, hoping he would read it.

"Please," I said, holding the Quran with my hands. "I want you to read it for yourself."

He softly said thank you and took the Quran.

I watched his taxi turn to the main street. I looked at the sky, breathed the fresh air after the rain and rang the bell of the one story house.

The next morning when my friend and I were still chatting after breakfast, the doorbell rang. It was the taxi driver who stood behind the door.

"I am afraid I needed to return your Quran." He paused, looked down at the Quran in his hand and said, "I spoke to my Muslim friend. He thinks this is terrorism against Islam."

I hadn't expected to see him distressed with doubt. I smiled at him and put out my hands for the Quran. He disappeared quickly, as if a shadow cast across the alley. Ironically, reading the Quran exposes the severe corruption in the Islamic world. It clearly shows that the misery of Muslims is the result of their following many nonsensical laws created by religious leaders.

The following year, in stunning Southern California, on the left side of a hill in Turtle Rock, I adjusted the camcorder on the heavy tripod, checked the scene through the viewer, and asked James, who was now just my friend, to take my position behind the camera.

I covered myself in a long black chador while walking through the dusty road to the hilltop.

While James's tall body was bent over the camera and his eyes were fixed on the viewer, he repeated in a very loud voice, "Go on, go on, it's great, go on…" and I thought, "James speaks like a Texan."

The wind was blowing mildly when I arrived at the peak of the hill and found the right spot to stand. If I did not know where I was, I could have believed this road followed by the soft rise and the dirt I was standing on could be in a village around Borujerd, where a cluster of simple homes, packed together, would appear after a few meandering curves.

I fixed the chador on my head and covered my eyes with a blindfold. The long black chador waved in the wind. I wished the time would not pass so quickly. I wanted to have time to concentrate on my thoughts and feel the moment. I wanted to imagine how the prisoners felt on the top of the hill in Evin, while waiting to be executed. I wanted to remember the past and what we experienced in the "Grave" for months under the chadors and blindfolds.

Finally I waved my hands to James and he started to film. "Under Thy Gentle Wing" was a short movie I made in remembrance of more than 2,500 young political prisoners who were hanged secretly in 1988 in Iran's political prisons. Among them there were my cellmates, Shekar and Sohayla.

In the cold, pale fall, in the last moments of their time on earth, they had left together, dissolving into the deep dawn of faraway heavens. Neither the world nor their mothers knew to cry for them. None received the news until the trees dropped their leaves, shivering in the autumn breeze.

Standing behind a few others in the movie section in the Gallery, I leaned against the wall to get a better view of the screen. The wind blew and the black chador moved. The symphony reached its falling moment; the waving of the chador slowed down and loads of green leaves fell on the ground from the top of a tree while a hanging noose appeared for a few seconds on the screen.

The film ended. My friends walked towards me, wiping tears from their faces.

In November of 2007, in the hushed early morning when the sun peeked through the backyard, I sat on an old wooden chair in the kitchen and reviewed my thoughts. The thoughts that would never leave me alone until I talked with an open heart about the time I was lost in the darkness.

Looking through the blinds, I watched a bird hopping back and forth in the water that had collected from the last night's rain. I started writing my story after twenty-one years, with the dream of world peace and happiness as "One nation under God, indivisible with liberty and justice for all."

AFTER WORDS

My friends were released in the same month as I.

In Iran, Lily lives a challenging, emotional life with her good-natured husband and his son. Hanna happily gave birth to two children from a man she married, a man "as soft as honeycomb in her hands," she proudly told Lily. Sister-in-law lives with her husband, writes poems and struggles under heavy medication.

Abroad, Roya lives with her American husband, raising her two stepsons while she teaches math at her own school. Marjan happily married a kind Iranian gentleman. Seena married one of the regime's men to wash away her sins for opposing the religious government while she was a communist. She divorced him later to promote free sex and prostitution openly and publicly in Germany, where she lives.

All, more or less carry the shadows, and the pain of their time in Iran's political prisons.

Hossein Ali Montazeri, who was expected to replace Khomeini, was put under five years of house arrest for disagreeing with government policies and criticizing the regime for denying people's freedom and rights. In June of 2009 Montazeri supported Iran's democratic Green Movement before his death.

ACKNOWLEDGMENTS

After I was certain I was ready to write about all that happened to me in prison, I received love, kindness and assistance from wonderful people who showed up in my life one after another and supported me in different ways, by God's grace.

My words are not strong enough to especially express my endless gratitude to Donal Brown with whom I met every Friday morning for over two years to work on the manuscript. I am thankful for his wise counsel in writing and his sense of integrity and respect for my individuality that brought me so much ease in penning my memoir in English. His contribution in forming my book wasn't limited in days, months and years of advising, editing, shaping and cutting, but his kind manner helped me rewrite the story over and over with confidence after inexhaustible reading and criticizing of new drafts. I thank Donal's wife and my dear friend, Brenda Brown, for her helpful editorial suggestions and corrections of my memoir. Their love and support for me and for freedom and human rights are a great blessing from God in my life.

I wanted also to thank those who generously spent time to read my story and advise me. I am grateful to Carol Hezelwood for her hard work with me every day for seven months; Lisa Spray for her wisdom, great suggestions, and copy editing the entire book. Wendy Coyle for her kind presence, excellent editing and suggestions about structure; Marina Nemat for her support and editing; Frances Gordon for her friendship and introducing me to Donal Brown.

I would also like to thank my dear friends and friends of my friends Loren Moore, Jeffry V. Shank, Steve Shank, Dr. Amana Ayoub, July Allecta, India Radfar, Pedrom Ghafoori and Gillian for their kind effort and support.

Mehri Dadgar